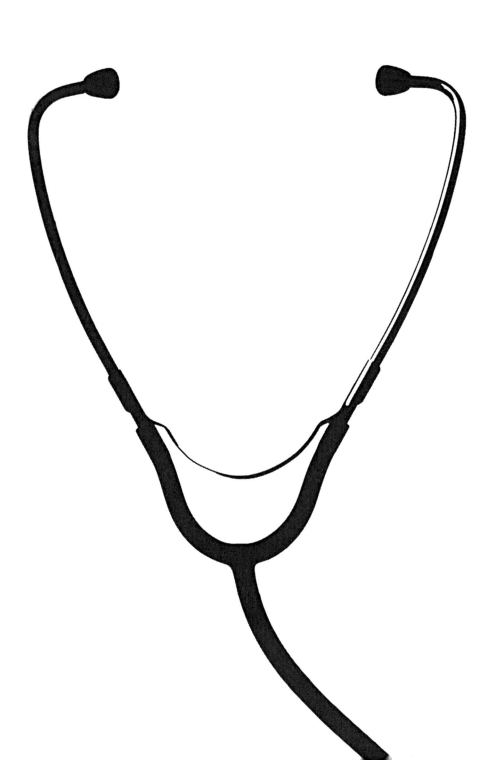

Dr Robert Lefever

Notes of a Private Doctor

BETRAYAL, CRISIS, BEREAVEMENT.

Edited by
Alex Rowe

RLB

Published by RL Books, a trading name of Doctor Robert
Limited, 58a Old Brompton Road, South Kensington,
London SW7 3DY, UK
Registered number 7852730.

First Published in 2013

10 9 8 7 6 5 4 3 2 1

A CIP catalogue record for this book is a available
from the British Library.

ISBN: 978-1-909449-00-8

Cover design by Agile Ideas
Typeset by Falcon Oast Graphic Art Ltd.

Acknowledgements

'No man is an island', says John Donne. I learned the deep truth of that in the pit of my despair. Friends first kept me alive and then gave me many reasons for living.

Tim and Ginny Bell and Anthony and Pat Mascolo gave us homes in their homes.

Canon Noelle Hall and Canon Peter Heartfield found us a home of our own.

Roger and Anne Pinnington, David and Rebecca Kerr, Theo and Louise Fennell, Paul and Gaynor Townley, David Greenhalgh and Kathi Kuhn, Robin and Annie Renwick, David and Judy Dangoor, Christopher Beaver, Guy Dellal, David Young and Hilary Haskell gave us heart-warming personal kindnesses.

Many of our former patients and staff stayed in regular contact with us to keep our spirits up.

Robin Lawrence gave us somewhere to work. Simon Heffer gave me the dignity and privilege of writing for him. Michael Dobbs and Jeffrey Robinson encouraged me.

Josh Dickson raised our spirits and supported us in our counselling work.

Alex Rowe gave me a thorough good shaking, which is exactly what I needed in order to focus on my professional future.

Pat Underwood loved me and brought me new happiness and a lovely home and found me a consulting room of my own.

Tony Mulliken, Fiona Marsh, Alastair Giles, Alex Rowe and Pat Underwood worked steadfastly to put this book together and keep me focused.

Working the Twelve Step programme alongside many friends in various anonymous fellowships kept me abstinent from addictive behaviour and as sane as I ever am.

My professional and personal life is blossoming and flourishing again. I am exceedingly grateful to all these wonderful friends who enabled me to see that, at seventy-five, my new life is just beginning.

'Robert Lefever is a remarkable doctor and remarkable man. In an age where people are increasingly afraid to take responsibility for themselves and their actions – and, indeed, are discouraged by the state from so doing – he shines with good sense and complete integrity.

Anybody facing a crisis in their lives, however big, will benefit from reading the account in this book of the series of blows that befell Robert, one after the other in short order, and how by his own resolve, determination and presence of mind he overcame them.

This book is the complete antidote to self-pity, and a testament to the importance, and vindication, of hope. He describes how to conquer even what appears to be the most serious adversity, and gives others a blueprint of how to do so. This is a visionary, but also rather humbling, book.'

Simon Heffer – Editor, *Mail Comment Online* and *Daily Mail* columnist

'I have known Robert Lefever for thirty years. He is always brilliant, sometimes bewildering and occasionally bonkers.

This is the story of his incredible journey, one that has visited soaring heights but also dark places that few of us could imagine.

He proves that the world can take almost everything from you – but so long as you have love and refuse to let go of your dreams, then you can survive almost anything.'

Michael Dobbs (Lord Dobbs of Wylye) – Best-selling author

To Meg and Pat
with love

Contents

Section 2: Crisis and Creativity

Section 3: Bereavement and Belief

Section 1

Betrayal –
the False Beliefs
and the Facts

False Belief: Betrayal is a fact rather than a perception.

Notes:
Throughout my life I have been betrayed and I have betrayed others. That's how it seems to me. But is it true? Is it real, like a clod of earth that I could shovel up and put in a wheelbarrow, or is it merely a perception – something that is entirely within my own mind? If it is real, there is nothing I can do about it but, if it is a perception, it can damage my relationships a great deal unless I do something about it.

Childhood abuse and abandonment are distressingly common. I did not escape that. I have to reflect that it did happen (I don't deny it), it was wrong (I don't buy into the belief that it was normal), and that it is over (I have better things to do than revisit those experiences and reopen those wounds again).

I carried, in my mind, the images of my abusers and the words they said, for many years. More fool me: I allowed the abusive experiences to continue to haunt me, instead of letting them become part of my history. In effect I was abused again, each time I thought about them. Now I can see that the abuse said a lot about the perpetrators but nothing about me. I have no reason to allow my self-image to be damaged by those traumas.

Also I see now that revenge is bitter. I never took any form of physical revenge – and I am glad of that because it would have reduced me to the same level as the abusers. However, I was scathing when I had the opportunity to be so. That hurt me. By wallowing in self-pity and blame, I made my own life miserable.

Far more significant betrayals occurred in my adult life but, by that time, I had learned not to damage myself. I did not stay in abusive relationships: I moved away. I did not retaliate when I was attacked: I did my best to survive and then move on.

I do not allow other people's actions to determine mine. I am totally responsible for choosing my beliefs and my behaviour.

Facts:
1 Betrayal is not something that can be specified. It reflects the way that each of us looks at things. Something that may be shrugged off by one person might demolish another.
2 If we perceive that we have been betrayed, we tend to focus on that issue to the exclusion of all else. We become utterly obsessed by it. When we resent someone's actions, it is as if we ourselves had taken a poison but hoped that the other person would be damaged.
3 We can choose what we put into our minds, in the same way that we can choose what we put into our mouths.
4 Some events are exceedingly traumatic and they may occur at an age in our lives when there is little or nothing that we can do to protect ourselves. These events may lead to deep and lasting imprints in our emotional memory (and cause post-traumatic stress disorder). Rational therapies are useless because our reactions are not rational: we may know perfectly well that we are no longer at risk – but it doesn't feel like it. We can be helped in other ways.
5 Retaliation can be as disastrous as allowing the abuse to continue: it commonly perpetuates the problems rather than resolves them. We need to find a way of protecting ourselves without risking further damage, either from other people or from ourselves.
6 A sharp tongue can hurt just as much as physical abuse. A cruel or inconsiderate spoken or written phrase can cause dreadful hurt – and be very difficult to recant.
7 Financial betrayals can have fearful consequences. People in positions of trust may still steal and defraud when they can. We have to protect ourselves against it by doing systematic checks, and not beat ourselves up too much when crafty theft or embezzlement does occur: we are the victims, not the villains.
8 Sexual infidelity is not insuperable. Both partners need to assess gently why the relationship deteriorated. Betrayal occurs when the infidelity is recurrent.

False Belief: My parents should never have had children.

Notes:
My parents were missionaries in India. My younger brother and I were both born there. At the time of my brother's birth, I was put into boarding school – at the age of four.

Three years later, at the end of the Second World War, we all went to the UK but, three years after that, my parents went back to India and took my brother with them. For the next four years I was farmed out to guardians.

Dad worked in the plains, where it was exceedingly hot, but Mum lived in the hills, where the climate was kinder. It is a wonder that my brother and I were ever conceived. My brother subsequently told me that, on one occasion, Mum put him on a train to travel back to school on his own – a journey of six hundred miles. He was six years old.

When the four years were up, our parents and my brother came 'home' for a year but I remained in boarding school during that time. When I was fourteen, at the time that they all arrived at Victoria Station, I ran up to my father and kissed him. He turned away, embarrassed. Subsequently our parents went back to India for a further three years. They left my brother with me under the care of successive further guardians but he went to a different school so I hardly knew him at all.

When my parents finally came 'home' to the UK for good, I was eighteen and on my way to do National Service in the Army before going up to Cambridge and then getting married. My parents missed the major transitions of my school life and played virtually no part in my home life, such as it was. But I survived.

Why did my parents have us if they didn't want us? Did they betray us when they did?

When my parents decided to become missionaries, should they not also have decided to forgo having children?

Isn't it time that I got over all this anyway?

Facts:

1 My father's father was alcoholic. He refused to let my dad take up a scholarship to grammar school when he was fourteen, saying that he was old enough to be supporting his mother – which Grandpa never had. He betrayed all his family. Dad worked as a secretary and, from night school, got into London University. Later he got a PhD in Philosophy in Germany.

2 My mother's mother was alcoholic. Her father died when she was six. In those days there were no social services. My mother brought up her younger sister and brother. They did exceedingly well academically. My uncle got starred firsts in everything at Oxford and subsequently entered Parliament and became Foreign Secretary. My Aunt read English at London University. My mother's skills were in painting and cooking.

3 In India my mother ran a hostel for soldiers on leave from the Burma campaign. She sent me to the convent boarding school, on the other side of the road, rather than have me share my home with thirty drunken Tommies. I was well taught and excellently cared for.

4 In my generation, many children were in boarding school when their parents were abroad in the Armed Forces or in business or the diplomatic service. My experience was no different from that of many others. None of us was betrayed.

5 I can look back at my early childhood with self-pity, if I so wish – but it won't do me any good.

6 My parents had far worse childhoods than mine. In due course they gave me a wonderful set of ethics, principles and values. My guardians did the same and they looked after me well. Was I betrayed? I don't think so – not at all.

7 My schooling was rather ordinary – but I did not make the best of it.

8 I worked very long hours establishing myself in medical practice. My children wondered if I should have had them. Did I betray them? Possibly: it's for them to judge.

False Belief: Spare the rod and spoil the child.

Notes:
I remember being caned. It hurt. A lot. I don't remember what I had done to merit that vicious punishment but I do remember that two weeks later the bruises were still present. My parents saw them when I was having a bath at home on a week-end leave from the London school that I attended when I was ten. My father took me out of the school (which specialized in caring for missionary children) and I was sent to another (that specialized in nothing whatever – not even in teaching – but it was a happy place).

I was naughty right from the start but I never did anything worse than bouncing on the bed springs, on the top bunk, so high and so hard that I went right through them. I was late for everything. I was cheeky and generally disobedient. I was grubby and always disheveled. I was punished – of course I was – but not brutally.

I sang in the choir as the lead treble and, with other boys on the small island in the pond, I built a den made from corrugated iron sheeting and tree branches and constructed a raft made of oil drums and wooden planks. In our games, I won over one thousand marbles. I did only enough work to get through the entrance examination to the main school.

When it came to the time to go to the main school, I remember hearing two of the masters saying 'Put Lefever into Collinson House – they'll beat it out of him'. I was clearly intended to overhear that comment but it mystified me: I didn't know what 'it' was. Years later I knew, from other experiences, what it is that my elders and betters find so threatening: my enthusiasm. In Collinson House, in the main school, they did their very best to beat it out of me. They failed.

To this day I am excited by creativity – doing new (even crazy) things. My critics are my friends. They show me where a new idea might lead me.

Facts:
1 Lots of other boys did very well – academically, socially and in sports – in all the schools that I attended. I did not. The betrayal, in this respect, was mine rather than the schools'.
2 I held the school records for all punishments: writing out lines, detentions and beatings. There was a very good reason for this: I was the naughtiest boy. For that reason I was never made a prefect. In my final year, studying for University entrance, I was punished by prefects who were two years younger than me. That was a betrayal of adult responsibility for children in their care – but I cannot complain: I knew the rules and I disobeyed them.
3 One question is whether the rules and the punishments were sensible and just. I didn't think they were and I took every opportunity to say so. Interestingly, the rules were changed soon after I left. I had my own influence on the school in a bizarre way. Even so, I asked for the trouble that I got.
4 The central issue is whether savage physical punishment should ever be meted out to children by anyone – by adults or by other children. I believe that it should not: it creates a savage society.
5 Retrospectively, there was one particular advantage in not being a prefect of any kind: I never punished anyone.
6 Correspondingly, I suffered a lot of sexual abuse from older boys and from one of the masters but I never abused anyone else. I attach no importance to being abused: my childhood is over: it's gone, finished. I do attach importance to the wrong that is done by the abusers: they have to live with that.
7 I am proud of the fact that, in an abusive and violent school, I myself was not abusive or violent. I am ashamed of having been violent, with my hands and voice, towards my own children. They deserved better than that. I betrayed them. A violent childhood does not inevitably lead to a violent adulthood. There is no excuse for violence.

False Belief: Music is for homosexuals.

Notes:
Believe it or not, that was the way my headmaster dismissed my request to study Music. He went on to say that there were no homosexuals in the school. I knew that he was wrong on that: the head boy was one, for a start.

Be that as it may, music was all that interested me. I was good at mathematics and English but music was the centre of my life. Sadly, in a school where the primary interest was rugby football, I had virtually no training in music: I had to pick it up as I went along – and my pickings were casual and haphazard. This was educational betrayal.

My successive guardians were at a loss to understand my passion: all three of the men were tone deaf. My Foreign Secretary uncle had to be dragged to his feet when they played the National Anthem – which was quite frequently in his profession.

Eventually, when I had passed sufficient examinations to get into university (if any would have me), I was allowed to study Music for three months and I was entered for a Music scholarship to Cambridge. I handed back the papers – blank, other than for my name at the top. On the strength of that, I was offered a place to read Engineering. I declined. My head-master was furious. His boys rarely got into Cambridge – and they certainly did not turn down the opportunity. But I did: I wanted to be a musician.

Three weeks later I entered myself for a singing scholar-ship and I got one. This time it was the Music Master who was flabbergasted: 'You haven't got a note in your head', he said, somewhat less than encouragingly. My housemaster was also completely taken aback, having tried all along to discourage me. When I eventually went up to Cambridge to read Music (after getting myself the standard academic qualifications), I was thrown out after one week: I wasn't good enough. My heart broke.

Facts:

1 I carried my headmaster's homophobia and prejudice against music for at least twenty years. He may have been dead by then. More fool me for allowing his behaviour to clutter up my head.

2 I do not have the natural talent to be a professional musician. Anyone can see that – except me (and I wouldn't look or listen).

3 The chances of all three of my guardians being tone deaf are astronomical. Was I being guided by the spiritual world? I think not: it was just chance. Nor was I betrayed.

4 My determination to carry through my own beliefs is still a major asset of mine – but I need to be sure that I am facing in the right direction before I set off on any future project or quest. If I do otherwise, I betray myself.

5 I have a right to do what I want with my own life. I am not a statistic for school examination results nor a unit of university or government policy. My life is mine.

6 The aim of teaching should be to enable students to learn. However, not all teachers have that gift – any more than all doctors have the gifts of compassion and common sense. Do I have those gifts? Would I have been a successful teacher, any better than my own teachers? I don't know. Anyway, I don't think I was betrayed.

7 Throw-away comments may sear the soul – but we don't have to be hurt by them for the rest of our lives.

8 I would have had a wretched life as a musician. I have had a wonderful life as a doctor (my kind of doctor), doing the personal and imaginative work that I enjoy. Being a psychodramatist is really no different from conducting an orchestra. Helping individuals to discover their own gifts is the same in counselling as it is in music.

9 Broken hearts can heal – if we give them the time and the opportunity to do so. Broken hearts make great plays, films and operas but it is the next (usually un-portrayed) act that is the real story: the triumph over adversity.

False Belief: The Army will make a man of you.

Notes:

The Army and I understood each other very well. We were required to spend two years with each other. Neither of us wanted that but it was the law and therefore we got on with each other as best we could.

Because I had done Mathematics and Physics, I was put into the Royal Signals. After basic training in Catterick Camp in Yorkshire (I never want to be cold again in my life) I was selected for officer training and went to Mons Officer Cadet Training School in Aldershot. It was a matter of honour in the Royal Signals that no cadet from any other corps would beat us over the assault course or at boxing. The assault course was no problem but boxing is difficult for me because I am very short-sighted. After three minutes in the ring, with punches landing on me from I know not where, I survived – but my opponent was limping for days: In my determined retreat I had trodden on his foot. I reckon I won.

Marne Lines, in Catterick again, was savage. Laying telegraph lines across the moors in three feet of snow for three days and two nights with no sleep taught me – in due course – that the pressures of being a junior hospital doctor were a doddle. I was learning appropriately that I had to earn the respect of men under my command in battle. The Army would have betrayed the men under my command if I had not been rigorously trained.

The first six months of my second year were spent in a secret signal centre under six foot of concrete. It was said to be 'atom-bomb proof'. (Where would we go if we did get out?) I shared my twenty-four hour, seven-day week, job with two others so we had to work a sixteen-hour shift every third weekend in order to get one thirty-six hour break. In the second six months I was responsible for one hundred and twenty cooks and drivers. I was aged twenty. Again this is the real world: no betrayal here.

Facts:

1 The Army taught me how to survive – but I had been to a British private school and I already had that skill.

2 My school housemaster, who never made me a prefect, said to me, when he learned that I had been made an officer, 'I always knew that you would do well'.

3 The Army and I parted on the same terms that we had agreed at the beginning: mutual tolerance. Working in the National Health Service is far more dogmatic and dictatorial.

4 The Army trains people to obey orders and to kill. Officers know that lives depend upon decisions learned and taken at the sharp end of the action. I understand that and I accept that someone has to fight for us. However, I do not believe that knowing how to kill makes me a man. Even the Army itself seems to understand that: in the Manual of Military Law, food may be condemned as being 'unfit for troops or for human consumption'!

5 There is every reason to fight for what we believe in, even when the odds are stacked heavily against us – but not when they are impossible. Retreat may sometimes be the best form of defence.

6 Stamina is a mental attitude, not a physical attribute. Military and medical training should be tough – to weed out the incompetent.

7 Respect can only be given; never demanded.

8 The Army taught me to respect and care for people. In medical school I merely learned about diseases. The Army didn't betray me; medical school did – or, rather, it betrayed patients through this deficiency in our training.

9 Young people are perfectly capable of taking significant responsibility, if they are trained properly and given an appropriate opportunity to develop management skills.

10 A 'gap' year, before going up to University, is a valuable step towards personal maturity. National Service in the forces achieved the same.

False Belief: There is nothing special about Cambridge.

Notes:
My girlfriend dropped me, saying that I wouldn't be able to take her out if I was going to Cambridge. A week later I was back at home when the Music Department at Cambridge dropped me as well. It was suggested that I should study some other subject. In two weeks my life had fallen apart.

A school friend, who had also been in the Royal Signals, had decided to study Medicine so I did the same. I was told that I had to pass the necessary entrance subjects (Botany, Zoology, Inorganic Chemistry and Organic Chemistry) in one year from scratch and then I would have to do the standard three-year course in two years (as many students do, prior to doing a special subject in their third year). As long as I sang in the college chapel choir, I could keep my place.

Corpus Christi College, and Cambridge University in general, were very kind to me. I was taught brilliantly and I had a lot of fun at the same time. I sang in the University Madrigals but, sadly, I was not able to sing while being punted down the river in May Week (the first two weeks in June) because I was taking an exam at the time. In college I made life-long friends, who mostly studied English, and I put on a series of recitals, keeping my music alive. My work did tend to get in the way of my social life – but not much!

At the end of my first term, a friend invited me to join her in London for the second night of West Side Story. I did so and I loved it. The following day we went to the Royal Academy to see the Russian art exhibition. We walked around the gallery separately. A beautiful girl got between me and a really dreadful 'heroic' picture and I said to myself 'She's the one'. I had some difficult explanations to make to the girl who took me to the gallery but I did the honourable thing: I later married the one I left with – although, since then, I was reluctant ever to take her to another gallery.

Facts:

1 I would have been miserable with my first girlfriend. I was wonderfully happy with Margaret. In fifty-one years, the longest time we were apart was one week. She visited me in Cambridge every weekend and played an active part in College musical life.

2 I consider myself to be primarily a product of Corpus. This is where I learned to think and reason, as best I can.

3 Cambridge never betrayed me but I could have done a lot better. I larked around too much. I could have taken more advantage of the fabulous opportunities to learn. I betrayed the chance that I had been given to get my mind into top gear.

4 The cleverest man I ever met in Cambridge was also one of the most humble. As a contemporary, and a top scholar, he helped me to grapple with Chemistry. (The lecturers were too far above me.) After graduating, he stayed on at the College and later became the Master. I know my place: I am not in his league.

5 Twenty-five years down the line, my elder son met someone at a party who said, 'Your father dumped my mother'. There is no answer to that – but I don't think I betrayed her: we would not have been suited.

6 I never had a vocation to be a doctor. I just loved my work as a GP and, in particular, I loved my patients. I developed this sense of absolute commitment when I was at Cambridge.

7 Throughout my life, whenever I have been given a choice – such as between Music and Medicine – I have always answered 'Both'. I refuse to be categorized. Cambridge gave me self-determination as well as everything else.

8 I got into my secondary school on a London County Council grant. I was supported in Cambridge by my scholarship and a local authority grant. This form of elitism, based upon selection by competition, is never a betrayal. Equality of opportunity does not require a levelling down.

False Belief: London medical schools are among the best.

Notes:
I looked forward to coming to London. Cambridge was too rarified for me. I love the hustle and bustle, the noise and the sheer pace and variety of London. The Middlesex Hospital was near Oxford Circus, right in the centre of town. I felt I belonged there and indeed I very much enjoyed my time there. I was in the dramatic society and the choral society and I took part in the Christmas Concert (the student review). I spent more time on stage than I did on the wards or in the lecture theatres.

I had got married soon after leaving Cambridge so I gave myself a lot of time to settle into married life and enjoy London to the full. I sang in Christchurch, Lancaster Gate, alongside other choral scholars from Cambridge and later I sang in The Temple church and St Margaret's, Westminster. I deputized in Westminster Abbey, St Paul's Cathedral, Westminster Cathedral and the Brompton Oratory and I sang in the Monteverdi Choir and other semi-professional groups.

I did sufficient work – at the very last minute – to get through the examinations but my finest hours were in producing the Christmas Concert and in creating the United Hospitals Operatic Society, for which I put on and conducted three performances of Puccini's opera La Bohème.

I was rewarded by being given both my post-qualifying appointments in my own teaching hospital – much to the understandable irritation of those of my contemporaries who had spent all their time working.

I disliked my time on the wards: I was more interested in people – in what made them tick – than in their physical and so-called mental diseases. I learned what I had to learn but I rebelled against the concept of 'interesting cases'. I am a people person.

Facts:

1 From my limited observation, London medical schools did not compare favourably with those in the USA or in other advanced countries – but it has to be said that they produced many fine doctors who were more disciplined than I was: in addition to my musical activities, I played too much poker. However, I can say that I lived life to the full and I think that this made me a better GP in due course: I had learned the diseases by then but I knew instinctively what human beings are.

2 It is often said that Medicine and Music go together. They don't. From each of the thirteen major hospitals in London, I found only three really competent musicians. Doctors tend to be more interested in golf, travel, food and wine.

3 I believe that the prime purpose of teaching hospitals should be to teach aspiring doctors about common ailments so that they become competent in treating the clinical conditions they are most likely to see in practice. What they tend to be shown – with pride bordering on conceit – is clinical conditions that they are unlikely to see ever again in their professional lives. This betrays them.

4 Doctors have to be competent but they must understand the perspectives of their patients. They cannot do this if their heads are stuck in academic clouds.

5 Did my medical school betray me or did I betray it or was there a bit of both? As with Cambridge, I think I could have made a great deal more of my training opportunities than I did. Even so, 50% of medical students subsequently become general practitioners and there is often poor training for the work that they will be doing in the rest of their lives. For example, they learn how to prescribe rather than how to provide human comfort and give help in order to heal. They give their NHS dictators and paymasters the (sometimes fake) numbers that are required for statistical surveys. O brave new world!

False Belief: Marriages are made in heaven.

Notes:

My father, a clergyman, said that if any couple can survive the first year of married life, it is proof of God's existence – because it is a miracle. My own view is that marriage needs to be hard work; it decays if it is taken for granted. It is never too early or too late to work on improving it.

I had a strange childhood. Margaret had a dreadfully abusive one. People who believe that they are tainted by childhood experience would never believe that we could have been as happy as we were for so long. The secret was that we never stayed the same: we were always learning new things about ourselves and about each other. We were always changing. Sometimes she would be ahead of me and then sometimes I would be ahead of her – but we always caught each other up.

We had a blissful honeymoon in an Austrian alpine village in the middle of the summer. We returned to London totally penniless and with nowhere to live. We were both still students and Margaret's grant was stopped because her county council refused to believe that she would do any more work. The two of us lived on one student grant. It was a wonderful way to begin our married life. La Vie de Bohème indeed.

Sometimes at night Margaret would wake up screaming, after dreaming of her childhood torments. A psychiatrist offered antidepressants. A clinical psychologist told us – after we had been married for six weeks – that we should not have sex. This did not give us confidence in competence and human understanding being necessarily allied to letters after names. One year later, our first child was born.

The early years of medical careers are demanding. By the time I was a doctor, we had been married for three years and could take the strain. Some of my contemporaries who had married later in their careers did not.

Facts:

1 Relationships are never easy. They have to be created afresh day by day.

2 There are three things that need to be said by those of us who suffered abuse of one kind or another in our childhoods: it did happen, it was wrong, it is over.

3 The most exciting thing in life is constant change. We die – or fossilize – from the moment that we stabilize.

4 We betray ourselves and we betray each other if we do not live to our full emotional and intellectual potential – and encourage each other to do the same. The worship of physical prowess in fitness clubs or on the sports field is healthy but trivial.

5 Despite having some expensive tastes (antiquarian books and mediaeval manuscripts are not cheap but they do not wear out), I am fortunate in having many pleasures that cost nothing. My student days taught me a great deal about human values.

6 Centralized organizations, such as local or national governments, have no power to vary their policies and procedures to take individual circumstances into account. Through being obsessed with following their rules, they betray the individuals who don't fit their mould – as in Margaret's case over her student grant.

7 Childhood trauma can be healed by various therapies, such as Eye Movement Desensitizing and Reprocessing (EMDR) and Neuro-Linguistic Programming (NLP). By contrast, Cognitive Behavioural Therapy (CBT), and other seemingly rational approaches, betray patients through the sheer arrogance of professionals failing to see that irrational problems (such as childhood trauma) cannot be resolved by rational approaches, let alone suppressed by medications.

8 Marrying young may help both the marriage and the career. Education authorities make their own policies on grants without taking this into account.

False Belief: Do what you love rather than love what you do.

Notes:
After qualifying as a doctor, I enjoyed my six months work on a surgical team. I did not enjoy the following six months in cardiology. As the junior member of the heart team, I was responsible for starting all resuscitations (after cardiac arrests) in the hospital. In those days we had little technical skill, nor the right equipment or drugs, for this task. One hundred people died under my hands, day and night, in six months. I had the stamina but not the enthusiasm for that work. I am not a physician by nature or by inclination.

After that experience, I did not want to be a doctor of any kind. I decided to try my luck again with my first love: music. To earn money, I took a job as a 'trainee' in general practice. I wasn't actually trained at all. I covered the partners for their holidays but otherwise I worked only two days a week and spent the rest of my time singing and conducting.

The senior partner told me that what he really liked about general medical practice in the community was finding out 'Who was sleeping with whom, don't you know'. I didn't.

I conducted part of one rehearsal of the Croydon Symphony Orchestra. They were excellent. I was useless. At the Royal College of Music, I was awarded a performer's diploma (ARCM), as a counter-tenor (alto), the only voice I have. One examiner told me 'We're going to pass you because you are obviously musical – but we don't want you to think that we like it, because we don't'. The other said 'Singing is about sex – and one can't imagine having sex with a counter-tenor: it sends shivers down the spine'. Subsequently, I gave a solo recital in the Purcell Room on the South Bank, sang a major part in an opera at Sadler's Wells and understudied at Glyndebourne – but I was still no good. I lacked the skills that would be necessary in a professional musician.

Facts:

1 I may be 'musical', and I love music passionately, but I do not have the talent to be a professional musician.

2 I do have the talent to be a doctor but I had to find out which type of clinical practice suited me. I loathe psychiatry: I think it is inhuman. I don't believe the pharmaceutical industry stories about medicines. Nor do I believe that surgery is always appropriate. I am no pathologist or academic: I like people – live ones.

3 I am familiar with death – too familiar and from too young an age – but it didn't put me off my medical work. I like patients. I find doctors and health authorities more challenging.

4 Some doctors are weird – but so are some anythings.

5 I was definitely betrayed by my GP trainer – but I chose him as much as he chose me.

6 I have no quarrel with people giving their opinions on counter-tenors or anything else. What does concern me (did betray me) is when the target of the attack (me in this case) is in no position to respond. I was put in a similar situation when the chairman of my local education committee (a local headmaster, two of whose pupils I had beaten when I got my singing scholarship) informed his colleagues that the state financially supplements only 'proper' scholarships. These stings can hurt – but more fool me if I let them hurt me now. They say more about him than they do about me.

7 I am very proud of my failures – I have had many failures in many areas – because I have given life a great try and done some very exciting things. I prefer that to a life in which I would merely earn my living, pay my rent, play rugby or golf, get drunk, bed a bird and watch TV.

8 I need both my head and my heart. I need both my right (feeling) brain and my left (thinking) brain. Some people are comfortable with one or the other. I am not: I want to use both at the same time, to think and feel equally.

False Belief: Lawyers and parents work things out fairly.

Notes:
The godfather of our daughter gave her two Premium Bonds, one for her birthday and one for her christening. Three months later one of them came up with a major prize. We decided to use the money as the deposit for buying a house. The lady who owned it gave us a personal mortgage, saying that she wanted the house to continue as a family home. We stayed there for twenty-four years so we didn't betray her trust. Those two pieces of good fortune made an enormous difference to our lives. Our children had a stable home and we had lovely neighbours, with children of the same age, so they all grew up together in each other's homes. We had many happy times.

We sub-let the upper floor until we needed it ourselves as our family grew. Later on, when I set up my own NHS practice on the ground floor, we dug out the basement and my wife and I moved into it. Finally, when the children left home, we stayed in the basement and made the house itself into a halfway house for addicts who had completed their initial treatment with us elsewhere. At each stage we remortgaged the house to finance our professional lives.

How much of the value of the house truly belonged to our daughter? How much of the improvements belonged to her? How much of my professional income, funded by mortgages on the house, belonged to her? We asked lawyers to sort all that out and they did – to nobody's real satisfaction, except perhaps their own. What was done was to imagine that the initial sum had been invested in equities on the stock market. I have never in my life bought a stock or a share so I know nothing about that. I have only bought property. At times I have done well and at other times I have been wiped out. Presumably this variability accounts for the caution of the lawyers. Did they betray us? Did I betray my daughter? I really don't know – but I never felt comfortable over this episode in my life.

Facts:

1 Bringing up a family is difficult. It costs a lot of money. Establishing a business costs a lot of money. In the absence of family inheritance, where is all this money going to come from?

2 The standard advice is that one should never risk losing one's home. Nowadays banks insist on taking personal guarantees to secure any significant borrowing. Thus, any substantial loan inevitably risks the family home.

3 The only safe investment is to work for the state and own nothing, owe nothing and create nothing. I myself would not count that as a life well lived. It would be a betrayal.

4 I remember a lawyer telling me that, if I wanted life to be fair in the sight of the Lord, I would have to go to the court of the Lord. His answer was as pompous as my prior statement had been – but it was true: we never get all that we want or consider to be fair.

5 Lawyers can never please all the people all the time. Where family issues or disputes are concerned, there are bound to be hurt feelings and resentments. In this instance, concerning my daughter, what she got was legally right. However, I got huge benefits from the initial cash injection. I suppose I could have been stupid and lost it – so the lawyers were sensible in their caution. In the end, my wife and I both felt that our daughter deserved more. In time she got it.

6 As parents we do the best we can – but we always wish we could have done better somehow.

7 We each have our own ideas on what we feel we deserve from our parents and what our children deserve from us. We may at times be damaged by receiving too much or giving too much. There is potential betrayal both ways.

8 The most important things we could ever learn at school are rarely taught: how to make a successful long-term relationship, how to bring up children happily and successfully and how to make a profit in business.

False Belief: Assistantships are opportunities to learn.

Notes:
My first assistantship in general medical practice was with a doctor who was a leading light in the British Medical Association. He employed no staff whatever. He used a mapping pen for his notes so as to save the expense of paper. I resigned when he ticked me off for collecting, from the chemist, some medicines for a lady in her nineties. He said that this would encourage patients to request home visits.

My next post was with a group of three doctors who worked partly in affluent South Kensington and partly in the poorer North. I worked mostly in the northern office, where there was no washbasin and therefore no opportunity to examine patients properly. On one occasion I was allocated two home visits at opposite ends of the practice area: I spent two hours in the car. When I became a partner, I was required to put my first year's income into a 'capital' account to cover unexpected costs. I earned my living – to provide for my family – by working from 8pm to 2am most nights for the Emergency Call Service. In my holiday I covered another practice in rural Kent – and loved it. I saw what a GP's life could be. I resigned my partnership on my return.

I then set up practice on my own in my own home. On the first morning I saw nobody. In the afternoon I saw one patient – a singer friend of mine. I continued to work in the evenings, I set up a daily clinic in the Royal College of Music and I worked every lunchtime for a two-doctor practice in South Kensington. In due course, we formed a partnership. Before I had time to argue with the health authorities that we could choose whichever partners we wanted, rather than stay within their boundaries, the junior partner emigrated. Then the senior partner failed to come back from holiday and, when I discovered more about what had been going on in the practice, I think I knew why the junior partner had left.

Facts:

1 In practice, assistantships tended in my time to be slave jobs, doing whatever the senior partner instructed. There was no training and, in that, I was betrayed. I learned as I went along – from patients.

2 The British Medical Association is a trade union, focusing its attention on obtaining – for its members – more pay for less work, rather than on improving patient care.

3 When doctors were paid a standard fee for each patient, regardless of the work involved, they earned more by spending less.

4 The poor standards of care – such as are inevitable if there are inadequate facilities for examining patients – were commonplace in my early days in practice. At our next meeting, I drew this to the attention of the Inner London Local Medical Committee of the British Medical Association. I resigned from it when no attention was paid to my concern.

5 The NHS prides itself on the standards of care in areas such as Oxford or Exeter, where there are stable populations and plentiful, well qualified, staff. The majority of the population of the UK live in major cities where the standards of care, and the qualification levels of staff, tend to be poor. These populations are betrayed.

6 The NHS is not free: it is paid for from taxation. It takes too much and gives too little. It does not rob Peter to pay Paul: it robs Paul (on middle incomes), messes around at great expense, and then gives him back less than he could have bought for himself and his family in the first place.

7 Like it or not, health care is a business: it has to be run properly by those who are doing it. Failure to run a business effectively results in a vast waste of resources.

8 Creating a general medical practice from scratch is hard work but also a lot of fun. Large health centres tend to achieve a low common standard of ability and enterprise.

9 Doctors have the same mental health problems as the rest of the population – but they have no prior screening.

False Belief: Bringing up children is women's work.

Notes:
While I was establishing myself in general medical practice, Margaret was working as a physiotherapist in Hammersmith Hospital and also in Wormwood Scrubs prison. She also taught herself secretarial skills and worked for the Friends of Hammersmith Hospital and, of course (says I), for me.

Our elder son was born four years after our daughter and our younger son eighteen months later. All our children were born by the time Margaret was twenty-nine. In addition to continuing work, only a few weeks after the birth of each child, she also looked after our dog, an Afghan hound who had ten puppies in a box in our hall – some months after being mated underneath the grand piano in our living room.

When our children went to primary school, Margaret became a teacher so that her holidays coincided with theirs. She first gained a Montessori diploma and then, from the University of London, a Bachelor of Education degree in the subject of Education. Later on, to help me in my private medical practice, she returned to physiotherapy and also trained as a medical laboratory scientist in haematology. Subsequently, in our addiction work, she trained as a Rogerian person-centered counsellor and headed our Family Programme, in which she had a superb talent and total, loving, commitment. Her piano playing (at concert standard – she obtained a distinction in Grade VIII of the Associated Board examinations at the age of thirteen) continued as her daily commitment to what she described as her 'breath of life'. Together with her sister, Hilary, and a friend, she played in a piano trio. Sometimes with her brother, Peter, and a friend, the trio would become a quartet or quintet. She observed that the piano part was always the hardest. Despite all her achievements, she always believed herself to be the dunce of the family!

Facts:

1 Margaret was incredibly versatile and skilled and always willing to do whatever might be helpful for other people. When there was a conflict of interest, such as between what she felt I might want and what she believed might be best for our children, she found it very difficult to decide what would be the most appropriate course of action. When our children were grown up, she told me that she had made a conscious decision to follow my wishes for her to work with me. She regretted not spending more time at home with our children.

2 Despite knowing many families where the mother had stayed at home, but the children had developed similar problems to those of our children, Margaret still believed that she had betrayed our children. I am left with the feeling that I betrayed her.

3 I wanted to make something positive with my life – and I did – but I still wonder if I abandoned (betrayed) my children in a manner similar to what I had experienced from my parents in my own childhood. I suppose this is something with which many professionals grapple: if we build a career we have the money to spend on our families but we may have less contact with them.

4 Margaret's love of her counselling work with families was based on a fundamental love of people of all ages, races, creeds and other distinctions. She had a particular empathy for those families who suffered the ravages of addiction problems, as ours had done. She spoke from personal experience and with profound human compassion. My own view is that she never betrayed anyone in her whole life: that would have been against her entire nature.

5 We gave all of our children some wonderful educational opportunities but the final tally of results was one A level for our daughter and none for the boys. I cannot believe that children can ever 'betray' their parents so that lash falls again on me – and on some of the schools.

False Belief: The NHS is the envy of the world.

Notes:
At the age of thirty-three, I became the senior partner of a group medical practice – the first in the South Kensington area. I designed new premises and chose two junior partners and we selected six members of staff.

In an affluent area, we rejected all private practice. We took on sixty new patients each week (there was a forty per cent turnover of residents each year in this part of London, which was mostly bed-sit land) and we also saw sixty 'temporary residents', who were just visiting London, each week. We were busy – and we loved it. I began to take medical students, allowing them to sit in on consultations. I enjoyed that because they kept me sharp. I gave lectures in medical schools… but my enthusiasm was gradually eroded by the failures of the NHS itself: in central London – and in other major city centres – it doesn't work.

At a lecture in 1976, I met Professor Lawrence Weed, from the University of Vermont in the USA, and I learned about his Problem-Oriented Medical Information System (PROMIS). I was captivated from his first statement: 'Maturity is fatigue: when you're getting old and tired and can't fight the battles any more, you turn to those who are still fighting and you say, "You're immature"!'

His system of medical records, medical education and patient care has been the bedrock of my clinical practice ever since. He puts his patients at the centre of care, saying that they are the most important members of his staff – because there is one to every patient and because they are well motivated! He looks at the significance, to the patient, of each problem rather than solely to the medical interest of the doctor. I had my first doubts that the NHS might not be what it is made out to be in the UK. The envy of the world had not been copied anywhere else … and it was becoming old and tired.

Facts:
1 In a GP partnership, doctors are jointly responsible for all that is done by any of them. I asked my medical insurance company what I should do over my former senior partner's inappropriate clinical actions. I was told that this was up to me. I reported him to the General Medical Council. His wife then committed suicide. Some senior doctors in South Kensington told me that I succeeded professionally only by treading on my partner's neck.

2 There are no 'green field' sites in South Kensington. All medical premises are conversions. They therefore do not fit the required specifications and, hence, not even the 70% allowance of our rent was fully paid by the NHS.

3 The allowance for staff also resulted in a significant short-fall that had to be paid by doctors. The result of that, in South Kensington, was that there was one part-time staff member to every three doctors and one full-time member of staff to every five. Our six staff had among the highest salaries in the UK so our own income suffered. We were penalized for providing good service.

4 Communication between hospitals and GPs was awful. We did a survey (published in *The Times*) that showed – for eighteen hospitals – that initial discharge chits, after patients had left hospital, were received for only 60% and the full medical summary of the patient's admission was received, on average, six weeks later.

5 Diagnostic services were poorly supplied to GPs by the local hospitals. If we wanted a blood test, cardiograph and chest X-ray, we would have to send the patient to three different hospitals. We had no facilities ourselves. We were betrayed by the NHS.

6 The dean of the local teaching hospital used to tear up GPs' letters unopened – in the presence of the patient – saying that they were not worth reading. Without test results, that was largely true.

False Belief: Governments make the world a better place.

Notes:
I am a political animal. My parents were not politically active but, in my formative years, I was brought up primarily by my uncle, Michael Stewart, a Socialist Member of Parliament. He entered the House of Commons under Clement Atlee, in the heady election after the Second World War. The welfare state was born and I was very proud to be a supporter of it, even though I was one of only three boys who would have voted Labour in a school of four hundred and twenty. I was once knocked unconscious for my political views. That fixed them in.

In my medical student days in London, I was an active member of the North Kensington Labour Party and I also helped my uncle in his Fulham constituency. I was totally committed to the National Health Service and to the welfare state in general. In my years as a junior doctor, I joined the British Medical Association and the Royal College of General Practitioners and I served on various committees in order to further their organizational and educational aims.

Later, after four years in my medical practice, I felt betrayed: I became totally disillusioned by the Social Contract brought in by Harold Wilson between his (Labour) government and 'all useful people'. As a medical practice with high expenses (we had excellent premises and plentiful staff) we found that, under this contract, our expenses would rise by thirty per cent and our income by only five per cent. Clearly we were not 'useful'. I resigned from the Labour Party and joined the Liberals.

I wrote the Health section in the Liberal Candidates Handbook and I wrote the Parliamentary speech for the 'pay beds' debate. I fought the February 1974 general election (called by Edward Heath on the issue of 'Who rules Britain, the government or the trade unions?'). I lost. We lost. Labour got in again and I thought of emigrating.

Facts:

1 I was never a firebrand: I did not march or shout or throw things. I preferred to fight bad ideas with what I considered to be better ideas – and then demonstrate their effectiveness in practice.

2 If an idea does not work in practice then, however good it sounds, it is a bad idea. The NHS clearly did not work in general practice (its gateway) in cities (where most people live) – and it is therefore a bad idea. Its problems were not due to under-funding (it had plenty) or to bad management (it wasn't that poor) but to the inadequate ideas upon which it is based. I wrote out my challenges to the basic principles of the NHS – but nobody would publish them: it was a sacred cow. These ideas are now reproduced in the final pages (98–100) of this section.

3 My belief in a compassionate society has not changed over the years. However, political parties have changed: tolerance and discussion have given way to pressure groups and direct action.

4 I have come to agree with the Russian/American writer and philosopher, Ayn Rand, that the difference between a welfare state and a totalitarian state is merely a matter of time. Her book *Atlas Shrugged* shows why.

5 After losing the election, I resigned from the medical practice that I myself had created. I could see that it would never create new ideas – and I was not interested in doing anything other than that. My wife, understandably thinking of our children and of our mortgage, asked what we would do next. I replied that I did not know – but that I could not continue as I was.

6 We visited Canada and the USA. We saw amazing general medical practices and we were offered wonderful new opportunities. We saw the full extent of the betrayal of ideas by the NHS in the UK. But we decided not to emigrate. We love London. We resolved to bring the best clinical and management ideas back home, rather than run away.

False Belief: The value of something is what you paid for it.

Notes:
Every time property prices went up, I remortgaged our home and bought an additional property. The first was a fourteenth-century cottage in East Kent. The facilities were slightly more modern. We absolutely loved it. Because I worked so hard during the week (in one year I used to visit a Saudi prince after midnight – at his request – every night except Saturday: it was exhausting but it paid the school fees), the cottage became, in effect, our family home. We used to walk in the woods, search for wild orchids, cycle to the seaside, toboggan on the hills, talk to the local cows and generally have a blissful time.

In due course I remortgaged the cottage and bought two tumble-down cottages by the sea, modernized them and sold them. Then I bought two cottages in even worse repair in mid-Wales and did them up. On some weekends we went to Wales instead of Kent. Three young children and the two of us and an Afghan hound would fit into an MGB. We knew that – we did it.

Then I bought the undeveloped farm next to our cottage in Kent and took on the sheep and New Forest ponies as well as the manager. Then, with the help of an architect, I designed a pig unit and, at night, I visited pig farms all over southern England. I failed to get planning permission. My expenses went up and my income went down.

Then I bought... disaster. Property prices crashed and so did I. All our property had to be sold but our friendly bank manager (they did exist in those days) allowed us to stay in our London home, even though we owed more than it was worth. Our children had to come out of private schools and go to the local state schools. They were bullied for being 'posh'. Our elder son (who beat me at chess) was said to be not up to the academic standard of a two-thousand pupil comprehensive school.

Facts:
1 All investments are gambles. I wanted a gamble in which I pitted my skills – such as they were – against those of other people. Maintaining safety never creates anything.
2 Gamblers eventually lose everything if they believe that luck – or markets – can go only one way. That is called stupidity.
3 I've experienced ups and downs. The ups were as wonderful as the downs were disastrous. If I betrayed my wife and children in our bad times, I also gave them some fabulous good times.
4 The Saudi royal family is nocturnal. That's the down side – but they can also be very generous. Again, I may have betrayed my wife by my odd working hours (the children were asleep by the time I went out) but we all got the financial benefit – and we had some extraordinary parties.
5 Property development is a profession. So is farming. They are not hobbies.
6 State schools in London did not compare favourably with those in rural areas – academically or socially. I tried to earn money, on top of my medical earnings, so that I could give my children a good education. I did not give them any stability. They suffered as a result of that. Whatever my good intentions, I betrayed them by failing to deliver this basic provision of parenting.
7 Nowadays GPs make a lot of money. We didn't in those days. I don't think the NHS betrayed me: I knew the score. I could have moved to the countryside if I had wanted to – but I was on a crusade (at my children's expense) to show how general medical practice really could be run. To do otherwise would betray myself.
8 Bank managers may be individually friendly even today but they are ruled from above and have no discretionary powers. I have no complaint against banks: I don't like them but I know how they function. Nobody betrays anybody in an open trading relationship.
9 Our son's headmaster definitely betrayed him.

False Belief: The effects of childhood trauma last for life.

Notes:

Neither Margaret nor I had any significant previous relationship. Although I had spent two years in the Army, I was still only a boy emotionally. At the age of sixteen I had kissed a girl once on the cheek – and then I ran away. My concept of a girlfriend was a friend who happened to be a girl. Margaret's experience was no more profound than mine.

We both recognized that our childhoods were over and that we wanted to create our present and future with each other. We also realized that we had to do the necessary work if we wanted to grow: to develop individually and to become closer together. This was not going to happen by itself merely as a result of getting older. We wanted to get something out of life by putting something into it. We never lost this sense of wonder or, in any way, diminished our love of adventure. Life is for living.

In our early years together we were focused on building a home, raising a family and creating a business. Later on we wondered what we really wanted to make of our lives – and we found out: we wanted to stay together (as far as we could) and keep our homes and our businesses together. On occasions, just surviving was enough of a challenge. We never lost our sense of fun, nor our commitment to loving each other, loving our children (exasperating though they, like anyone else's children, could be at times), loving our work and loving other people. There was a great deal of love in our lives.

Some friends had told Margaret that we were bound to break up if we worked together. We did work together for almost all of our lives and we didn't break up. I don't suppose that our problems were any less challenging than those of other people – but we decided to work through them and we succeeded. Not only that: we had a great deal of pure, glorious, hilarious fun.

Facts:

1 Different phases of life require different approaches and attitudes. The first requirement is to get over the abuse and betrayals of childhood. There is no point in carrying all that baggage for the rest of our lives and then damaging our future relationships through being obsessed with the past.

2 Some people imagine that it takes a lot of time to get over the hurts of the past. It is in therapists' financial interests to get us to believe that. The truth is that we may need a bit of help in changing our direction but, ultimately, we ourselves have to make the decision to move on – and then do so.

3 'Survivors workshops' tend to perpetuate self pity and blame. The 'inner child' needs less attention than the inner adult.

4 Innocence is no bad thing.

5 There are many things that we have to do all at the same time in early married life, when we are trying to settle into the relationship as well as build a home, a family and a business.

6 It is a miracle that any relationship survives. Even sexual infidelity does not have to destroy a relationship. Recurrent sexual infidelity, however, needs treatment: a common long-term end result is suicide as a result of the inevitable loneliness.

7 We get out of a relationship whatever we put into it.

8 We may have had poor examples of building successful long-term relationships and we are commonly taught nothing whatever in school about this crucial aspect of our future lives. But do the teachers themselves know how to create long-term relationships? They betray us if they try to teach something they themselves cannot do. We have little choice but to find our own way – and to have confidence that our way is probably as good as any other, provided that we remain kind and considerate.

9 Daughters are difficult. Sons are worse. No betrayal there: just reality.

False Belief: Government departments innovate.

Notes:

Margaret and I came back from Canada and the USA inspired by what we had seen in general medical practices: diagnostic facilities (pathology laboratories, X-ray and ultrasound units, cardiographs for heart tests and spirometers for lung function tests) and physiotherapy units. We decided to copy them and try to persuade our own government and the British Medical Association and the Royal College of General Practitioners that these would be more cost-effective and more clinically efficient than traditional health centres (which had chiropodists and district nurses providing valuable social services but no diagnostic facilities that would help in clinical diagnosis of the early signs of significant illness).

I bought the adjacent flat to my previous group practice premises, employed an architect to design the premises (an almost unheard-of concept in general medical practice in those days) and selected the diagnostic equipment. Planning permission took one year and converting and equipping the unit took another year. Meanwhile I earned a fortune (because my expenses were so low), working from a single room in the back of my former premises.

I employed – at my own expense – a radiographer, a medical laboratory scientist (assisted by my wife who got yet another professional qualification) and a nurse practitioner (whom I sent over to the USA for training and who, I believe, was the first in the UK). I gave all my 3,500 NHS patients free use of my diagnostic and therapeutic services (the cost of the X-ray films and the laboratory reagents were minimal). I began to take private, fee-paying, patients for the first time in my life but this meant that the more I earned from private practice, the less I was paid by the NHS for my premises and secretarial staff.

After four years I had convinced nobody – so I left the NHS.

Facts:

1 The cost of converting and equipping the premises was three times the purchase price of the original flat but no equipment decayed and very little went out of date. It was a very sound investment.

2 The government paid nothing whatever towards the cost of the conversion or the equipment or the salaries of the specialist staff. However, this did not stop the government's own Central Office of Information from using my premises as a demonstration of the wonders of the NHS. The one journalist, from *GP Magazine*, who came to our open day reported that 'There seems to be no demand for Dr Lefever's swanky, North-American style practice'.

3 I was getting virtually nothing for looking after my 3,500 NHS patients (after I calculated the proportion of my premises and staff time that they used). Eventually, when I resigned from the NHS, I was told by one of them – an accountant – that I had betrayed my NHS patients by depriving them of my services.

4 Mine was not the first such unit in London. I was not the only innovator. However, we pre-dated NHS general medical practice by thirty years.

5 I paid for consultants to report the X-rays and to supervise the laboratory. Yet, even then, the costs of my services were far less than those of a traditional health centre – because our staff were flexible (everyone covered reception) and our premises were well designed (saving lots of very expensive space). My blueprint was intended for larger units.

6 Working in our unit was wonderful fun for us. The patients obviously valued the service (even though my former NHS group practice was still next door), partly because it was so personal and partly because it saved them so much time – and time (although the NHS did not realize it) is money.

7 I did not feel betrayed by the NHS because it was made clear in advance that my ideas were not wanted. Health officials described them as 'the thin end of a wedge'.

False Belief: Medical partnerships are made in heaven.

Notes:
In choosing my own partners, rather than joining an existing partnership, I was exceedingly fortunate.

My first partners, in my group practice, were both Cambridge graduates. One was a professional musician and the other played the trumpet but was more interested in sailing. We could hardly go wrong – and we didn't. The general difficulty with three-person partnerships is that all the contentious decisions split two-to-one, so someone always feels aggrieved. That didn't happen to us because we didn't do anything contentious: we enjoyed our work and we worked hard. When we split up, it was over the age of our children. Clearly, we were going to go bust under Harold Wilson's Social Contract. Either we would have to cut our staff and services or we would have to start taking private patients (which would require us to work in the evenings because none of us was prepared to reduce our hours for NHS patients). My children were at boarding school. Theirs were still at home.

My subsequent partner (a former student and assistant of mine) in fully private practice was with me for ten years. We had similar attitudes towards clinical work and investment of time and money in the practice and we liked each other's friends and families. These potentially divisive issues commonly break up other partnerships. Eventually we parted over our diverging clinical interests. I was smitten by my new insights into the nature of, and appropriate treatment for, addictive behaviour, while he was more interested in physical ailments, being a much better doctor than I was in this respect. We agreed to separate. He took over the next-door premises when my former NHS partners moved to larger premises that became a health centre. Neither of them stayed in practice for very long. They became disillusioned with the NHS. My private partner is doing well.

Facts:

1 Partnerships in small practices are difficult. In larger practices they are even more difficult – because nobody feels
heard. A group of small practices working alongside each
other in a large building that has diagnostic facilities and
other communal services, appears to me to be ideal.

2 We should remember that Dr Harold Shipman, the mass
murderer of his patients, worked alongside other doctors
in a large unit – but the fact that he was not picked up was
the fault of the Home Office for not monitoring pharmacies for prescriptions of large quantities of dangerous
drugs and also the fault of the Department of Health for
monitoring only the cost of drugs, when morphia – his
killing drug – is cheap. The government used the Shipman
case as an opportunity to drive through its opposition to
small practices (that are less easy to control politically) and
allowed the General Medical Council to take the blame for
not monitoring doctors more tightly. Subsequently the
GMC membership became predominantly lay people
rather than doctors. This betrayed the medical profession.
Another consequence was that the GMC was criticized
for not striking off Dr Shipman when, as a young man, he
appeared before them for abusing drugs. This resulted in
the impression that he killed because he was an addict.
This is a gross betrayal of doctors who suffer from addictive disease. Few asked for help after that: they remained
addicted while treating patients.

3 It might be best for government to be divorced from the
provision of health care, while still paying from general
taxation for specific services. The same principle could
apply to educational services.

4 The fundamental issue is that governments betray the population they are elected to serve. Fiddling Parliamentary
expenses is trivial, as is the failure to deliver on party election promises when in government. The real political
betrayal is failure to monitor the outcome of their policies.

False Belief: 'Good' ideas should not be challenged.

Notes:

My first published article was in the *British Medical Journal*, written when I was aged thirty-seven. I wrote about the new academic departments of general practice in teaching hospitals and about the fledgling Royal College of General Practitioners. I was very much in favour of both. GPs need to be as professional as hospital doctors. However, I now feel a bit betrayed by both these institutions because I believe that they have become wings of the NHS and have lost their independent spirits.

Nowadays I see myself as a writer: my journalism and broadcasting has taken over from music as my creative channel, although I am still, first and foremost, a clinician. I became a full member of the Medical Journalists Association. I was the medical editor of *Medical News* and *Mims Magazine*. Both died. I was the weekly doctor for *Good Afternoon* on Thames Television and *The Saturday Morning Show* on London Weekend Television. Both the shows died and so did both the TV channels. I don't think I was entirely responsible for that. I wrote regularly for *GP Magazine* and *Woman's Own*. I once contributed to five TV shows in one day, when the press thought I was looking after Michael Jackson. It gave me an opportunity to put across some ideas on treatment for addiction.

When I wrote *The Diary of a Private Doctor*, with three strands (clinical, personal and political), fifteen publishers said they were interested. One said that I could be 'the Herriott of the medical profession'. However, they all said that I should 'drop the politics'. I refused. The NHS will never improve its services while it is a sacred cow. One publisher asked me to write a book on the sex life of Arabs. I suggested that he should examine his palms to see if there were tufts of hair. Eventually I published my own book – but vanity publishing is unrewarding.

Facts:

1 General medical practice is an art. It cannot be made into an academic subject. To my mind, it primarily involves the early diagnosis of significant physical illness and the appropriate (non-medicinal) treatment of the emotional problems of today so that they do not become the physical problems of tomorrow. I see GPs as skilled clinicians, not as failed hospital doctors, as Lord Moran – Sir Winston Churchill's (hospital) doctor – described them.

2 Health centres – the holy grail of politicized health care – provide a valuable social input, through the services of district nurses and social workers but social concepts betray all who want to do serious clinical work in general medical practice. GPs should not routinely work alongside these professionals. Each has his or her own specialist work to do. Nor should they work alongside hospital doctors – as a sorting office so that the Great and the Good consultants are not troubled by 'trivia'. Specialists need familiarity with the common man and with common clinical conditions.

3 Social problems require social (political) solutions. The medicalizing of social problems – with consequent vast over-prescription of antidepressants and tranquillizers and sleeping tablets – is a clinical betrayal of the first order.

4 Institutionalizing general practice changes its nature: the relationship between GPs and patients is primarily personal.

5 In forty years as a GP, I did a total of a quarter of a million consultations, but in one published article I could reach many thousands of doctors and in two minutes on ITV's *News at Ten*, I could get across a couple of points to six million viewers.

6 The public tend to be most critical of journalists (they rank lower than politicians in polls on honesty) when they themselves are least informed on the subject in question. In this respect the public betray the journalists.

7 Sticking to our beliefs can result in paying a high price – but can be the right thing to do to avoid betraying ourselves.

False Belief: Private practice is for fools, thieves and charlatans.

Notes:
When I resigned from the NHS, only a very few of my former patients asked to stay with me in my private practice. I was given a few stern lectures by True Believers in the NHS but these were offset by some people who used private practice for the very first time when they came to me.

In my first year I made a tiny profit. I was very proud of that. I offered a service that was in direct competition with the NHS practice that I myself had created next door. People chose to see me (and to pay my fee and the cost of medications) when they had a free alternative. By contrast, some others said to me that they could see no point in having a private GP because an NHS GP could always refer them to a private specialist whose fees would be covered by private insurance.

After three years I was so busy that I took on a full-time assistant who subsequently became a partner. That was an excellent decision and we worked happily together for the next ten years. We remain friends and we respect each other's skills.

I became a private doctor by conviction, not because I wanted to have more time for patients or for myself. I worked the same long hours that I had done previously. I wanted to innovate and I did. I could never have built my GP unit in the NHS. Nor could I have built my addiction rehabilitation centre without funding it entirely myself or through a charity.

I had no interest in making vast amounts of money. My former partners were, eventually, comfortably off in the NHS but I would not have had the freedom to create. I loved my work as a GP, both state and private. I loved the patients equally: I am a people person – it makes little difference which people. I feel that I have been immensely privileged in my chosen profession.

Facts:
1 Some patients followed me when I entered private practice but the vast majority did not. NHS and private populations are different. Financial strength is obviously an important factor but, in general practice, the average total cost of private care in a year would be less than many people spend on alcohol, cigarettes and gambling.
2 Over the years I contributed (without charge) to the training of many medical students. They owe no subsequent allegiance to me or to the private sector. Nor do I belong to the NHS simply because I was (rather patchily) trained in it. I did not betray it.
3 NHS patients who had benefited from the use of my own private X-ray and laboratory facilities did not betray me when they stayed with the NHS after I left it.
4 My views on the NHS changed, from being those of a True Believer to being a critic, as a result of observation that it did not work in major cities – where most of the population live. General practice is the gateway to the NHS and early diagnosis in general practice is therefore vital. Without facilities and staff to achieve this, general practice is merely a social service.
5 A private service that looks after a privileged few has no base from which to criticize the NHS. The challenge is not how we can look after some people excellently but how we can look after large numbers of people at all.
6 There are as many crooks and charlatans in the NHS as in the private sector. There are as many dedicated and hardworking doctors in the private sector as in the NHS
7 Making a profit in private general medical practice, where there is no reimbursement of fees by insurance companies, indicates that it is providing a service where the NHS fails.
8 All doctors should be interested in diseases. GPs also have to be interested in people – seeing their idiosyncrasies and foibles as well as their housing and employment conditions.

False Belief: Doctors should relax by playing golf and partying.

Notes:
I have no interest in horses, nor in playing golf, nor in parties. I have travelled all over the world in the course of my work but I tend not to travel for holidays – or even take holidays at all. It is amazing that I am a doctor of any kind, let alone a private one.

I love opera, ballet, theatre, film, literature, art, architecture and sculpture. My active interests have included singing, politics, farming and property development. I would do almost anything rather than get on a horse, play golf or share an evening with people who are getting progressively more drunk. Do I betray my profession or even my gender? I think not.

Our cottage in Kent was sheer heaven. When it was totally destroyed by an arsonist who, I believe from the graffiti left behind, disapproved of my contribution to a television programme on Sex and Love Addiction, I wept. It was our own personal paradise, our opportunity to be off-duty, even if the telephone was always with me. Evidently the arsonist said that he had been told by God to destroy our cottage. His psychiatrist said that he was depressed but made no mention of the possibility of schizophrenia. The arsonist was sent to Broadmoor Hospital and was discharged after three years. We rebuilt the cottage, making it even more beautiful but with modern facilities, a study, a larger kitchen and an extra bedroom.

I do not relax by watching television. I rarely watch it at all other than for the news or for an occasional comedy show or for a national event. I prefer to read or write or lie in a hammock.

I don't smoke or drink alcohol or caffeine or eat sugar or refined flour or take recreational drugs or any mood-altering medicines, such as tranquillizers, antidepressants or sleeping tablets. I do not find any of these substances relaxing. They would injure my peace of mind, spontaneity, creativity, energy and enthusiasm.

Facts:

1 A study done by one of my contemporaries in medical school showed that twenty per cent of us did everything. We ran, or performed in, the music and dramatic societies, the Christmas show, the chess club and various sports. Some doctors have chosen careers in the arts. They betrayed nobody: they enrich our society.

2 Medical students are selected, appropriately, on being good at science. When they have few other interests, this is a betrayal of the emotional needs of their future patients, who should be seen as much more than diseased or disorganized machines.

3 There are significant risks in taking on unpopular work, such as the human-spiritual (rather than pharmacological) care of addicts of any kind. Do I betray my family by doing this work?

4 The reluctance of some doctors to diagnose schizophrenia betrays the victims of psychotic attacks.

5 An initially unpleasant event can be mentally reframed as an opportunity for creative development.

6 Adults in the UK generally watch four hours of television a day. Children generally spend a similar amount of time on computer games, Facebook and Twitter. Our society appears to be withdrawing into itself.

7 Mood-altering substances are taken and prescribed precisely because they alter the mood. This betrays the integrity of the mind. Some people have a depressed mood, a sense of inner emptiness. When they discover the effect of mood-altering substances and processes, they are understandably reluctant to give them up. In this way they become addicted. Other people have moments of crisis and use (or are prescribed) mood-altering substances. In both cases, there is a risk of causing a dependency on substances which are ineffective, dangerous in overdose and which delay starting effective behavioural treatments that give patients responsibility for their own well-being, when shown how they can do this.

False Belief: Addicts are a waste of doctors' time.

Notes:

A young girl asked me whether a particular drug was 'mood-altering'. She described herself as 'a recovering heroin addict' and said that she went regularly to Narcotics Anonymous. I asked whether that meant that she held hands under Waterloo Bridge. She asked whether I had ever been to a meeting of NA and, if not, how I could be so sarcastic.

She took me to my first meeting – where I promptly met three more of my patients. I asked them why they had not told me that they were addicts (because that was surely something that a GP should know). They replied, 'You're a doctor. You wouldn't understand'. From that moment on, I decided to do what I could to increase my understanding of recovery from addiction and to help addicts of all kinds to become free from their shackles.

Every evening after work, during that summer, I went to an addiction treatment centre and learned from the patients what they had done to become addicted and what they were now doing to be rid of it. They suggested that I would learn more if I became an in-patient myself, even though they did not suggest that I was an addict of any kind.

I enrolled on the 'professionals in residence' course in Hazelden in Minnesota. This took the form of opening the door to one of the residential sets, ushering me in, and then closing the door. For a week, I worked alongside a Chicago cop, a Kentucky horse thief, a New York stockbroker, a Mexican drug-runner, a Maine insurance broker and other men with whom I could see nothing in common – except that I felt that they were 'my people'. In all my life, even at Cambridge or at the Royal College of Music, I had never felt so much at home. In the subsequent year I went to Hazelden five more times, spending all my holiday time there. I learned a great deal about myself as well as about their work.

Facts:
1 My medical school betrayed students by teaching us nothing about addiction, other than how to treat the medical consequences.

2 Subsequently, even my medical partner described my work with addicts as being 'not really medical'. I asked him if he would say the same about helping people to give up smoking. This illustrates the division in attitudes that we had towards what GPs should do with our time. I felt that we should try to intervene in emotional and social issues before they had medical consequences. Sixteen years in the NHS had given me that perspective, alongside my personal experience in Hazelden, where I saw addicts becoming totally drug-free and happy and constructive – their real selves.

3 Another private GP was totally dismissive, saying that I 'let the side down'. I feel that he betrayed his addictive patients, just as I myself had done previously.

4 I learned more from patients than I ever learned from other doctors, psychiatrists included, or from psychologists. I now learned a basic principle of counselling: if we look we shall see; if we listen we shall hear. The 'counselling' usually done by medical and nursing staff is little more than giving factual information – interesting but not curative. Frightening people doesn't help them. It betrays Nurse Edith Cavell's Crimean War instruction to her staff – 'First do no harm'. Addicts already know that what they are doing is harmful but they do not know how to stop doing it or stay stopped.

5 By spending so much time with addicts, I was thought by some of my general practice patients to be betraying them – and they left, which is their right. I certainly betrayed my wife and children, giving them no family holidays while I followed my personal, self-aggrandizing, passion.

6 Margaret later felt that she had betrayed our children by spending so much time working with me. She never betrayed them: I did. I was the addict. I dominated the decisions.

False Belief: Staying married is easy.

Notes:

At the time that Margaret and I got married, I was thin. Within four years of my qualification as a doctor, I had put on fifty pounds. Every so often, on crash diets, I would take it off – but then it would creep back on again. It was not until we had been married for twenty-three years that I finally acknowledged that I had an eating disorder and that I was also a compulsive gambler (on property ventures rather than in casinos), compulsive shopper and spender, and workaholic. In addition to all this, I was also a compulsive helper doing too much for other people and not enough for myself and my family – because of my need to be needed by everyone else and my preparedness to take severe risks in the process.

Margaret told me that I was hell to live with. I knew that I had a fiery temper at times (I thought that apologies would neutralize the effect), but I paid the mortgage and the school fees, I did not get drunk or use drugs, and I did not hit her. I was not a model husband but I simply did not see how awful I was. When Margaret told me that she had been attracted to someone else, I asked our GP, who knew us well, what was wrong with her. He said, 'It's not her: it's you'.

I agreed to seek help in a mental nursing home. It housed seventeen old ladies. I was in a side ward. There were no pictures on the walls. My only human contact was with the lady who brought my meals. The consultant psychiatrist did not visit me once: he did not need to do so in order to get paid by my private medical insurance company.

After three days of sensory deprivation. I discharged myself and told Margaret that she could have the houses and the children and half my income but not have me at that price. She took me home again. Subsequently I paid her back by becoming briefly infatuated with someone else: the mark of a self-pitying addict.

Facts:

1 The principal psychopathology of any active addiction is denial. The sufferers from any form of addictive disease simply do not see it. We justify, rationalize and explain our behaviour – to ourselves as well as to everyone else – but we do not see its true nature.

2 The early years of married life, or of any relationship, are difficult. As I have said, building a long term relationship at the same time as building a business and a family, is extremely demanding.

3 The outlets for addictive disease come in clusters. It is rare for addicts to have just one outlet, such as alcohol, without at the same time being addicted, say, to nicotine and caffeine. All outlets need to be addressed.

4 The best definition of addiction that I know is 'the inability to predict what will happen, in any day, after the first use of a mood-altering substance or process'.

5 Through my addictive behaviour, I betrayed my wife. She did not betray me by falling in love with someone else. I drove her to it. I betrayed her by retaliating.

6 Addicts tend to see our own behaviour only when we are in pain. Compulsive helpers, who take away our pain, make it less likely that we shall seek help in order to change our behaviour.

7 Compulsive helping is perhaps the most destructive of all addictive behaviours – particularly in the hands of politicians.

8 Apologies can be repeated a thousand times – and they often are – but they mean nothing without a change in our behaviour.

9 The consultant psychiatrist betrayed me and also his profession. The private medical insurance company betrayed me by taking all consultants on trust.

10 With good will, relationships can survive anything.

11 Any concept of 'levelling the score' in a relationship – as I did – can lead only to further destruction. We betray ourselves and other people when we play psychological games.

False Belief: Rehab lets addicts off the hook.

Notes:

After my experience in Hazelden, I was still not aware of my own addiction. However, I knew that I wanted to work with addicts even while continuing my general medical practice. I liked that work and I liked my patients and I wanted to keep my feet on the ground, rather than lose my sense of perspective on the behaviour of the general population.

For my training in addiction treatment, I visited rehabilitation centres all over the USA as well as visiting the few, rather basic ones, in the UK. I met the giants in the field, such as Betty Ford, Father Martin, Patrick Carnes, Claudia Black and Geraldine O Delaney – who knew Dr Bob and Bill W, the co-founders of Alcoholics Anonymous personally and who was still running a treatment centre in her nineties. With their encouragement, I became determined to bring back to the UK the best of what I had seen.

I went to SECAD, the major addiction conference in the world and I met even more greats, such as Governor Hughes who was responsible for the amendment to the Constitution of the USA that established alcoholism as a disease, rather than as a weakness of will or a depravity. Out of curiosity, I attended a meeting of Overeaters Anonymous and saw myself in the mirror of others. I have attended these meetings and those of other anonymous fellowships, including AlAnon for family members and friends of alcoholics, several times a week ever since.

Returning to the UK, I established a charitable trust to raise money for a rehabilitation centre. The board members were the Greatest of the Good. After a year, we had raised not a penny: nobody would believe that a private GP could have charitable intentions. Margaret and I therefore remortgaged everything and raised the money for a rehab of our own.

Facts:

1 Denial is amazingly persistent. My own addictive nature was obvious in my childhood yet I myself did not recognize it until I was forty-seven.

2 I believe that only addicts can help other addicts to get well. We understand each other instinctively and we do not get put off by the abusive attacks that we get from the very addicts we are trying to help, nor by the haughty dismissals from other people, especially doctors and other health care professionals.

3 It is very easy to lose our judgement when overflowing with enthusiasm. My general medical practice protected me from that. Even so, other doctors generally described me as a maverick.

4 The USA is thirty years ahead of the UK in the understanding of addictive disease and its treatment. In Europe there is nothing of significance outside the UK, Scandinavia and Portugal.

5 I could not have had better training. First I had to unlearn what I had been taught in university and medical school, which wasn't very much. In six years I had been given no lesson at all on human psychology. I was educationally betrayed.

6 Our insular arrogance is extraordinary when there is such a wealth of experience and skill just the other side of the Atlantic. We are culturally betrayed by looking back in history instead of forward to those who make it.

7 I believe that an addictive nature is genetically inherited. I go to anonymous fellowship meetings to keep mine at bay and to protect me from betraying myself and my family and others through a relapse.

8 Nobody betrayed me by not giving me money for a rehab. Anyway, by using our own money, Margaret and I determined our own therapeutic principles and policies.

9 Addiction is the most rewarding condition to treat. The Twelve Step programme enables a resurrection of spirit.

False Belief: Time is short.

Notes:
I am often asked how I find the time to do so many things. My answer is that I do only those things that I enjoy. Consequently I don't get tired. I was born with creativity, energy and enthusiasm. That certainly helps. Above all, however, I married the right wife and we worked very closely together – and had a lot of fun doing so.

Constant change protects against boredom and against going stale. New ideas kept me young – and they still do. Disciples are not my friends: I need people to challenge me. That's how I grow. Settling down is a false security: the world moves on all the time and I would soon be overtaken if I were not to move with it.

I have never bothered about personal or professional status. I am not interested in social or professional advancement. I am content simply to be me. Throughout my career as a GP, I have never been in a more 'important' position than I was when I started. As the head of my own treatment centre, I was more concerned with what I learned than who I was.

I have written over twenty books – because the process of writing clarifies my own ideas. I am not frightened of failure: I do not acknowledge the concept. I 'succeeded' in all sorts of things – simply by trying. It's just that they didn't all work out as I had hoped. Other people might see these events in my life as failures but, in many ways, I learned more when things went wrong – because I had to think through my ideas all over again.

I feel that our educational and cultural environments betray us by categorizing us and putting us into boxes with labels on them saying 'doctor' or 'musician', 'success' or 'failure'. I want to be both or all – and more. I overcome this betrayal by ignoring it.

I define myself as 'Robert', nothing more precise than that. This gives me the advantage of never being tied down to one activity or trapped in one set of ideas.

Facts:

1 'Down time':

Bedroom and bathroom	8 hours
Dining room	2 hours
Sitting room	2 hours
Entertainment	1½ hours
Travel	½ hour

This still leaves ten hours for creative work each day, ie a seventy hour working week. I myself tend to cut meal times and sitting times below this, ie there are a huge number of hours in every day. My great privilege is that I work only on what I enjoy. Other people have less privilege and different priorities. We betray ourselves if we waste time through sloppiness.

2 Working with a spouse can enrich the relationship.

3 Change generates more enthusiasm: the stimulus of new challenges maintains energy and a youthful outlook.

4 We need critics – not sycophants – to keep us sharp.

5 Settling down spells o-s-s-i-f-i-c-a-t-i-o-n of the mind.

6 Trying to improve our own self-esteem through particular achievements, by comparison with others, or by association with others (eg the rich and famous) is doomed to failure.

7 Status is for circus artists. Competitions are for racehorses.

8 The twin goals of becoming more skilled in our work and more kind and considerate in our relationships are enough.

9 Mankind is a thinking animal, with greater capacities than merely eating, drinking, excreting and reproducing. Hunter-gatherers had lives that were nasty, brutish and short. Modern man has wonderful opportunities for greater fulfilment.

10 Success and failure exist only in the mind.

11 Don't *try* again at something that doesn't work: *think* again.

12 We are all betrayed when work is seen as a chore that has to be endured or avoided.

False Belief: Good work is its own reward.

Notes:
We looked at buildings for a treatment centre. London was too expensive. East Kent was beautiful, as we knew, and we found a lovely place that already had the necessary planning permission. I found a builder to do the conversion work on plans that I drew up.

We looked for staff and found local people very keen to help us – except the consultant specialists, whom I approached out of politeness to tell them what I hoped to do. The head of the local psychiatric hospital told me that private medical practice is against God's law. The head of the local services for alcohol problems told me that I was not welcome in the area. Local GPs were equally unimpressed and were very reluctant to provide services, even for a high fee.

Finding counselling staff was exceedingly difficult. There were no training programmes in those days so I had to recruit from other centres (people who wanted to leave them) or from the anonymous fellowships (people who had no training at all).

Eventually, I got a team together and I paid for twenty-four of us to go to the USA, to see what really can be done and to get basic training, over two weeks, in getting a programme started. A charity wrote to me and said that they would give me the money for that trip and therefore I was able to borrow the money from my bank on the strength of their letter.

The training was more on paperwork than on practical skills and it was not worth the investment. The proposed head of our family unit resigned on our return and the doctor, whom I had persuaded to join us, told me that his wife would not let him work with addicts. The charity told me that they could not give me the money after all. The bank therefore closed down all my accounts – on the medical practice and the treatment centre.

Was I betrayed? I think not.

Facts:

1 Working for the state is nothing like as demanding as working in the private sector. I know: I have been the senior partner of significant practices in each.

2 Getting planning permission for an addiction treatment centre is very difficult. When I subsequently tried to get permission for follow-on facilities (where the patients would already be clean and dry) in Kent and in London, I was opposed by three hundred and fifty local residents in each case. I was very fortunate to find the treatment centre building, with its existing planning permission.

3 Consultants own their local patches and do not like interloping GPs. Some have direct lines to the Almighty. NHS GPs were keen to get private work – at their price, which was higher than mine.

4 Counsellors can be God's gift at times. I was told by my own staff that my job was to find the patients and that I was not to interfere with their work as counsellors.

5 Working with charities can be dangerous. Borrowing from banks is even more so. Paying for professional training does not guarantee skill or even competence.

6 When staff moved on, I learned to be grateful that they had not stayed. Working in an addiction treatment centre is very demanding. Staff have to be fully committed to that work. None of them betrayed me by leaving: they would have betrayed me by staying, if they were not up to the job.

7 People are understandably frightened of working with addicts, or of having addiction treatment centres in their locality. Newspaper stories tend to focus on disasters associated with active use of drugs or alcohol. NHS clinics that supply drugs to addicts are the worst example of what people imagine rehabilitation clinics do, whereas we actually do the opposite: take the drugs away. We do have disasters but we are trying to clean up the local community (there are drugs everywhere) rather than bring drugs in.

False Belief: Addiction comes from a disturbed childhood.

Notes:
My own childhood was odd, in my separation from my parents, but no more so than that of many other boys. The abuse I had at school was more, but not much more. My own addictive nature was obvious already. My wife had a dreadfully abusive childhood but never became an addict of any kind, other than being a compulsive helper – caring too much for others (even in her early childhood) and not caring sufficiently for herself. I am not the one to judge whether I was abusive to my children. Certainly I did a lot of shouting and, at times, hitting. Also we did have many reversals of fortune that were very unsettling for the family.

I am sad and ashamed over all of this but I am not convinced that this caused my elder son's addiction, although it may well have caused all sorts of insecurities. I think I handed on my addictive genes to him. I know a very large number of addictive families and I have found no common pattern of abuse or abandonment. And when looking at individuals in those families with an addictive nature (including alcohol, drugs, prescription drugs, eating disorders, nicotine and risk-taking) there was no direct correlation between abuse and abandonment and addiction.

Against that, we had a lot of fun. In London we went to the parks and to the shows and our children had many friends of their own. Five families in our immediate area used each other's homes as communes. In Kent we enjoyed every aspect of the countryside – the fields and woods and the seaside. In Wales we went wild – and fitted in well with the locals.

We had cats and dogs, hamsters and gerbils in London and sheep, ponies and a couple of cows in Kent. In Wales there were fan-tailed kites and buzzards. We had (I had) a rich life.

Some (not all) of our son's friends took drugs.
So did he.

Facts:

1 An addictive tendency can be diagnosed in childhood on these common characteristics:
   - They come from an addictive family.
   - They tend to feel separate from other people.
   - They have big mood swings.
   - They try to control everything with reasons and excuses.
   - They are easily upset.
   - They are easily bored.
   - They often feel lonely, angry, sad and misunderstood.
   - They often feel resentful for being picked upon.
   - They may stop doing things that they previously enjoyed.
   - They do not do as well at school as they did previously.
   - They get into more trouble than before and they pick new friends who also tend to get into trouble.

2 Sometimes it is difficult to distinguish these features from those of normal adolescence – but the addictive child tends to have them excessively.

3 These children are commonly misdiagnosed as suffering from depression or attention deficit disorder.

4 Early diagnosis, as happened with our son, could save many years of emotional turbulence and physical and social damage..

5 School doctors may betray their pupils by paying more attention to physical illness than emotional problems that are associated with an addictive family.

6 My wife and I did not learn these things from a book. Like many other families, we learned through personal experience.

7 Addictive children tend to be highly creative and very imaginative. They are high achievers in things that interest them, such as computer games and rolling the perfect joint.

8 I may have betrayed my family. It is for them to judge.

False Belief: Sit back and let the money roll in.

Notes:
Our counselling director never turned up. Even so, we did a dummy run in the treatment centre, using 'patients' from friends in AA. We found out how to run the treatment programme smoothly and the 'patients' got a week of free treatment. Then, on our first real day, I put in three patients I had been saving up from my medical practice, including one who was the first anorexic patient to be treated in a Twelve Step treatment centre in the UK. Even my own staff felt that this was a step too far in my madness. The assistant counselling director, in recovery from alcoholism, said to me 'Nobody has ever been arrested for being thin in charge of a motor vehicle'. In due course it was the other patients who changed his mind, saying that the emotional processes were identical to those in any other compulsive behaviour. I was mocked by the staff at the major psychiatric hospital but they changed their tune when they thought that there might be money in it for them.

The next patient to be admitted to the centre came in six weeks later. I had no choice other than to take in some free patients, just to keep the staff active. This irritated those patients who were paying the fees. It also resulted in other people wanting free treatment. The family counsellor made no attempt to find appropriate ways of helping family members. He said that was my job. Two counsellors formed a lesbian relationship, to the dismay of the husband (one of the other counsellors) of one of them, and they left in order to explore their own feelings rather than those of the patients. One other counsellor could not take the strain and had to be admitted to a psychiatric hospital. I reflected on what another director had told me in advance: my major problem would always be staff.

Financially we survived by traders very kindly giving us credit, and by remortgaging, but we lost £1,000 a day for a year.

Facts:

1 Throughout the whole time that my wife and I ran the treatment centre, we never paid ourselves any salary other than the cost of the mortgages. Our income from our medical practice was used to keep the treatment centre afloat. We invested our entire assets and lost them. Our indebtedness constantly increased. Despite all of that, there was never any shortage of people to tell us that we were morally wrong to take money for providing clinical services and that we must be making pots of money. These people betrayed us by making false assumptions.

2 I do not feel that any of our counselling staff betrayed us. Counselling addicts of all kinds is the most demanding (and rewarding) clinical work that I know. Burn-out, which I believe is due to unaddressed compulsive helping, is common. Relapse is common when counsellors believe that their daily work with patients helps their own recovery. I give personal, if not professional, respect to anyone who tries to do this work.

3 In addition to our pioneering work with eating disorders, ours was the first treatment centre in the UK to treat nicotine addiction, compulsive shopping and spending, compulsive gambling and risk-taking, sex and love addiction and compulsive helping.

4 Despite our continuing goodwill towards AA, there are always some members who resent the existence of treatment centres, saying that we make money out of recovery that has been given freely to us. This certainly underestimates the psychological work that is done in treatment centres, overestimates the recovery potential of the anonymous fellowships on their own, and also may reflect the unwillingness of some members to examine their own widespread addictive tendencies. For me to talk of betrayal, in these circumstances, would be ungenerous.

5 Local traders trusted us and helped us through. It was the professionals who let us down and, maybe, betrayed us.

False Belief: Abstinence is unnecessary and obsessive.

Notes:
Addictive disease runs in families. It probably has both genetic and environmental causes and therefore needs both continuing behavioural and initial social changes. In my own family there is no history of cancer or heart disease or diabetes, except in old age when we all fall apart. However, we are riddled with addiction in every generation. My wife's family was similar. Our children therefore were born into, and grew up in, an addictive family. Problems were inevitable.

Grateful patients used to give me bottles of whisky every Christmas. There was a lot of gratitude – which was nice – but I never kept track of the whisky. Years later I was told by my elder son that he had been drinking himself to sleep since his early teens. My own difficulties meant that he changed school many times – but he also had a part to play in that. He left school early and became a commodity broker in the City of London. His addiction really took off in that environment.

On discovering what we were up against, my wife and I asked for medical help – and got none whatever. It was assumed that we were the problem and that we had to change our behaviour in order to help our son. That was in fact true. We learned from the anonymous fellowships that we had taken too much responsibility for him, rather than too little. When he was seventeen, we gave him the choice: to live with us without his drugs or live elsewhere with them. He replied, 'I am an orphan' – and walked. It was a difficult time for us, knowing the risks he would be running but we simply let him go so that he learned for himself that his addiction problem went with him, wherever he went. We made no attempt to find him. We educated ourselves on the AA Twelve Step programme, that came to revolutionize our family life – for the better.

Facts:

1 Addictive disease is an illness that runs in some families but not in others. Those of us who are troubled by it need to learn what it really is and how it can be treated appropriately though the Twelve Step programme. We learn best from other families like ours. They have the necessary practical experience and human understanding.

2 Other than those who are addicts themselves, doctors tend not – maybe cannot – have any understanding on what to do that will really help addicts and their families to change their behaviour.

3 Our son knew perfectly well what his risks were – but that did not alter what he chose to do. He was driven by an inner compulsion. He had to find out about that for himself.

4 My wife and I were also driven by an inner compulsion to help him compulsively, beyond caring into care-taking, and to deny our own emotional needs. We had to learn about all that from seeing other people who were like us and by observing how destructive that behaviour could be.

5 We can be remarkably blind to something that is happening under our own roof (literally, when someone is growing strange plants), perhaps – in part – by not wanting to see it.

6 Some environments are toxic to feelings and behaviour.

7 We did not betray our son by giving him the choice – and the consequences – of his own behaviour. We helped him to make the discovery of his own addictive disease and what he needed to do for it in order to get into recovery, one day at a time, for the rest of his life. We knew the risks. The risk of doing nothing was greater.

8 Addicts have a way with words.

9 'Geographical cures' – going somewhere else in the hope of escaping from addiction – do not work.

10 When families try to learn all about addiction, it gets in the way of the addict getting better. We betray our loved ones by doing so. We need to learn about – and treat – our own compulsive helping.

False Belief: Doctors should look after their own families.

Notes:
At the time that our son had addiction problems there were very few addiction treatment centres in the UK. We wanted the best for him so we sent him to Hazelden in the USA.

I focused my own attention on learning as much as I could about treating addicts of all kinds in a Minnesota Method treatment centre, employing psychological ideas. I visited all the major centres in the UK and many in the USA, where I also attended numerous conferences. There were no Twelve Step conferences in the UK or anywhere in Europe. When we established our own treatment centre, it took us years to catch up with the Americans but eventually we were able to offer them some ideas of our own.

Margaret trained in Rogerian person-centred counselling and, in due course, ran our family programme. She did wonderfully. She loved the families and they loved her. She understood them instinctively as well as from her personal experience.

The general hostility, by the medical profession and the health authorities, towards Twelve Step ideas and treatment centres continued. We were tolerated but not respected. The most bizarre comment came from a Director of Social Services who expressed the opinion that my centre was a money-laundering front, supplying arms to Saddam Hussein. However, when the government required local authorities to say what they were doing in their local areas to help addicts, we were given pride of place – as if the NHS had created and funded our centre!

In due course, when our son told us that he had decided to go back to drinking alcohol, it was only a matter of time before he went back on drugs. As with any other addict, he had to learn that the brain sees alcohol as just another drug. My staff treated him in our own centre. I stayed well away.

Facts:
1 A common attitude in the UK is that we have nothing to learn from Americans, other than how to make profits from the sick. This keeps us thirty or more years behind their clinical progress and practice. In a psychology conference that had over eight thousand delegates, my wife and I were two of fewer than ten from the UK. Our educators and politicians betray medical students and patients dreadfully by their arrogant isolation. Far from being the envy of the world, the NHS is way behind other developed countries in mortality rates of many common clinical conditions.

2 AA is not run by doctors. Therefore doctors tend not to be interested in it and think that it is for religious nuts and pathetic has-beens. This is a fundamental betrayal of their patients. Although there are two thousand four hundred groups of AA each week in the UK, they are very rarely attended by doctors who are not alcoholics themselves.

3 Counsellors betray their patients if they believe that they need no training beyond their experience in AA.

4 An instinctive love of addicts and of their families should be at the heart of treatment. Otherwise their exasperating behaviour is seen merely as stupidity and belligerence, rather than as an illness.

5 The most forthright critics of the abstinent philosophy of AA are often addicts themselves.

6 Addiction is a chronic relapsing condition. It is like diabetes rather than appendicitis. It has to be managed on a day-to-day basis for life. There is no cure. Education and all forms of medication (common sense and pills) are ineffective – and they are dangerous if they keep the addicts away from seeking more effective treatment. Doctors and social services betray their patients/clients when they persist with clinical approaches that do not lead towards total abstinence and happy and productive lives.

7 We should not work on the addiction problems of our own family.

False Belief: Things settle down in time.

Notes:

After surviving the initial traumatic year, I had hoped that life in the recovery centre would settle down. It didn't.

Managerially, it remained an immense challenge. The patients – addicts of all kinds – were generally much less troublesome than the staff. One significant issue is that East Kent is a peninsula. Staff cannot be recruited from the Thames estuary, the North Sea or the English Channel. We had to take the staff we could find in the local area. For ground staff, chefs, house staff and administrative staff (other than in accountancy) this was no problem. Nursing staff generally wanted to run the place their own way and counselling staff even more so. I appreciated the skills that they did have but there was a general reluctance – perhaps endemic in the UK – to learn new approaches.

We trained our own staff but then they were often bribed away by the big hospital groups that had no training programmes (because they are expensive to run).

The local health authority, with whom we had to be registered, was a hindrance rather than a help. Their inspectors never observed a group therapy session, our major work. They were interested only in the nursing department.

Their tick-box forms had no category for treatment centres so we had to satisfy their criteria for old people's homes. In due course, this meant that bedrooms had to be a certain size. We therefore had to change our bedrooms to offices and build a new bedroom wing. The local planning committee supported us because they said we were doing good work. They had the courage to go against their own regulations for development in an area of outstanding natural beauty. The costs were added to our mortgage.

Despite all this, we loved every minute of the work.

Facts:

1 Choosing to establish the treatment centre in East Kent was a mistake. It is an area of high unemployment for very good geographical reasons. I should have stayed within the boundary of the M25 but I couldn't afford it.

2 Nursing staff are trained within the NHS and they tend to have NHS attitudes. They learn that addicts have to be shown the error of their ways and that they have to be given medication – or counselled sensibly with Cognitive Behavioural Therapy – to help them. Yet again the NHS betrays patients by categorizing them, rather than by treating them as individuals. The NHS also betrays its nursing staff by giving them such narrow training. I would prefer to recruit staff from the private sector or abroad.

3 Counselling staff tend to believe that they know everything that they need to know, simply as a result of being addicts (in recovery) themselves. Such arrogance betrays their patients. A bit of humility would not come amiss.

4 Local health authorities are a destructive, rather than creative, force. Answerability to the government can never be a stimulus towards creating anything original. Local individuals should be trusted to spend their money for their own local benefit. Governments – local or national – betray the population that they are elected to represent and serve.

5 In strong economic times, when property prices rise, costs can be added to mortgages. This increases very real debts but the financial assets that secure this borrowing are illusory. Short-term benefits (beloved by governments because they themselves think only in the short term until the next election) can lead to long-term disaster.

6 I borrowed. I risked. I betrayed. I shall not do so again. The costs of answerability to government are too high. There are other ways of being creative and of loving my work.

False Belief: Charity begins abroad.

Notes:

As the son of missionary parents, I respected them for their beliefs but I have to say that it was difficult for me to be separated from them during my formative years. In my adult life I have been more moved by the neglect of our own people by our own government than by those in countries betrayed by corrupt and nepotistic despots. I believe in giving to individuals rather than making up for deficiencies in government funding.

In the recovery centre we received gifts from some individuals and from one organization and we gave free treatment to many patients (who often assumed that they were being funded by the NHS) but we had no charitable funding because we were not a registered charity. We had, immaturely, tried that route but failed to raise any money.

We took no income other than reimbursement of the expenses incurred in our work. That was a personal choice – just as my parents made theirs. We earned our living in our medical practice. We were happy with that.

I wrote and published many books on various aspects of depression/addiction and I hoped that these would carry our ideas to people who could not afford our treatment. My (forlorn) hope was that these books and my media work would also influence doctors and even the Department of Health.

On a personal basis, Margaret and I gave annual prizes to young musicians at Glyndebourne and the London Symphony Orchestra. These institutions are not funded by the state. Musicians give wonderful pleasure to many people. Margaret described music as her 'breath of life'. We hoped to foster that in others.

We took on the ethics, values and principles of our families, even if our way of expressing them was our own.

Facts:

1 The greatest evils in the world are perpetrated – with the best of intentions – by governments. The smaller the government the lesser the chance of evil and the greater the opportunity for private investment in worthwhile enterprises, as in the foundation of schools and hospitals by Victorian philanthropists in the UK and by individuals in the USA today. We betray these individuals when we allow governments to take over responsibility for the provision of education, health care and welfare. The proper function of government is to uphold contracts and to make it unnecessary for individuals to carry arms.

2 Donations to foreign countries rarely get through to the population in need and often fill the coffers of dictators.

3 Making charitable donations to nuclear powers, as we do today, is crass and it is a betrayal of the hard work of tax-payers, from whom 'government' money is confiscated by force and with significant threat for non-compliance.

4 We may patronize people when we assume that they are not able to look after themselves or capable of creating new productive work .

5 We should each be free to make our own choice on how we spend, or give away, our own money. There should be no sense of obligation and no emotional blackmail. That false morality comes from people who sponge off others, or who wish to control others, when they themselves produce nothing.

6 The only beneficiary of compromise between good work and bad, or between productive work and dependency, is the person who does nothing creative for self or others.

7 The only way of surviving betrayal by the state is to oppose it by producing something better. Despite the welfare state, the public contributes many millions to charity. Kind and generous people are the norm, rather than the exception. The state is not irreplaceable.

8 We betray ourselves when we do not live by our values.

False Belief: Good work will be supported and rewarded.

Notes:
Once the in-patient treatment centre was established in Kent, we needed somewhere in London (from where we got most of our patients) to assess them before treatment and follow them up afterwards.

We could not afford to buy more property but we did have a large home that we no longer needed for our grown-up family. We further excavated the basement and moved into it. We housed twelve patients in the lovely rooms in which we had previously lived. In the five years that we ran it as a 'half-way' house (between treatment and the real world) we lost £1,000 a week – but over ninety per cent of the patients stayed abstinent so it was very well worthwhile.

A change in government regulations on room sizes for residential units (for old people) also caught us. I pointed out that our patients were mostly young and fit and spent most of the day in sports or education. I also showed that we already provided the total amount of space required but used it in a way that was appropriate for our patients. These submissions were rejected: regulations are regulations and we should close five of our twelve beds. That would take us right down so we closed altogether. There was no similar facility in the area so the bureaucrats got their ultimate dream: the regulations were satisfied but there was no work to do.

We opened an out-patient facility in rented premises in South Kensington, near our medical practice and we moved our home to a nearby flat. This was much more convenient and pleasant for us: living underneath twelve pairs of feet is no party – or, rather, that is exactly what it is: constantly.

The out-patient work was just as challenging financially. South Kensington property is expensive and so are staff. We made a significant loss – but many patients and their families got well.

Facts:

1 The major expense of any treatment facility is staff salaries.

2 In central London the second greatest expense is premises.

3 In the private sector these expenses cannot be charged to the taxpayer. The owner of the business pays all. A high gross income (total number of patients times the weekly charge) does not always lead to a profit. The only way that we survived at all was through remortgaging our property each year when the value increased.

4 The standard financial advice is that one should not risk losing one's own home. As I have emphasized previously, my experience is that banks will not lend money without a personal guarantee so one's home is on the line anyway.

5 The only way to take no risk is to work for the state – but then one cannot innovate: the state calls all the shots.

6 The Twelve Step ideas that underpin my work are not accepted by the Department of Health in the UK, who prefer a cognitive behavioural approach (common sense education) – which doesn't work for addicts. The Department betrays addicts in this way.

7 I do believe that I was betrayed – and so were my patients – by the registration authorities. They ticked boxes rather than made sensible judgements based upon the clinical and social needs of particular groups of patients.

8 A significant factor in patients remaining abstinent is the length of time they stay in treatment. This inevitably leads to financial challenges, either for the individual patients or for their families or for someone else who is paying for them or, in our case, for us.

9 The personal rewards of running a treatment centre are enormous. The patients of most doctors get worse in time, through progressive illness. Many of ours got completely well and stayed well, through working the Twelve Step programme on a daily basis for life.

10 The professional rewards are few. Many of my colleagues think of me as a maverick – or worse. That's up to them.

False Belief: Private patients come from the patient tree.

Notes:
In the NHS patients do come from the patient tree: there is no shortage of supply. The private sector is a competitive market: patients have to be found – and kept. They always have the option to seek a further opinion from someone else. In my private general medical practice, I worked next door to the NHS practice that I myself had designed and created.

I had also chosen the doctors in my own style. Very few patients came with me when I went private. I had not anticipated otherwise. There was no betrayal on either side: NHS and private patients are essentially two separate populations, not simply divided on income but on belief in the self-correcting virtue of one or other system.

In the treatment centre I had to market my services. To the wider public, I wrote articles and I paid vast amounts of money on advertising and public relations. Despite being promised dramatic results, absolutely none of it had any effect. This was not a betrayal by those professionals: all marketing is smoke and mirrors – we all know that.

Eventually our patients and their families told their friends. Word of mouth was always our best marketing, exactly as in my private medical practice.

Five years down the line, I remember meeting a doctor who lived near the treatment centre. He knew nothing about it but he did remember our cat, Beetle, who got a *Blue Peter* badge for walking from London back to where he was born in Kent.

If I had worked full-time in the treatment centre, I would not have survived: I needed my medical income. If I had stayed in full-time general medical practice, I would have missed out on the most challenging and professionally rewarding work that I have ever done. I stayed doing both – and loved both.

Facts:

1 The three 'A's of private practice are availability, affability and ability. When the telephone goes, you say 'Yes'. Be polite and considerate. Have something special to sell.

2 All health care is a business. If the NHS gives no thought to its budget, it could bankrupt the entire country.

3 NHS doctors are well paid, relative to teachers and many other professionals except bankers, accountants and lawyers. Private medical specialists can earn a great deal – especially in plastic surgery, cardiology and gynaecology but rarely in paediatrics. Few private GPs earn more than their NHS counterparts. Most earn less.

4 The rewards of the private sector are primarily those of being free to develop one's own ideas.

5 There are semi-private doctors – with an NHS income and pension scheme to support them – who say that what they value is to be able to spend time with their patients. I do not accept that: time is a product of careful organization and delegation. Doctors who see a few private patients while neglecting their NHS patients are creeps. They betray their NHS patients and their NHS paymaster

6 To anyone hoping to establish a private medical practice of any kind (other than in the successful disciplines I have mentioned), I would say that advertising, marketing and public relations are a prodigious waste of money. Get a cat.

7 I very rarely got patients directly from my television appearances but these gave me 'name recognition', which is important. When patients did eventually come to us, they had often heard of us from three different sources.

8 I have often wondered if I could have made more of my work in addiction if I had left my general medical practice – but I could not afford to do so: I had no financial support other than what I earned. Also I did not want to betray my patients, many of whom had stayed with me for decades.

False Belief: Training is for the benefit of students.

Notes:

I was very much aware that, despite being a career GP, I had received no training in counselling. I had been taught about diseases, not about human beings. In the treatment centre, I found that the counsellors knew a great deal about human beings but very little about counselling techniques as such.

I set about getting some training for myself. I did not want my staff to know more about the subject than I did. I spent eighteen months on a one-day-a-week course on analytical psychotherapy. I'm glad I did that so that I could learn for myself how inhuman it is. Then I did basic courses in Gestalt, Transactional Analysis and Choice Theory and I learned a lot. Then I got some exposure to Rational Emotive Behaviour Therapy and Cognitive Behavioural Therapy. I wasn't much impressed with them. I wanted to know how to help people, not simply how to educate them. However, I now had more familiarity with counselling approaches than most of my staff and I could hold my own in group therapy sessions – which are much more challenging (when really using the group, rather than merely being in it) than one-to-one sessions. My training really blossomed when I had repeated training in the USA in Psychodrama, Neuro-Linguistic Programming (NLP) and in Eye-Movement Desensitization and Reprocessing (EMDR).

In due course, with the professor of psychology who headed our research department, we established a counsellor training course in a university, leading to an MSc in addiction psychology. I should have known better: the lecturers had their own ideas and told my staff that they were addicts because they had not been breast-fed. I took my staff – and my money – away. The second university was no better: my staff were told that our Minnesota Method of treating addicts was misguided. This time I myself left: I gave up on universities.

Facts:

1 The consultant psychiatrist William Glasser says that universities exist in order to prevent the spread of human knowledge. That certainly fits with my own experience outside Cambridge. They betray their students.

2 Counsellors themselves can be remarkably resistant to gaining new skills. They merely want paper qualifications. In their narrowness of vision, they betray themselves as well as their patients.

3 State institutions and professional bodies are also obsessed with paper qualifications. These rarely give any guarantee of practical skill or personal commitment. Self-satisfied grandees betray their students and subsequent employers.

4 As Professor Lawrence Weed of the university of Vermont points out, more care is given to the training of airline pilots, where achievement is the constant and time is the variable, than to the training of medical students. The same is true for counsellor training.

5 Sigmund Freud caused a lot of suffering. So do his followers. They betray their patients by analyzing them into a stupor.

6 There is a wonderful array of psychotherapeutic methods nowadays. I am constantly learning new skills, most recently in Cognitive Dialectical Therapy, Positive Psychology and Mindfulness. Counsellors who believe that they know all that they need to know are missing out on fabulous adventures.

7 We need to value our own minds (at whatever level of intellectual and emotional competence) and our own professional life. When people care primarily about appearances on paper, this shows an extraordinary lack of self-esteem and an equal lack of esteem for others. The betrayal is then total.

8 Our society is sick in mind and in heart. Through loving others we come to love ourselves and through loving ourselves we come to love others. This should surely be the yardstick by which counsellors should measure ourselves and each other.

False Belief: Good ideas and good examples will spread.

Notes:
When I created my private medical practice, with its own X-ray and ultrasound unit, laboratory, pharmacy, physiotherapy room and nursing unit (with facilities for testing the function of ears, eyes, lungs and hearts as well as for minor surgery), it was one of the first independent diagnostic centres in London. In due course other doctors, mainly from outside central London where capital costs and salaries are high and where there is easy access to private diagnostic centres in the Harley Street area, developed similar ideas. Some did very well by franchising their ideas. I could have gone down that route but I see myself as a clinician, rather than as a businessman.

My own private medical partner did not take on this idea – nor those of my addiction work – when, after ten years, he left to set up his own practice after the NHS practice next door left for larger premises (with no diagnostic facilities but with district nurses and health visitors, along the standard health centre model that I had moved away from many years previously). I do not believe that I was betrayed by any of my former colleagues. They had the right to implement their own ideas.

Thirty years after I had established my diagnostic centre, the principal advisor to the Department of Health came up with the idea of housing diagnostic facilities in large general practice units of thirty doctors or more, with each of them developing particular expertise in one or another medical discipline. In effect he would recreate the Soviet polyclinic idea. As a hospital doctor, he would inevitably see general practice as a way of relieving hospitals of 'trivia'. He would not see it, as I do, as a specialty in its own right – looking at the emotional and social contributions to physical and mental illness, as well as having the diagnostic facilities to make early diagnoses. He got only half the answer to the challenge of care in the community.

Facts:

1 Early diagnosis of significant physical disease makes a great difference to the outcome. General practice is the gateway to the health services. GPs therefore must have easy access to diagnostic facilities. In my days in the NHS I did a survey that showed that GPs in my area of London arranged, on average, for one pathology test – of any kind – a day, one X-ray – of any kind – a week and one ECG a month. This is clinical neglect of dramatic proportions. No wonder the survival rates from cancer and other significant illnesses in the UK are behind those of other developed countries.

2 Doctors speak about the value of their own time but there is little evidence that they value the time of their patients. By having simple diagnostic facilities on the doctor's premises, the patients can have all the tests done straight away. Saving time saves a lot of money. Failing to do so betrays us all.

3 The cost of the salaries of specialist staff is saved by getting them to do other things as well. In my private general medical practice, I did not employ receptionists or nurses. My radiographers covered reception and did all the tests for the function of ears, eyes, lungs and hearts. They also did all the accounts. They enjoyed the variety in their daily work and they were never hanging around waiting for the next patient. Trade unionists betray their members when they insist on professional demarcation, other than where real safety issues would be concerned: obviously a laboratory scientist has to do the complex tests but anyone can be trained to test a urine sample or to run off an ECG.

4 Soviet polyclinics were dire. The novels of Solzhenitsyn should have influenced the Department of Health. Clearly they did not.

5 General medical practice tends to be an unpopular specialty for young doctors unless they can see it as an easy option to earn more money and have more time off. The NHS has betrayed its doctors and its patients by allowing this bizarre situation to develop.

False Belief: Families have to be told what to do or not do.

Notes:
The man I appointed to be our first 'family counsellor' sat in his office for three months until I dismissed him. He expected me to find patients for him. The woman who succeeded him was scarcely more proactive. I do not recall her ever having more than five family members in her Sunday afternoon sessions, even though she was the wife of one of the senior counsellors.

I asked Margaret if she would do that work. The prospect frightened her because she had no training as a counsellor and she felt overawed by those who did. What she did have was an alcoholic father who had committed suicide, a mother who was the compulsive helper from heaven or hell (depending upon a point of view on whether one wanted help or not), an addictive husband and three behaviourally challenging children. She also had a naturally loving and gentle nature. She got the formal training for herself and she took on the task. Very soon we had family groups of thirty every weekend.

Many families asked Margaret if they could see her also in London during the week so she set up weekly groups and then some five-day workshops in which individual family members worked on their own compulsive helping. This is the addictive tendency in which they need to be needed and tend to do too much for other people – who are led to dependency – and too little for themselves. Margaret would say that her job was primarily to 'guide the traffic' – keep things ticking over while the family members did the work. Heads of major legal firms, doctors or redoubtable housewives would all bask content in Margaret's kind gaze. She understood them from the inside but she never patronized them by saying that she knew how they felt. She knew how to love them as they were and she did so. And they loved her. She had a natural gift, as she did for playing the piano. It was as if she 'played' people – with lovely results.

Facts:

1 Counsellors who believe that they are God's gift, simply because they themselves are in recovery from their own addiction or because they come from an addictive family, have a great deal to learn – but, in my experience, they rarely have the humility to acknowledge that. They betray the families who ask for help.

2 Humility can never be acknowledged in oneself – to do so would be a sign of arrogance – but we can see it in others.

3 In the course of my own addictive behaviour, I betrayed Margaret in many ways – primarily through taking full advantage of her kind and willing nature and getting her to do work, such as medical laboratory science, that she really did not want to do. Against that, I can say that I provided her with a superb piano and I introduced her to the art of family counselling which she loved and which brought out the very best in her. She herself never betrayed anyone. It would be totally contrary to her whole philosophy.

4 When teachers have natural talent, their pupils flock to them because they feel comfortable and they want to learn.

5 Training can bring out the best in people only if they have natural talent in the first place. My own musicianship was never up to the standard of my training. I neither betrayed my teachers nor was I betrayed by them: I lacked the talent.

6 In the UK there are nowadays more counsellors than there are doctors. It takes twelve years to train a brain surgeon. Some counsellors launch themselves onto their patients' emotional brains after twelve weeks' training – or even less – yet, in my view, they can do just as much damage as surgeons. Training courses that are superficial betray the patients whom the counsellors will soon see.

7 Cathartic moments, when patients cry, are not a sign of effective counselling. Mentioning the magic word 'mother' will do that. This betrays the trust of patients. Quietly effective counselling makes huge demands on patients and counsellors equally.

False Belief: Directors direct.

Notes:
Margaret and I were the founding directors of the treatment centre and the counselling centre. To the directors of individual departments, this often meant no more than that we paid the wages. The Counselling Directors took on counsellors and counselling assistants and the Nursing Directors took on full-time nurses, agency staff and care assistants. We built a mountain of staff. Running everything from London, I had little direct control. That was a major error. I had thought that my senior staff would have the same concerns for the business that I had. I betrayed them in this respect: I gave them management trust and responsibilities beyond the level of their professional competence. They all came from a welfare state culture. They did not have private sector experience like mine.

I remember looking at the possibility of employing a Finance Director but the salary that I was quoted was astronomical. In retrospect, I think it would have been worth it: we could have saved a great deal on wages, our major expense. However, I wonder whether that director would have done the work any more competently than the other directors.

It seems to me that the source (apart from myself) of all these problems is in our schools. The general population is betrayed by an inadequate educational system. We teach subjects that have no practical value and we teach little about economics and business management. In the adult world we create further problems through a dependency culture. We teach people their entitlements rather than their responsibilities.

I should have recognized all this myself and kept a firm eye on our profit and loss account, rather than looking at assets and liabilities. I was strong on paper but fragile in reality. In my blind ignorance, I betrayed my staff, my family and myself.

Facts:

1 The title 'Director' can be the kiss of death to responsibility. Repeatedly, it led to the distribution of personal and professional favours by those people – at my expense.

2 'Hands-off' management is fine if one has money to burn – and burn it will.

3 There is no reason why salaried staff should have any of the financial and management perspectives of the owners of a business, be it in health care or industry. In fact health care is a very risky business, precisely because of the common belief that all health care should be free. The inevitable consequence of that belief is slack financial management and control.

4 My business experience was minimal: I had run a large NHS practice but the real control was in the hands of the government. I ran a significant private medical practice but I delegated all financial matters to my accountant while I looked after the patients. In my addiction work, I built up my business so that eventually I employed one hundred and twenty staff. I betrayed them all – including an over-promoted Managing Director – by being totally out of my depth. My skill was in the counselling work, in its various forms, and in caring for staff and for patients but not in monitoring and managing a business. I should have brought in a money man. However, my fear was that he would cut the things that I most valued – such as the family programme and the research and training departments.

5 Our state schools are as weak as our state hospitals. By international comparison they are expensive failures.

6 As I mentioned previously, I believe that the three most valuable subjects that should be taught in schools are how to build and keep a long-term relationship, how to bring up children to be happy and creative and how to make a profit in business. Instead we teach children politically correct attitudes. There is no greater betrayal than that.

False Belief: Compulsive helping is helpful.

Notes:
At school I remember taking punishments for other boys in the hope that they would appreciate me. They didn't. They saw me as an idiot. When they were made prefects before me, they punished me. In the army I was fairly relaxed at times over the behaviour of the men under my command. They did not respect me for that. As a junior hospital doctor, I tolerated appalling working hours and grim living conditions. As a father, I paid off my son's debts – perpetuating his addiction – and I wondered what I had done wrong to get an addict in the family.

In each of these examples, I was either doing too much for other people or doing too little for myself. Either way, I caused myself and my family a lot of damage.

Professionally, I overworked and overpaid. I took too much onto my own shoulders and I rationalized, rather than criticized, when I was let down. Financially, I was particularly careless. I trusted my staff to be honest in their expenditure of my time and money. Most were; some were not – and the few betrayed the many. It never occurred to me that people to whom I was kind and supportive would rip me off – with a smile. Through my lack of responsible supervision I betrayed my good staff.

As someone who is both an addict and a compulsive helper, I never have any doubt about which I am being at any particular time. I was always the addict to my wife and always the compulsive helper to my son. My wife was a compulsive helper to both of us. My son was always the addict to both of us. I believe that each tendency – being an addict or a compulsive helper – is the exact mirror image of the other: we are fatally attracted to each other through our genetic make-up and emotional drives, although the environment of our upbringing does influence how our addiction or compulsive helping expresses itself in practice.

Facts:

1 My compulsive helping is seen in caretaking for others (going beyond normal caring and into patronising molly-coddling, regardless of whether I was actually being helpful in practice) and self-denial (often putting the needs of other people ahead of my own, regardless of the cost to myself).

2 There is no betrayal of self or others in being an addict or a compulsive helper – that's just the way we are. But we still have free will and we are still responsible for our behaviour.

3 Betrayal comes from insensitivity to the effect that our actions have on other people. I betrayed my wife in taking too much trust from her. I betrayed my son in giving too much trust to him. In my primary addictive behaviour, I often betrayed other people by riding roughshod over them. In my compulsive helping, I betrayed myself in doing too much for others and not enough for myself.

4 To be kind and considerate to other people is a lovely thing. It is very un-lovely when we patronize people by assuming that they could not manage to do things for themselves. We may hinder their ability to build their self-esteem on their own achievements. We may sentence them to a self-perpetuating dependency culture.

5 Some people – not all – will steal time or money when they can. In a responsible society we have to prevent them from doing that. We have to live by the rule of law (as few laws as possible), because otherwise we would have to take the law into our own hands. But this means that we have to protect people from perceiving that they need to steal time and money in order to survive or have any form of life that is worth living. This is the great challenge for our politicians – how to create a framework for a compassionate society that is equally considerate to those who produce the goods and services, upon which we all depend, and to those who have little or no capacity to produce anything. Politicians betray us all when they fail in this even-handed task.

False Belief: Trusting staff is kind and creative.

Notes:
In my private medical practice, I employed only a handful of staff. We were a family – yet one staff member, who worked for me for many years, stole from me consistently until I compared what I knew I had earned with what she had paid into the bank. Persistent small thefts added up to a huge total. I remember walking my daughter down the aisle at her wedding, wondering if we would be met at the altar by the bailiff rather than by the priest. When caught red-handed with notes that had been marked by the police, my staff member asked if it meant she would lose her job. She did. She went to prison.

I should have learned my lesson but I didn't. In the treatment centre the same thing happened but the amounts were more substantial. Cheques were altered after they had been signed. Extra tens of thousands were not picked up by the Managing Director or by the accounts staff or by the external accountants and auditors. More significantly, they were not picked up by me. Even though all the debts were in my name, I did not see it as my job to do anything as menial as to look at numbers.

In due course, this massive theft lead to me having to borrow vast sums of money – at twenty-five per cent over base – to plug the gap and pay my taxes. At that rate of interest there was no shortage of people prepared to lend money to me – including the merchant bank arm of my high street bank (that had refused to extend my routine overdraft which was the equivalent of only one month's trading income). I was asset rich, being only about sixty per cent borrowed on the current valuations on our properties, but that didn't save me. For eighteen months I paid my way because we had lots of patients asking for treatment. However, the accounts were in such a mess that I could not present clear statements to Companies House or to the Inland Revenue. My financial life unravelled.

Facts:

1 A family business is no protection against theft or against incompetent financial management – not even by family members or, above all, by the owner. The business and the staff are betrayed when accounts are not the first concern.

2 Thieves – of time or money or goods or anything else – betray everybody. They put the whole enterprise, and therefore the livelihoods of others, at risk. They also betray themselves when they take something that belongs to someone else.

3 Families, teachers, social workers, probation officers and politicians, and everyone else who supports the idea of an entitlement culture, betray the whole of society. Credit should be given to the producers, not to those who demand the right to the product of someone else's work.

4 Governments take by force and they distribute to their own chosen recipients. Then they expect to be given credit for doing that – when they themselves have actually produced nothing.

5 Despite the welfare state, our population gives millions to charities every year. American tax laws enable donors to set off charitable gifts against tax. In the UK only charities can reclaim the tax paid on gifts. Donors themselves get no tax relief, because it would lead to people recognizing that the state is not indispensible. They might even see that the welfare state is wasteful in the extreme and that it becomes progressively more profligate and totalitarian each day. It betrays every one of our precious individual freedoms.

6 The avarice of bankers knows no bounds. Bankers serve no interest other than their own. The same applies to professionals in general.

7 Balance sheets are based on fiction. Profit and loss accounts are based in reality. Cash flow is everything.

8 The Inland Revenue does the job that it is required to do by Parliament. Their staff have no knowledge of what it takes to run a business and we should not expect them to do so.

False Belief: Medical insurance companies want to help.

Notes:
In my private medical practice my own fees as a general practitioner were never reimbursable by the private medical insurance companies. Patients were able to get reimbursement for the cost of some tests because we employed consultants to oversee the laboratory and also the X-ray and ultrasound unit. When we first set up the treatment centre, we were able to receive payments from the private medical insurance companies because our patients were under the care of our consultant psychiatrist. All of this gradually changed when the companies ceased being provident associations (recycling profits for the benefit of their subscribers) and became profit-making.

In the short term, treatment for addiction is expensive. In the longer term, when it is successful, it is very good value because of the medical complications that are avoided. However, as with governments, medical insurance companies think only in the short term. One company never did cover addiction. One made so many requirements on reporting back to them that it became (intentionally, I believe) too much of a hassle for us. The third said that they would cover treatment of depression but not addiction. All our patients suffered from depression – that is precisely why they used mood-altering substances and processes – but the insurance company insisted that depression must be treated with antidepressants. I was not prepared to prescribe these drugs because I believe that they are addictive to people who have an addictive nature. We couldn't win so we stopped taking patients on insurance.

I believe that behind all this was a battle fought against treatment centres like ours by consultant psychiatrists. They referred NHS patients to the private hospitals where they worked. They also advised the medical insurance companies. We were upsetting the system by being outside it.

Facts:

1 Private medical insurance companies have the right to run their own business any way they like (within the law). They do not betray their members by trying to limit the liability and reduce costs. Equally, they do not betray GPs like me when they cover only consultant specialists. That's business.

2 There comes a time when the cost of insurance is greater than the cost of treatment. Insurance companies know this. Therefore they may offer reduced premiums to those who voluntarily exclude the treatment of addiction and other clinical conditions (commonly mental illness) from their policies. That is business, not prejudice.

3 Saving lives does not save money. When people live longer, the costs of their medical care over the years goes up. The long-term cost of medical care – state or private – is a bottomless pit. The funding of the NHS can only be brought under control by deciding what it will not cover. Politicians betray the population at large when they fail to clarify this and pretend that everyone could be treated for everything all the time if it were not for financial 'cuts'.

4 Medical insurance companies betray doctors by insisting that they follow particular clinical approaches (which protect the companies themselves through establishing rigid protocols) rather than allowing doctors to make their own clinical decisions.

5 Advances in clinical care rarely come from the centre, the establishment. More commonly they come from the periphery, the individualists who think for themselves and who dare to say 'I disagree'. The power of the medical establishment – the Department of Health in particular – is considerable. To come up with an unorthodox approach is fraught with professional risk.

6 Consultant specialists who, in effect, refer NHS patients to themselves in private hospitals betray their profession.

7 Maybe there is a place for provident institutions after all. Perhaps the trade unions could lead the way again.

False Belief: Regulation makes better doctors.

Notes:
Dr Harold Shipman probably murdered over two hundred of his patients. The government blamed the self-regulating General Medical Council, rather than the local health authorities and the Home Office for not doing their duty in monitoring prescriptions for dangerous drugs. The government took its long-awaited chance to get control of the medical profession.

The GMC now has a majority of lay members. Doctors may not be 'the enemy' (as they have been described by the head of a community healthcare trust) but they are certainly not friends. The expectations put upon them nowadays are virtually demanding that they know everything about everything. More worryingly, the expectation is that doctors must do what their colleagues customarily do. Clinical and managerial innovation is stifled. The Department of Health makes all the rules.

The Care Standards Act 2000 was brought in to reform clinical standards of doctors and in care homes. It was a politician's and bureaucrat's dream and a provider's nightmare. We had to draw up policies which would satisfy twenty clauses of the Act that are applicable to medical services and a further twenty-six clauses specifically applicable to mental health care. For each policy there had to be a procedure for implementation and for each procedure there had to be monitoring of outcome.

It all seems to be fair and proper but I wrote nothing else in two years other than this two hundred page legally-binding document. If I had written it too loosely or too tightly, it would be my fault. This is a government's and bureaucrat's ideal situation: the provider is in the wrong – at any time and on any issue – until proved otherwise. That principle keeps dissidents in their proper place – underfoot. However, as subsequent scandals showed, it does not lead to better health care.

Facts:

1 Dr Harold Shipman betrayed his patients in the most damaging way possible. He also betrayed the whole medical profession by creating fear in patients' minds and also by creating fear in doctors' minds that they would for ever more be thought by the General Medical Council to be guilty until proved innocent of any charge brought against them. This, in turn, betrayed all patients because fearful doctors are more likely to make mistakes.

2 Local health authorities betrayed doctors by not monitoring all prescriptions for content rather than merely for cost. Morphia is cheap and therefore the authorities did not see what was being done by Dr Shipman, even though he was prescribing vastly more morphia than other doctors.

3 The Home Office has an established duty to monitor the dispensing of dangerous drugs by pharmacies. The vast over-prescription by Dr Shipman was not seen. This betrayed the patients who were murdered and it betrayed all doctors by enabling the government to blame the General Medical Council (who could never have monitored all doctors in everything they do) rather than one of its own departments.

4 The Government betrayed all doctors by taking its chance to regulate them even more by making the General Medical Council become dominated by lay people. Previously there had been a majority of doctors monitoring the behaviour of their professional colleagues. This meant that doctors are now largely judged on the perceptions of lay people who may have false impressions of what doctors could ever do in the reality of clinical practice.

5 The standardization of medical procedures, under the dictates of bureaucrats implementing the Care Standards Act 2000, betrays the innovative skills of all doctors. The population at large is betrayed by this process because it will inevitably lead to UK medical services resembling those of the Soviet Union.

False Belief: Bankers alone caused the credit crunch.

Notes:

An inspector from the Healthcare Commission told us that we had to join our three buildings together so that our patients did not get wet. Some of our patients had been living under hedges. Also we had to box in the fire escape and change all the handles on doors and windows so that patients could not hang themselves. I hesitated to point out that there were trees in the garden. We had to change all the baths to showers so that patients could not drown themselves. I said that we were close to a railway electric line but the inspector said that his concern was only with what patients did on our premises.

So that was it: he had no interest in whether patients lived or died but only in whether he might be blamed for inadequate supervision of our services.

The total cost of implementing these 'recommendations' was over one million pounds. When I said that this might take us down, he replied that when one centre closes another opens.

My bank said that they would not lend me the money because the value of the premises would not be increased. As with the fraud, I therefore raised it from smaller lenders. They took charges over all our properties and over the contents. They charged us twenty-five per cent over base rate.

We were busy and we managed to pay our way for eighteen months but then the credit crunch led to us losing eighty per cent of our patients. Our total income fell disastrously and so did the value of our property. I had thought that I would be safe because I had borrowed only sixty per cent of the paper value of my assets but, as property values fell, they were overtaken by my increasing debts. I tried to sell but there were no buyers. I tried to make arrangements with my creditors but the banks and one small lender refused. I was made bankrupt and I lost everything I possessed.

Facts:

1 Governments make laws. Civil servants draw up regulations. Agencies enforce them. Each bureaucrat in turn makes life progressively more difficult for the provider – who pays the taxes that fund the welfare state from which they are paid. While building up their fat pension pots, these jobsworths betray the entrepreneurs upon whom they – and everyone else – depend.

2 I am not the first person to come to grief – in part – on health and safety considerations that seem to be lacking in common sense. The inspectors betray us all while protecting themselves. I doubt whether they ever save lives.

3 Lawyers can be guaranteed to make any situation worse.

4 The 'recommendations' of state agencies cannot be ignored without risking being sued out of existence by people with a grudge or by those who are trying to avoid paying a bill. This leads to a significant betrayal of creative enterprise.

5 No Minnesota Method treatment centre has replaced the major centres that have been forced to close. The gratuitous comments of non-combatants in the war against drugs betray those of us who are fighting on the front line.

6 Balance sheets are works of fiction. Profit and loss figures are more realistic but cash flow is all that really matters. Any director who does not understand that betrays his or her employees as well as the shareholders or other lenders.

7 I borrowed too much and I paid the price of that. Each lender – other than the banks who were secured creditors – lost money on me. I know that business is business but I feel that I betrayed people who trusted me and also those whose livelihoods depended upon me. I should have closed the treatment centre some time before the banks forcibly closed it.

8 The Government also borrowed too much and they betray us all when they don't admit it. The same applies to many of us.

False Belief: Gamblers know when to stop.

Notes:

I stopped playing poker after I lost three months' income on the turn of one card. I have never gambled in casinos or betting shops or at race tracks. I seemed to be very virtuous – but I gambled on property values and I didn't know when to stop.

I have never gambled on stocks and shares or on commodities or on insurance at Lloyds. I put everything I had into property, most of which I used for professional purposes, but I bought more than I needed. I glowed when a bank manager said that I appeared to have a real talent for property ventures. Of course I did: all property values were going up at that time. I had no talent whatever in knowing when to sell.

When I was bankrupted, I watched as our car was collected and driven away. I always had second-hand Volvo estates: I took no financial or other risks there. Even so I felt humiliated at being dependent on public transport for the first time in fifty years.

Losing our home and our cottage, which we had bought over forty years previously, was a great wrench. More specifically it meant that we had nowhere to live. As the empty treatment centre had not yet sold, I was still the titular owner of property and therefore could not be considered in law to be homeless.

Margaret and I stayed with friends, the first for five months and the second for three. We lived out of suitcases. Our friends were very generous to us. Another friend lent us a car. But it was all pretty wretched.

Eventually, on the strength of my father having been a priest in Canterbury and because we had helped a lot of people in the area, we were given two small rooms in a Church of England almshouse. The care assistant who welcomed us said, 'You can die here'. I felt that she was right.

Facts:

1 Gambling is gambling – whatever form it takes.

2 I justified my gambling on property by saying that I had tangible assets. Eventually, that rationalization came totally apart.

3 Priding myself on what I did not do is a 'not yet', like alcoholics saying that they don't drink in the morning or drink spirits.

4 Yet again I was trying to do other people's professional work. I am not a property developer any more than I am a musician or farmer or politician.

5 In telling my story, I make it look as if all the disasters were happening only to me. The truth is that my wife was right beside me through every one of these experiences. I dreadfully betrayed the person I loved most of all.

6 In some ways I am very cautious – such as in the car I drive, even though my children would say that, with my standard of driving, I need to be cautious and so does everyone else. Even so, this shows that gamblers don't always gamble on everything.

7 Even though I had worked all my adult life in Kensington, I was not entitled to council housing because I still owned a house, even though I had no power over its sale. Later I was told that my residence in the almshouse meant that I would be declaring myself homeless if I were to leave it. This attitude of the council was not a betrayal of me after all the work that I had done in the area. It is the truth and I had to live with it. Nobody betrayed me but myself.

8 Some people spend their whole lives living out of suitcases – or even less. It does me no harm to have shared their experience (at a comfortable level) for a time. It would be a betrayal of them if I were to cry only for myself.

9 It was a privilege for us to be able to stay at the almshouse, rather than continue to live as transient guests in the houses of friends. At least we had some dignity and also a sense of security that I had previously failed to provide.

False Belief: Professional advisors are on your side.

Notes:

We were offered a reasonable price for our counselling centre and our home in London, provided that we exchanged contracts within ten days. I accepted the offer and told my lawyer. He went on holiday and did not get a partner to take over. The offer lapsed and property prices plummeted.

We marketed the property again – but not through the big local estate agents. Each time someone expressed interest, these agents were asked for their opinion. They said the property was worth only half what we were asking. Eventually it did sell at our price – but not before I had been declared bankrupt.

In Kent I asked local agents to sell the treatment centre and they put it on the market at a far higher figure than I had anticipated. At that price we would have survived. We had no offers. The agents got our business but we got nothing.

The accountants acting for us arranged for two informal voluntary arrangements with our creditors. This cost a fortune but neither was successful. The same accountants then offered us a very low sum to buy one of our properties for themselves. Presumably they had thought that they were on to a good thing when I was so vulnerable. It sold for twenty per cent more than their offer – even in those dreadful times.

A property developer offered me a quarter of a million pounds in cash if I would accept a low offer. He said this could help me during a bankruptcy. I refused. My architect worked for one of the other bidders for that same property and got them a deal with the planners so that they were able to sell on for a profit of one million pounds within a month when the market was still down.

My bankers called in all my loans and charged me twenty-five per cent over the base rate, which they knew I could never afford.

Facts:

1 At the very start, when I called in the liquidators for the first company, a friend – who had himself been bankrupted previously – recommended me to declare myself bankrupt immediately. He said it would save a great deal of grief and get it all over with much quicker. He was right – but I couldn't do it. I fought for what I loved. Maybe I betrayed my wife by fighting a losing battle and distressing her so much – but I do not know whether her distress would have been any less if I had bailed out earlier voluntarily.

2 My lawyer was unprofessional. He betrayed me but I could not prove that the sale would have gone through.

3 The estate agents did what some estate agents do. At that level of financial behaviour, I don't know that I can say that anyone betrays anyone: maybe it is the norm.

4 Maybe the Kent estate agents were also desperate for business. They did nobody any favours by over-valuing the property. They harmed me by their incompetence – but there was no betrayal.

5 Informal voluntary arrangements are a gamble. Sometimes they don't come off. There is no betrayal in that.

6 I suppose my accountants would argue that I was fortunate to receive any offer at all in that time of financial free-fall. I think they betrayed my professional trust.

7 The property developer did what some property developers do, just as some agents, doctors, politicians or other professionals do what they do. These professionals betray their clients, constituents or colleagues – but not all members of those professions are like that.

8 Some bankers are the overall champions in the avarice and corruption competition that seems to characterize much of the City of London. They betray those who are honest.

9 I cannot escape my own responsibility for my financial affairs. I had all the privileges in the good times. I cannot complain about losses in the bad times. I betrayed myself.

False Belief: Responsible officials behave responsibly.

Notes:
One of the smaller creditors told me that his policy is always to bankrupt anyone who did not pay his debt in full. It is illegal to pay one creditor selectively. I therefore entered no defence when I received a summons from a court. The day of the hearing came and went. Ten days later I received formal notification that I should attend the office of the Official Receiver in Bloomsbury and bring all my financial documents.

Margaret and I lugged four large bags of lever-arched files into the office of the nominated inspector. He was surprised because he anticipated that we had gone down only for the amount mentioned in the court papers. Four hours later, after many many tears, Margaret and I emerged from a gentle – but firm – grilling under oath. My professional life was over. I had no office, no staff and no money. When we moved to the almshouse we lost all our familiars and all our social culture.

A Trustee in Bankruptcy was appointed to oversee all my financial affairs. For a full year I had to answer one query after another, week after week. My pensions were taken, apart from the statutory state pension that gave us £1,100 more for a year than our rent. A legacy from an aunt who died at precisely the wrong time (for me as well as for her) was taken.

When our property in London did not sell, I was taken to court – and judgement was entered against me – for non-payment of council tax after the six months period of leeway for selling a property had expired. My explanation that I had no power over the sale was disregarded. The Citizens Advice Bureau (after a queue for an hour for an appointment one week later) told me that I should brief a private solicitor. I had no money to do so. The Inland Revenue continued to hound both me and my wife.

Facts:

1 The creditor who bankrupted me had every right to do so. I had not paid my debt. He did not betray me; I betrayed him.

2 The nominated inspector for the Official Receiver was very kind and understanding. He did his job with a human touch. During the interview I thought of my father and my uncle and of Margaret's mother. I had betrayed their trust in me.

3 By reducing Margaret to penury and taking her away from everything that she loved, I betrayed her terribly. My creditors now chased her for our joint debts, as they were entitled to do. On her seventieth birthday, when other husbands would have given her a family party, I walked her up to the county court and paid five hundred and ten pounds (that I borrowed from my brother and subsequently repaid) to make her bankrupt. My betrayal of her was complete.

4 My Trustee in Bankruptcy was doing his job. Later he didn't: he forgot that my wife and I owned a strip of woodland. He said that he had to take us to court to prove his right to its ownership. He did so despite the facts that I was clear of bankruptcy by then. He betrayed his duty to me, as someone in his care, but it was just a slip.

5 The council tax people eventually agreed that I had nothing to pay. I received no apology for their error. It is a criminal offence to harass a bankrupt – but evidently not if the bully is a government official. I was betrayed by 'the system'.

6 The Citizens Advice Bureau were doing a very difficult job. I was fully appreciative that their volunteers do the best they can to help people in need. The fact that they were not able to help me with my complex issues does not indicate that they betrayed me.

7 The Inland Revenue were doing their job but I did not like their hassling. My wife had declared all her income to our accountants but she was given the third degree and it distressed her dreadfully.

False Belief: Acts of God are acts of God.

Notes:

Insurance companies call natural disasters 'Acts of God'. This is very unfair to God. When my wife and I met, it was the most wonderful experience of my life. When our professional and social lives were destroyed, it was the most tragic. With the exception of the death of my infant brother, I had not suffered any family bereavements other than from old age. I do not believe that God was involved in my losses. They just happened.

When our lovely cottage was totally destroyed by an arsonist, with whom we had no connection whatever, he said he had a message from God to torch our home. After I was bankrupt, the empty building of our treatment centre – which we had created with much love and in which so many people had been given hope of a new life – was also totally destroyed by fire, probably by vandals. I believe that the fact that we were twice targeted by arsonists was coincidence and that this had nothing to do with God or the devil.

In the course of my life I have created many things. I have also destroyed many things, most commonly as a result of my compulsive helping. I have many natural aptitudes and even more ineptitudes. I do not see these as gifts or faults from God or the devil, other than as part of my genetic make-up.

I believe that God and the devil exist inside each one of us and that we create our own heaven and hell on earth in our relationships. We each have the potential for good or evil.

Also we each have the capacity to make or break our lives by taking advantage of, or ignoring, chance as it occurs. I have had my share of both good and bad fortune. When good things happen, I have tried to capitalize on them. When bad things occur, I do my best to minimize their effects. From my personal experience of betrayal, crisis and bereavement, I try to grow.

Facts:

1 Some insurance companies do their best to avoid paying out on any claim. Some injured parties do their best to inflate their claims. Each of these groups betray themselves and they betray each other.

2 I do not believe that the loss and destruction we had suffered was a betrayal by God or a curse from the devil.

3 My parents are dead. What and where are they now? I do not know. Some people have very clear perceptions on the answer to these fundamental questions and they lose no opportunity to share their insights. I believe that they betray the integrity of their own minds. As a musician, I am well aware that not everything can be explained in intellectual terms (why is some music so moving?) but I value curiosity over certainty: curiosity creates whereas certainty stagnates. I am sure that the intentions of these people are kind but I am content to leave the discovery of the answer to the great issue – of the true nature of life and death – until after my own death.

4 Other people have no doubt about what my parents would wish for me now. I feel that this would betray their individuality. They had highly independent minds and this was one of the many things that I valued in them. I would betray their true essence if I were to second guess them now.

5 When coincidences occur, I see no need to postulate the influence of God. They simply happen. It betrays the integrity of the human mind when mental function descends to the level of superstition.

6 I am concerned more for the actions of man than of God. We do terrible things to each other in the course of our certainty over God's will for us and for other people. We betray the wonder and beauty of our individual existence, and our commonality with each other, when we impose our own will in our certainty of God's.

7 We each have the opportunity to make the very best of whatever comes our way. We betray ourselves if we do not.

Reminder: Coming through a betrayal:

Of course we have been betrayed at times: everybody has. When will we get over it? Ever? Do we become the architects of our own continued misfortune by allowing resentment to dominate our lives? Do we benefit from going on about it and letting it fester? Or do we live in peace and harmony with other people?

Of course we have betrayed other people: everybody has. When will we make appropriate amends to the people we have harmed? When will we understand and forgive ourselves for the mistakes we have made? Do we benefit from continuing to wallow in guilt for the bad things we have done? Do we benefit from continuing to curse ourselves in shame for being miserable wretches and condemn ourselves even more than other people might condemn us? Or do we judge ourselves on how we are now, live in peace and harmony with ourselves, and bring out our best potential?

Do we see the church and the state as supporters or enemies of our individuality? Irrespective of fine intentions and silky words, do we see them as forces for good or evil? Are they loyal to us or do they betray us? Despite the worthy behaviour of some individual True Believers in their religious or political creeds, is the end result in practice creative or destructive? Are they tolerant of those who disagree with their perceptions or do they use their supposed temporal or spiritual power to repress?

Abuse and abandonment, in one form or another and to varying degrees, are distressingly common. They say something very nasty about the perpetrator but they say nothing negative about the victim. We come through it by recognizing and accepting that distinction. We make it worse by reliving it in our own minds each day. There are psychological techniques that can dispel the lasting effects of trauma. By choosing to ruminate, we damage ourselves and we damage our current relationships.

The past is over. In 'Crisis and Creativity' and 'Bereavement and Belief' I shall tell the stories of my further losses. In this section I have told the story of various traumas in my life, some caused by other people and some self-inflicted. They are all over. I create a new life for myself today – an exciting, vibrant, creative and enthusiastic life – because that is what I want. I cannot predict my future but I do know that I shall love it (give or take the occasional inevitable disaster). I know how to survive but I also know how to enjoy. That positive feeling is my choice: it does not depend upon the actions of other people. I can choose my reactions as well as my actions.

The most difficult times in life are managed best without resorting to medication. Antidepressants, tranquillizers and sleeping tablets are a hindrance rather than a help. They are highly addictive to people who have an addictive nature. They lead to a psychological dependency in everybody – addict or otherwise. They solve nothing. They help nothing. They raise the spirits artificially. They do not help the brain to function more effectively. They cloud it. Small wonder that the time that doctors recommend for them to be taken gets progressively longer. Doctors know that life has to be dealt with on life's terms at some time – but they repeatedly put off that day of reckoning.

I found, in my time of despair, when one disaster came after another, that my mind was numb – understandably so: that is a healthy reaction. Now it is alert again – simply through the passage of time and through the love I give to other people and receive in return from them.

If we want to stay stuck in emotional troughs, we can. If we want other people to 'fix' us, we can. If we want to take tablets from doctors or moan to counsellors, we can. These are all choices – not necessities. I do not make those choices. I prefer to respect the integrity of my mind, to do life-enhancing things and to allow my tired, sad head to heal itself in time. Now, if you will excuse me, I'm busy – I have a lot of living to do.

The Philosophy of the NHS is wrong.

1 If the state takes over ultimate health care responsibility from the individual then:

a) Individuals come to think that they have rights, and hence can demand a service without at the same time having to recognize that the service is inevitably the product of the life and work and integrity of someone else.

b) Any thinker who allows himself or herself to be the property of someone else ceases to think. Doctors who allow themselves to become mere units in state provision of health care, rather than people who are responsible for their own philosophical and mental integrity, are not worth asking the time of day let alone their opinions on clinical or personal problems.

c) People often assume that the state will care for the less fortunate. When presented with evidence that it does not do so, they complain that it should – but do not feel obliged to take any positive helpful action themselves. Thus the state is the cause of the Inverse Care Law, whereby those most in need of help are least likely to get it. The state creates a cruel, arid, uncaring society that smothers individual compassion and human charity. The state cannot be relied upon to produce responsible clinical care at the time that it is needed. A true sense of commitment can only be the product of an individual mind and personal philosophy. It can never be instilled by rules, regulations and committees, nor even by Royal Commissions.

2 If resources are distributed according to need then:

a) People compete with each other to establish their need rather than their capacity to do well on their own account. The individual demands his or her so called 'rights' without any thought that it is at another's expense. The corporate body, answerable for its expenditure of public funds, spends its budget up to the hilt – or even overspends regardless of the needs of others – so that it can demand the same again or even more the following year.

b) Little attention is paid to the capacity of the recipient to benefit from the resource. An absolute need may be totally unchanged even after all the resource has been devoured. Meanwhile someone else with a lesser objective need is left with no possibility of the benefit that could have been his or hers because the resource has in effect been squandered.

c) Scientific assessment of benefit takes second place to the repetitive, mindless, arrogant hollerings of political pressure groups.

3 If services are free at the time of need:

a) Perceived needs become relative rather than absolute. Meeting a need does not satisfy: it merely shifts attention to another need.

b) Instead of the individual patient not being able to afford treatment, the state runs out of money so that either the individual cannot get treatment at all or, alternatively, the treatment that he or she can get is not worth having.

c) The proponents of the system point to a few people who have been dramatically helped 'at no cost' and:

i Play on the fear or pity of their listeners – and in so doing make them into supplicant pap.

ii Disregard what is happening in general to the NHS by focusing upon a few fortunate patients in particular.

d) The state comes in time to be thought to be indispensable and with that goes every last individual freedom.

If the ideas and principles of the NHS are wrong then the practice will inevitably fail. True compassion can only be individual. If I choose to help you or not, that is my affair but I shall reap the consequences. I have to earn my place in a compassionate society through my actions for others. By contrast, the state can never be compassionate: when A gives the life of B for the benefit of C, but A expects the credit for himself or herself, this is the essential prerequisite for totalitarianism. This is why Ayn Rand, the author of *Atlas Shrugged,* is right when she says that the difference between a welfare state and a totalitarian state is only a matter of time.

Section 2

Crisis and Creativity

Reminder: Caring for yourself in a crisis is life-saving.

Notes:
There is always something worth living for. Any crisis can be turned into an opportunity. We can survive bereavement. The more experience we have, the more we can learn. Shaping the future depends upon how we look at our present.

When I was made bankrupt at the age of seventy-two, my wife and I were left with nothing material to show for our entire professional lives. We had nothing except our experience, our minds and each other. The recent experience had been grim, struggling to retain something – anything – but finally losing everything. We lost not only our home and our office and our other properties but also our daily contacts with friends and with other professionals. We lost our entire social and professional culture. Our health suffered.

I felt too young to die. I had created things before. People who never create anything rarely go bankrupt unless they are gamblers or alcoholic or addicted in some other way. I could therefore create something again. Why ever not? Looking to the future, I would have no assets, no buildings, no staff, no money and no borrowing capacity. But one thing that could not be taken away from my wife and me was our sense of hope for the future.

We were fortunate in having each other but I am sure that each of us on our own would have the same sense of hope that life is for living, regardless of circumstance. We cared for ourselves. We had our own values. We shared many of them but essentially they are our own. We did not know what our future would be – but we did know that there is a future and it will be great if we choose to make it so.

Everybody goes through crises at some time or other in life. It may be a financial crisis or a problem with health. Everybody has crises in personal and professional relationships. None of us escapes. We therefore have to find ways to survive and flourish.

Principles:

1 Remember that you have come through difficult times before.
2 Starting again is a challenge but in time it can be wonderful fun.
3 Let yourself grieve appropriately and give yourself time.
4 Ignore the encouragement and advice of people who have not shared your experience: they simply wouldn't understand.
5 Defy your enemies by refusing to be put down. Never let them take away your sense of hope for the future.

Action:

1 Look after your physical health. Keep yourself fit. Eat well. Sleep as well as you can.
2 Get up at your normal time and establish daily routines of activity.
3 Do the simple things that you have always enjoyed.
4 Initially make no plans for the future: you need time to be able to see that the future does not have to be built on the past – it can be completely new.
5 Maintain your personal standards.
6 Stay in contact with friends.
7 Remember that the world is mostly a beautiful place, other than as usually presented on television or in the newspapers.
8 Don't drink or smoke or gamble or get involved in other addictive behaviour. This would only make things worse.
9 Keep your mind active by reading, doing puzzles and surfing the web.
10 Remember what Nelson Mandela endured – and look at what he then created.
11 Maintain or develop one special close relationship. This is by far the most important health factor of all, far more significant than giving up smoking, losing weight or getting fit.
12 Remember that you are not alone in your experience. Many other people have been where you have been.

Reminder: Believe it or not, to have hope is a choice.

Notes:
When things were progressively falling apart, I was carried along on the crest of a wave of hope. Each day I looked for possible good outcomes and I worked out what I might do to make them come true. But the wave broke and I was left floundering. So I got onto the next wave of hope – and then that broke. In time the waves became progressively smaller but still I lived in hope that something would work out well and that we would be left with something of our previous lives – but that wasn't the way it worked out. We lost absolutely every material thing.

But we didn't lose hope. That cannot be taken away by bailiffs or creditors. We could choose to despair – and believe that we had no future. Or we could choose to have hope – and believe that we could always create something new, even if nothing turned up out of the blue.

We never doubted our capacity to be creative and happy. We had created a great many beautiful things in our time – buildings, organizations, management systems, ideas. Why should this fountain of creativity suddenly run dry?

What we had lost were things that we loved and treasured – but why should we not create new things that we would come to love and treasure? We recognized that the future might well be very different from the past but we had hope that starting again completely from scratch would be an adventure which would take us forward in new and exciting ways that we would never otherwise have explored.

Hope is available to everybody. It does not depend upon particular environmental circumstances or opportunities. Anyone can choose to have hope, rather than despair. Hope really is a choice, not an attribute that is given to some people but not to others. Whoever we are or wherever we are, or in whatever state, we can make this choice.

Principles:

1 Some people are understandably sad as a result of distressing personal circumstances. Others may have the inner emptiness of an addictive nature. This leads to feelings of depression.

2 No one can make us feel anything. We feel sad when our good values are under attack. We feel happy when they are affirmed. Our own values determine our feelings.

3 Emotional pain leads to physical damage. It eats us alive. Hope dissolves it.

4 We came into the world with nothing and we'll go out with nothing. Everything in between is merely transient – but we might just as well enjoy it in whatever way we can.

5 Choosing to have a hopeful outlook on life makes solving our various problems much easier.

Action:

1 Treasure your own creativity. Never let it falter. Do something – anything – to keep it alive.

2 Make a list of all the things, however small, that you have created in your life. Remind yourself of your best moments.

3 Recognize that you have created something out of nothing many times – and therefore can do so again.

4 Do not waste emotional energy on your own frightening thoughts or on unpleasant people. They are like an infectious disease and there is no need for you to catch it.

5 Recognize that time is flexible. You can have as little or as much as you want in order to be happy and creative. It's a choice.

6 Note that the next world can take care of itself later on. There are still plenty of opportunities to live in this world to the full.

7 Recognise that you yourself can create your own future life in whatever way you wish. If you want to despair, you can. If you want to look forward to a brighter future, you can.

8 Beware of mood-altering substances, prescribed or otherwise.

Reminder: Freud was wrong.

Notes:
When I look back to my childhood I can see abuse and abandonment if I want to look hard enough for those things or I can see happiness and friendship if I choose to look for them.

I can look back at my life and see a whole series of failures: I failed in my dream of becoming a professional musician. I failed in a farming enterprise. I failed in property development. I failed in politics. And then I failed financially in my basic profession as a doctor and as an addiction specialist.

Or did I? One thing I can say for sure in all of these things is that I have given them a really good try. I have given life my best shot. I have done lots of things – and enjoyed them all while they lasted. I can do many more things now – and enjoy them.

If I want to look back or forward, I can be as miserable or as happy as I want to be. Given that choice, happiness wins every time in my book.

I choose now to follow the principles of Positive Psychology spelt out by Professor Martin Seligman of the University of Pennsylvania, USA. Each day I note three good things that have happened in that day and five things for which I am grateful. That keeps my head in a good place and enables me to think and act positively for the future.

My childhood experience established 'tapes' that occasionally re-play in my adult life as reminders of difficult times. I choose to recognize the tapes but not to act upon them. I've got better things to do than wallow in self-pity and blame. I have a life to live.

I do not accept that my childhood experiences determine my thoughts, feelings or actions for the rest of my life. Some of my childhood experiences were distressing, as for anyone, but I choose to leave them in the past and get over them.

Principles:

1 If you want to be miserable, you can be. If you want to be happy, you can be. It is all a matter of choice: it is not determined by childhood experience.

2 Childhood should be a time of adventure and learning. This aspect of your childhood can continue for as long as you want.

3 Psychology has moved on from the days of complexes and childhood imprints.

4 Thinking positively results in having positive feelings and taking positive actions.

Action:

1 Look up Positive Psychology on the web – and give it a try.

2 Make a basic gratitude list of all the lovely things in your life. See how many of them are completely unaffected by your present circumstances.

3 Search for your childhood 'tapes' and see how similar circumstances in the present can create emotional echoes. Recognize that they are not commands to take action of any kind. They are simply tapes that play. Identify them – smile at them – put them back in their childhood box, and move on.

4 Forget all the incomprehensible psychobabble that has unsettled so many lives in the last century.

5 Accept the oldest proverb in the world: 'Shit happeneth'.

6 Emotional competitions to see who has been abused and abandoned the most are no help to anybody. These things did happen and they were wrong – but now let them go.

7 'Therapy' involving beating cushions and screaming enables people to become better at beating cushions and screaming.

8 Remember that the traumas of your childhood are over. They cannot be un-done in reality, although perceptions can be modified through various psychological techniques so that they can be left to lie in peace

Reminder: Hope can be rekindled.

Notes:
I found myself looking at the ground when walking along the street. I had never done that. Generally, I look at the houses because their architecture interests me. I hold my head up high because I am curious to see what is going on. I see the familiar shopkeepers and newspaper sellers. When passing them four times every day, I chat to the charity muggers and the street beggars.

But all this changed. My head went down involuntarily. Telling myself 'Look up!' didn't work: my head stayed down. Saying 'Smile!' was even less productive. I had been hit with an emotional hammer.

At such a time, people generally ask for help from doctors and the help that they most commonly receive is a mood-altering drug, a so-called antidepressant. I didn't want any of that druggy stuff. I value the authenticity of all my feelings and I am not prepared to sign them over to the pharmaceutical industry.

I began to take a brisk walk early every morning (and I met a number of urban foxes). This deliberate exercise helped me to feel a bit better. I looked up. I smiled. And I kindled a sense of hope.

I had lost the habit of telling 'the joke of the day' to my friends. I had to relearn how to smile and laugh at a time when I had so little to smile or laugh about.

Time is the great healer – but we can do our best to help it along. Taking mood-altering substances, prescribed or recreational, gets in the way of that natural healing process.

I found that my head took its own time to clear. I couldn't force it. I had to wait until it cleared itself. Gradually, week by week and month by month, I was able to be more clear-thinking and positive. I saw this retrospectively, rather than at the time. I took positive action. My thoughts and feelings followed in its wake.

Principles:

1 Body and mind work together: hurting the one hurts the other, being kind to the one is kind to the other.
2 The brain is a physical, chemical and electrical organ. It has miraculous ways of generating its own healthy mood-altering chemicals, when given the encouragement to do so.
3 Simplistic instructions don't work.
4 The psychological and physical benefits of exercise and of smiling and laughing are well established in medical literature.

Action:

1 Take some physical exercise every day – sufficient to get you slightly out of breath.
2 Antidepressants and sleeping tablets are of questionable benefit. They create a problem of dependency and they do not solve any emotional or practical issues.
3 If you go to a hairdresser and sit around for long enough, you are likely to get a haircut. If you go to a doctor you are likely to get a prescription. It might sometimes be better to tell your problems to the hairdresser and get the double benefit: a listening ear and a haircut, without the side effects of a drug.
4 Never 'fake it to make it' – be genuine. Be the person you really are, rather than a shadow of your former self, weighed down and oppressed by fate.
5 Involve yourself with other people as often as you can.
6 Have some humour in your life. Even laugh at yourself. Remember the old joke 'Out of the gloom a voice said unto me "Smile and be happy: things could be worse". So I smiled and was happy and lo – things did get worse'.
7 Remember that time will tell. This too (whatever difficulty it may be) will pass in time.
8 Get out and about. Do something – anything. Best of all, create something

Reminder: Peace of mind is possible even in spite of unsolved problems.

Notes:
Feeling that my mind was no longer my own was the most difficult of all my experiences. I couldn't think straight. I shook my head but it didn't clear. On the advice of a nutritionist (I was desperate), I took fish oil and vitamins. My mind became more cloudy rather than less. A healer was very wise and kind but my stubborn head did not budge from its negativity. I could not see my way past the immediate problems and losses.

I tried a particular meditation course but the requirement that I should be vegetarian – and also give up onions and garlic – was too much for me because I am already abstinent from sugar and white flour. (These substances make me crave for more.)

Another approach to meditation – outlined in Deepak Chopra's book, *The Spontaneous Fulfillment of Desire* – helped to do the trick by getting me out of my slough of despond. The problems confronting me hadn't changed at all but my mind became progressively more clear. I had no solution to the difficulties confronting me but at least I could see that a solution of some kind would eventually be possible. I would come through.

I had previously written a book of 'prayers' for atheists and agnostics. I used them now, as ever, as psychological settlers and as reminders of the existence of a spiritual dimension. We are not merely atoms and molecules. Reason isn't everything.

I found a sense of hope by recognising that I could not simply pull myself together. I came to accept myself as a unit of a (non-religious) Universal Spirit, alongside others. I recognized that my dreadful experiences could be reframed as pointers to a new future.

From that starting position, all I had to do was to put one foot in front of the other each day and keep moving in the same direction.

Principles:
1 The mind heals itself.
2 Will power and determination don't work.
3 Hope is a spiritual quality, not a product of the intellect.
4 As John Donne said, 'No man is an island'.
5 Any experience can lead us to see things in new ways – if we are willing to do that.
6 Spirituality can coexist with religion or be independent of it.

Action:
1 Give up any search for a magic bullet. There is none. Drugging the mind with pharmaceutical or recreational substances simply clouds it and makes it less capable of finding a healthy natural solution that will be effective for the long term.
2 Try whatever you find works for you.
3 Eat healthily. The physical brain needs nourishment.
4 Trying to find solutions when your mind is still unbalanced will simply make things worse.
5 People who have not had this experience will tend to be exasperated when you say 'I can't think straight'. There is nothing that you can say to explain your mental confusion.
6 In practical terms you may still have a rational mind but your judgements may be hazy. Beware of making decisions on your own but also beware of blindly following the advice of others. Simply wait until your head is clear.
7 Well-meaning family and friends may have insights and ideas of their own but these may not necessarily be helpful to you.
8 Learn more about quantum theory and sub-atomic physics before making brash statements about spiritual ideas being unscientific. The worlds of science and spirituality are much closer than might at first appear.
9 If you so wish, study the psychological ideas of Carl Jung on the shared unconscious.

111

Reminder: Everybody builds castles in the air. Some people live in them.

Notes:

I am a dreamer. I have had wonderful dreams and, as a result, I have created some wonderful things. However, some of my dreams were merely fantasies, without any firm base in reality. When I tried to put them into practice, I caused mayhem.

My career as a musician was based upon wishful thinking rather than talent. My brief foray into politics was born of arrogance: I believed that I knew what should be good for other people. My farming venture was silly. I can see now that I bought the farm out of greed and kept it out of stubbornness. Inevitably, all these distractions fell apart. They were not my full time work and therefore I could not give them sufficient time and attention to make them successful. I was doing other people's professions as my hobbies.

Having made these mistakes in the past, I had no wish to make similar errors in the future.

The first thing I needed to do was to get a clear picture of how I came to be in my recent predicament. I could blame other people or the Government or the general economic situation. However, a great many people who worked in similar circumstances did not go down. I had to look at my rationalisations for my behaviour and see that they were built upon the quicksand of make-believe.

For the future, I had no choice but to accept the very real terms of bankruptcy and recognize that starting again with no buildings, no staff, no money and no borrowing capacity was really not going to be easy. It was no bad thing to have my hopes firmly based in this reality. I could then make sensible decisions.

But I could not make sensible decisions when my mind wasn't working efficiently. I had to do what I find most difficult of all: wait. Rushing things would only compound my difficulties.

Principles:

1 Being imaginative and creative is what life is all about – but living in fantasy and unreality is very destructive.
2 Renaissance man had wide interests and activities. The pace of life has changed since then and competition is fiercer.
3 Admitting mistakes is sensible. Repeating them is not.
4 Blaming other people is easy but it gets us nowhere.
5 Dishonesties, deceptions, distortions, diversions, delusions, evasions, rationalizations, justifications and psychological game-playing are the stock-in-trade of politicians. Those of us who live in the real world should have better things to do.
6 Nothing truly new can be built while looking over a shoulder at the past.
7 A truly original idea does not come from gradual changes.

Action:

1 Dream as many dreams as you can. Do not immediately put them into practice. Try to discover which of them have true creative potential and which are merely fantasies, doomed to destroy everything in their path.
2 Remember that the problems of today cannot be solved with the solutions of yesterday or even today. Otherwise they wouldn't exist. Think outside the confines of your standard way of doing things but do not assume that a new way of doing something is necessarily a better way.
3 Do not take decisions at night. Sleep on them.
4 See where you yourself were at fault, irrespective of whatever mistakes may have been made by other people and whatever general circumstances might have applied. This is the only way to avoid repeating the mistakes of the past.
5 Start again with a clean sheet. It's more fun that way.
6 Be gentle with yourself. Take your time. Allow your mind to heal at its own pace, exactly as you would for an injury to your body.

Reminder: Without dignity we are nothing.

Notes:
When one thing after another was being stripped away from me, it was very hard – but not impossible – to continue my daily work as best I could with diminishing resources. It was difficult to maintain my dignity when the credit cards were cut up, the car driven away, the companies put into liquidation and the vacant properties sold (and the contents left behind) or vandalized.

What mattered to me was that I should continue to be polite and respectful to other people, regardless of their behaviour towards me. I had to remember that receiving two or three telephone calls or threats in the same day from some creditors was simply the way that these particular people worked, trying to put pressure on me or my family to find money that we hadn't got. They would not have behaved like that if I had not got myself into this situation.

Observing the harsher elements of business practice did not make me want to copy them. Nor was I impressed by the avarice of financial vultures, circling their prey. I should never have put myself in a place to see them.

My hope for the future, whatever it might be, would depend upon the preservation of my dignity and self-confidence. This required me to recognize that I may be stupid but I am not innately a bad man. I took each day as it came. I behaved towards other people in the way that I wished them to behave towards me and my wife. I kept my feelings to myself. All this had the advantage of leaving me with no new apologies to make and no need to pick myself up from a moral floor that I was never on.

Just as I can look back at my school days in the certain knowledge that I did not behave towards others in the abusive ways that some masters and boys behaved towards me, I was determined now to maintain my dignity and my own standards of behaviour.

Principles:
1 Do as you would be done by.
2 Dog eats dog is the least of the laws of the financial jungle.
3 Living on credit is no longer at all possible when the credit stream dries up.
4 Professional advisors make a killing.
5 We choose our own behaviour. We are as responsible for our reactions as we are for our actions.

Action:
1 Remember that you have a prime responsibility towards people who are still paying for your services. Never let your personal difficulties damage your professionalism.
2 Remember that everything that is stripped away from you is a mark of how much you created. This should give hope that you can create again, if you wish to do so.
3 Observe that money really isn't everything, as can be seen in the unspeakable behaviour of people for whom it does appear to be the prime reason for living.
4 Take responsibility for your own mess. In that way, you will have the best chance of cleaning it up.
5 Look the part of the professional that you are. Don't let your personal standards slip.
6 Recognize that it would be dreadful to dig yourself deeper into a pit by doing things that might bring down further retribution upon your head.
7 Be careful of accepting help from people who may well have financial or personal agendas of their own.
8 Appreciate yourself for your good points.
9 Be kind to others, personally and professionally. Be honest and open in your dealings with other people. Be fair and generous. These are the ethical principles upon which you can build a good new life, irrespective of what you have gone through.

Reminder: We live or die in accordance with our values.

Notes:
If I were to betray my own values (listed in the last two pages of the middle section of this book) I would find it difficult to live with myself. I am no saint but I am also not the worst sinner that has ever lived. I can live comfortably with that.

Hope for the future always lies in maintaining my values (changing them if I find better ones) and doing the best I can to live by them.

Clearly my values are most under threat when I am under pressure spiritually, mentally, emotionally and physically - as I was in all these areas during this fearful time.

My wife and I walked to work, still arriving on time, when we had no car. I kept careful records in my medical practice right up to the last patient on the last day, with my wife typing them out in the evenings after all the patients had gone. These records belonged to the patients: they had paid for them. I gave them to my successors.

We destroyed the computer hard drives to protect our patients' confidentiality. We disposed of the oxygen cylinders and the radioactive elements of the X-ray machine so that there would be no risk to anyone else following our departure from the premises. All this should be taken for granted in any professional doctor.

We were very grateful to two separate friends who housed us for a total of eight months after we had lost our own home. Again it should be taken for granted that we did not abuse those friendships.

We made our staff redundant before we could not pay them for work they had done. As far as we could, we let people know before we were unable to pay for services. We made no underhand deals.

Throughout all this most humiliating and depressing time, we maintained our personal and professional standards. We would have destroyed ourselves if we had behaved any differently.

Principles:

1 Except in religions, there is no ranking order for saints and sinners.
2 When we live in accordance with our values, we feel good about ourselves. When we do the opposite, we feel bad. Our feelings are a very accurate indicator of the appropriateness of our behaviour at any time.
3 It is fatally easy to adjust our values to suit our behaviour.
4 Bankruptcy inevitably results in some people not being paid for goods and services that they have provided.

Action:

1 Establish your own hierarchy of values, spelling out what you value most and least.
2 Live up to your values as well as you can. Nothing more can reasonably be expected of anybody.
3 Recognize that spiritual, mental, emotional and physical pressure takes its toll but compromising your values would make matters indescribably worse.
4 Respect the generosity of friends.
5 Be considerate to staff.
6 Call in the liquidators or make yourself bankrupt as soon as you know that you will be unable to pay for services. A fall in property values may cause havoc with the final balance sheet and therefore with payments made to creditors. Take this into account, as best you can, in advance of any calamity.
7 Absolutely make no underhand deals. They will live to haunt you. By poisoning you, they will poison all your relationships.
8 Don't beat yourself up. You have enough to contend with already.
9 It would be easy to see bankruptcy as merely a part of the natural cycle of business. It is not. Innocent people get hurt. We have to spare a thought – a lot of thought – for them.

Reminder: People who are bereaved often die soon afterwards.

Notes:

I have been very fortunate. My parents both died in old age and no close family member or friend has died before the age of fifty. However, through my work as a GP and in my addiction treatment centre, I am very familiar with death, often in young people and even in children. Even so, I do not pretend to understand the feelings of people who lose a partner or child or close friend.

My own bereavement was over the loss of my professional and personal life. I had lived and worked in Kensington for the whole of my adult life and I missed it dreadfully when I had to leave it behind and seek sanctuary in an almshouse in Kent. In time I settled in and developed a new perspective, being grateful for what I have got, although still understandably sad over what my wife and I had lost.

During the six months between when we lost our companies and our home, and the time when we lost our medical practice and cottage and residual possessions, I lost twenty pounds in weight, my cortisol (stress hormone) went up, my PSA (prostate hormone relating to inflammation or cancer) went up, my testosterone (sex hormone) went down, I was constantly trembling day and night, I was passing urine between four and nine times every night, my sheets were drenched with sweat, the small muscles of both my hands were constantly flickering, my pulse became fast and irregular, I developed a fungal rash on my chest and back, my right shoulder became frozen and (through a viral infection) I lost 40% of the hearing in my left ear. All these medical conditions resolved completely over the next year, as I became less stressed, many of them sooner than that.

I have never doubted the close relationship between mind and body. I have observed it day after day in numerous patients in my medical practice and in my rehab. Now I experienced it in myself and I could do nothing about it.

Principles:

1 It is best not to say that we understand how people feel: we may not do so even if we have had similar experiences – and certainly we cannot say it if we haven't.

2 Familiarity establishes emotional 'anchors'. An anchor is a Neuro-Linguistic Programming (NLP) term that applies to sights, sounds, tastes, touches and other sensations that bring up reminders of feelings or people or places or events.

3 In time we establish new anchors in new relationships and in new places.

4 It is foolish to pretend that we ever fully get over any form of bereavement. It would be sad if we did – because it would be disrespectful to the people and other familiars we have lost. We learn to live with the loss.

5 Even with a normal healthy diet and looking after ourselves as best we can, we cannot counter the effects of dysregulation of the stress hormone. The interaction between emotional and physical aspects of our lives is total.

Action:

1 Count your blessings. Treasure memories of the good times.

2 Simply survive until the raging torrent of feelings subsides.

3 Physical symptoms resolve when the mind is healed – although you should always get appropriate medical check-ups.

4 Remember that there are many kind and helpful people in the world. They may lack professional qualification but their hearts will be in the right place and that is what matters, provided that they give support rather than specific personal advice. (This caution should apply also to professionals.)

5 Do anything rather than retreat into isolation. That would be the surest way to depress yourself.

6 You may believe that you are stuck in a pit of despair, where the bottom appears fathomless, but there is a way out.

Reminder: The bigger they come, the harder they fall.

Notes:

I had been used to running my medical practice and treatment centre over a seven day week. I had once been a junior hospital doctor in the days when we were very rarely allowed home. I did two years in the Royal Signals in the Army before I ever thought of doing Medicine. I survived the stupidities and cruelties of a British private school. I am very tough.

Yet, as I have just illustrated, I came crashing down. My wife fared better than I did. In fact she looked after me.

The medical practice and the treatment centre were my babies: I created them. My staff were my friends: I chose them and trained them and worked alongside them. My personal friends, mostly musicians, actors, artists and writers, were all creative people.

Now I had nothing – no work to do, day or night, and no regular contact with anyone other than my wife – and she had better things to do, rather than to be my full-time carer. She had her own life to lead and I had to remember that.

Somehow I had to pull myself together but I found that I couldn't. This was not through lack of will-power or stamina – I am an exceedingly determined individual – but it is simply a statement of fact.

Doctors might diagnose my clinical condition as 'depression' and then debate whether it was exogenous (caused by outside circumstances) or endogenous (within me). That wouldn't help me. Their platitudes and pills would be the last thing I needed.

The next last thing I needed was to be patronized by people telling me that they were sure that I would benefit from the experience. How could they possibly know that? Eventually I simply had to wait to get better but do positive things each day. Waiting is difficult for me at any time – but that's the way it had to be.

Principles:
1 All the practical experience in the world does not prepare us for the personal upheaval of bereavement.
2 Determination and will power are practical assets. They have little or no function in the world of feeling.
3 To enjoy our work, and be friends with our staff, is a privilege. Productive enterprises and happy professional relationships, that were once created, can be created again.
4 Personal partners may choose to occupy any number of roles within the relationship – but these roles have to be taken on by choice rather than as an expectation.
5 The inability to sort ourselves out and pull ourselves together is as true in bereavement as it is in addictive or compulsive behaviour. It is precisely this feature that makes these conditions so fearful – and also so little understood by other people, even by most doctors, including psychiatrists. It may be that we have to experience these mental states ourselves before we get a true understanding of them.

Action:
1 Remember that, as a member of the human race, you have the capacity for thoughts, feelings, actions and reactions and you are a member of various family and professional and social groups. When they all collapse at once, that inevitably causes significant trauma. Preserve whatever you can of your sanity.
2 Remember the business principle that expanding a loss-making enterprise simply results in making a bigger loss. Remember also the recommendation that, if you are in a hole, it would be wise to stop digging. It is counter-productive to be busy, busy, busy until you are in a sufficiently settled state to be able to make clear observations and sensible decisions. Do simple things each day.
3 Masterly inactivity can on occasions be the most effective strategy. As Buddhists sometimes say, 'Don't just do something – sit there!'

Reminder: Two legs good (sometimes), four legs comforting (mostly).

Notes:

My wife and I always enjoyed the company of four-legged animals, sometimes more so than the two-legged version. We missed them now.

Phoebe, our Bichon Frisé, has a mind of her own, such mind as she ever had. She had favourite human friends, especially among our house staff and counselling staff, and she was sometimes more obviously affectionate to them than she ever was to us. She also made her prejudices clear by barking at particular visitors. She had no sense of the requirement for affability in the private sector. She now lives with our former housekeeper, whom she always loved.

Cat and Cat (we couldn't tell them apart), whom we had had since our daughter's Burmese queen gave birth to a litter of half-moggies after an illicit assignation, lived in the country, half wild. They seemed to acknowledge us when they felt like it, the one (I don't know which) apparently visiting us somewhat more frequently than the other. Now we had them re-homed through the Blue Cross. Catching them (by deceit), caging them, carrying them off to distant parts and leaving them in strange new surroundings, was very painful.

Parting from the sheep (who kept the grass cut at our cottage) was less of a wrench, although they were certainly the most attentive audience that I have ever had when giving lectures.

Now the only cats and dogs and other animals that we had were china ornaments – at the very time that we could most have done with some live four-legged company.

We were not sentimental over our pets. Nobody who has kept farm animals could ever be sentimental. But we loved them. We enjoyed their company. Losing them was a dreadful blow. We missed them, in some ways, more than anything else.

Principles:

1 Although sentimentality can go too far, domestic animals can be very comforting at any time, let alone at times of particular need.

2 Animals have their own personalities and we need to respect that. They choose us, although we may fool ourselves into thinking that we choose them.

4 Dogs are essentially pack animals whereas herding cats is totally impossible.

5 Parting from beloved pets is incredibly painful, particularly as there is no way of explaining it to them.

6 Domestic animals usually have a shorter life span than humans and their loss can be a significant bereavement every time.

7 Human beings also have some good points.

Action:

1 Do the best you can to arrange for care for your pets if you have to leave them.

2 Do not underestimate the sense of loss that you will feel on the death of a pet or when otherwise parting from one.

3 Remember that dogs have to be fed and watered and walked whereas cats are more independent.

4 Remember that veterinary surgeons charge fees for the services that pets deserve. Do not get another pet unless you can afford one.

5 Maintain all the human contact that you can. Becoming isolated can be a killer.

6 Avoid becoming insufferably soppy over animals. They may at times appear to give us more love than our families but we should remember that animals have to love us in order to get fed. That trick is also played by children who are reluctant to leave the parental nest.

7 When the time comes to part with a much loved pet, our first concern should be the welfare of the animal, rather than our own.

Reminder: 'A dead man walking' refers to a person who is in denial of the seriousness of his situation. It is only a matter of time before he dies.

Notes:
Retrospectively, I can see that I was a dead man walking for almost two years before the final debacle. I thought I could survive all the mis-management, and even criminal activity, by working harder. I did not see the credit crunch coming. (Nor did the Government but they do not pay a personal financial price for that: the taxpayer pays it.) Those of us working in the private sector cannot afford the casual laxity of state enterprises.

Interestingly, a lot of the comments made to me were evidence that dead men were walking (in my shoes) all over the place:

> 'It will soon be over.' . . . No it wasn't.
> 'It's only money.' . . . No it isn't: the losses are far more widespread.
> 'You will wonder why you did not make this change before.' . . . No, I didn't.
> 'Things will be even better.' . . . Only if I make them so.
> 'You will be on your feet again in no time.' . . . Or on my back.
> 'At least you have your health.' . . . No I didn't.
> 'At least you have each other.' . . . Many relationships falter under this emotional pressure.
> 'Think of how much worse it could be.' . . . Thanks a bunch for that.
> 'Think positively: you're a long time dead.' . . . Really?

These gratuitous comments were intended to be comforting and supportive. I did not find them so, but that does not detract from their positive wish for our welfare.

Principles:
1 Serious situations require serious appraisal and serious remedies, preferably in advance of disaster.
2 The private sector funds the state, which cannot be trusted. Politicians get elected on saying what they will spend. In this way we get the Government that we deserve. In the private sector, we need to take that into account when running our own businesses.
3 Insensitive comments can be made, usually inadvertently, in any bereavement situation.

Action:
1 Take nothing for granted. At some time you will be bereaved in some way.
2 If you work in the private sector, you have to take on the responsibilities of the private sector.
3 Do not assume that your professional advisors and banks are working for you: they work for themselves.
4 Recognize that the insensitive comments of other people were usually well meant.
5 Try to avoid making insensitive comments to other people who are in some kind of difficult situation, particularly those remarks beginning, "You must feel . . ."
6 Be gentle with yourself. Hindsight is easy. Foresight is difficult.
7 Take the opportunity, on a daily basis, to observe your current behaviour. Note the good and bad things you have done and note the people who were affected by your actions. Put yourself on the list and see how your actions affected you.
8 Read Ayn Rand's novel *Atlas Shrugged*, the story of what drives the motor of the world. (I read it thirty-three years ago but I still forgot the personal, political and philo-sophical messages that are very pertinent today.)
9 Think long and hard before establishing a new business. Be very wary of any involvement with government.

Reminder: The first requirement is to survive.

Notes:
Following my financial and personal catastrophe, I was very fragile emotionally. Feeling guilty and shameful compounded my problems. The depth and pace of the changes that my wife and I endured were huge. Whatever my personal and professional skills and previous achievements, they counted for nothing. They were no use in the eye of the storm.

My medical problems, outlined earlier, indicated to me an increased risk of cancer, diabetes, a heart attack or a road accident. Successive losses caused successive deterioration. In some people, in similar situations, there is a significant risk of suicide.

I needed help and I was only too glad to ask for it from my professional colleagues. I often benefited greatly from their specialist expertise. Some, very kindly, simply gave me time and lunch and I responded warmly to both. Obviously these are difficult commodities for doctors to give to all their patients but I firmly believe they are more effective than the recommended standard treatments with medication and Cognitive Behavioural Therapy (which works very well for people who do not have significant clinical problems in the first place).

Psychotherapy can be very helpful in skilled hands – but I myself had trained many of the people whose clinical knowledge and understanding I respect. (Well I would respect them, wouldn't I?) However, two professional colleagues – a Jungian psychologist and a trainer in Neuro-Linguistic Programming – were very helpful to me.

Most of all I benefited from maintaining the loving relationship that my wife and I had continuingly created and shared for half a century. Also, on the principle that we keep what we give away, I reached out as best I could to help others. Taking my mind off my own problems, and focussing on theirs, actually helped me.

Principles:

1 As mentioned previously, a long-term loving relationship is known to be the most important factor of all (even above not smoking cigarettes) in achieving long-term physical health.

2 Guilt and shame cannot be wished away. However, in time, following any bereavement, broader perspectives on our previous circumstances become apparent.

3 Road accidents are the most likely cause of death in the surviving partner after a bereavement of any kind.

4 Suicide is distressingly common when people can see no way out of their difficulties and have little sense of hope.

5 Psychotherapy requires significant skill. It is understandable that brain surgeons are at the peak of requirement for clinical training. Brain manipulators often have very little training.

5 When one person reaches out to help another, it is the person doing the helping who gets the benefit (provided that the helping does not veer into compulsive helping, having a need to be needed and giving to other people a form of help that might get in the way of them finding their own path).

Action:

1 Do not smoke or drink excessively (or even at all) or use drugs of any kind. They are likely to make things worse rather than better.

2 Drive carefully or, preferably, not at all when you are in a stressful situation.

3 Talk to the Samaritans (or anybody) before making a suicide attempt.

4 Remember that human empathy and practical skill, rather than paper qualifications, are the essentials for psychotherapists or counsellors of any kind.

5 Find out some simple ways of reaching out to help other people appropriately and then do so on a regular basis – but respect other people's capacity to do well on their own.

Reminder: Mentally going over and over what has happened is not helpful.

Notes:
I felt I had to find the underlying cause that led to everything falling apart. I ruminated, chewing the cud like a cow.

Should I have left my medical practice previously and focussed only upon the treatment centre? Should I have employed, at great expense, a full-time finance director? Was I right to spend two whole years writing policies and procedures and monitoring systems, in accordance with new regulations from the Government, or should I have given up the unequal struggle with bureaucracy and found a way round it? Should I have been more cautious when times were good, expanding less so that I had what I needed rather than what I wanted? Was I wrong to hand over the management of the treatment centre while focussing upon the group therapy and counselling work and the training that I enjoyed? Should I have resisted the expansion into Europe? Did I over-promote and over-pay some of the staff? Should I have taken some part of every week to monitor the financial management? Should I have taken more note of the cynical but true observation that some staff will steal if they can? Was I right in calling in the liquidators (who were very pleasant before I signed their letter of appointment but who seemed totally aloof afterwards) or might I have struggled on somehow? Should I have recognized that estate agents initially put in a high valuation because it is in their interests to get the appointment? Should I have seen in advance the credit crunch and the crash in property prices? Should I have wasted time and emotional energy on an informal voluntary arrangement with my creditors (IVA)? Should I have got my head to rule my heart and sold out years ago? . . . and so on and so on.

Perhaps there was only one consideration that I really ought to have pondered: should I have listened more to my wife's concerns?

Principles:

1 Running a business is like fighting terrorism: just one mistake can be fatal. Most of us make plenty.
2 Staff need to be worth their salaries. Senior specialist staff may be well worth their high cost if they bring in specific expertise.
3 There comes a time in the growth of any business when it requires a formal management structure.
4 The person who takes the financial risk should also take the responsibility of supervision of the financial management.
5 Some staff will steal when they can. Monitoring systems are necessary in order to protect all the other staff from the criminal activity of these few.
6 Outside professionals still work primarily for themselves even after taking a fee.
7 Some professionals, such as accountants, lawyers and liquidators, do very well out of the misfortunes and stupidities of others.
8 The ideal situation is for head and heart to work together.

Action:

1 Stop playing God: accept that you are fallible.
2 Remember that the dead hand of accountability to the Government will always ultimately be destructive. Stay clear of it as far as possible.
3 Expect value for money from your staff and from outside professionals and recognize that competence – or even good manners – does not automatically accompany a high fee.
4 Take into account that greed has a stranglehold in financial markets.
5 Don't lose heart. Give yourself a break. Rumination over any form of bereavement embeds it. After an appropriate time for grieving, you need to focus upon moving on.
6 Always remember, at the peak of your activity, that another person, especially a spouse, may suffer every bit as much as you do.

Reminder: Timing is everything.

Notes:

As a former general medical practitioner, I am aware that long-term immunity against a disease depends upon the precise timing of inoculations: the second injection results in a dramatically increased response in a previously sensitized individual. Now, with one physical and emotional loss after another, the end result was that I had a progressively greater bereavement reaction.

I lost the counselling centre and our London home. That hurt. Then I lost the treatment centre itself. That hurt a lot. Then we lost our cottage, in which we had lived for forty-two years, and that was terrible. Finally, losing my medical practice and all our personal and professional contacts was devastating. I am not sure whether losing everything at once would have been easier but I suspect it might have been. The intervening moments of hope were almost more difficult to take – because they led to deeper despair.

Losing a loved one, human or animal or material, is inevitably painful. Losing several is more so. Dragging out the process over several months or more was utterly soul-destroying. Just when I was getting up, I was knocked down again – time after time after time.

I had hoped that going bankrupt would be an end to the inexorable series of losses but my wife, as a co-signatory for our securities, had to follow me into bankruptcy. This was not what I had anticipated giving her as a present at that time in her life. It made little practical difference to our situation but it was another painful humiliation for both of us.

We walked up the road to the Crown Court and went into the insolvency office. The clerk took my wife's details. I paid the fee with money borrowed from my brother. In due course the judge declared my lovely wife bankrupt. She wept. I wept.

At some stage the bereavements had to stop. I wondered when.

Principles:
1 We are none of us the master or mistress of our fate.
2 Successive bereavements cause progressively deeper emotional reactions.
3 There is no law that says that losses (or benefits) have to stop.
4 Giving a partner a sense of security through co-ownership can be a two-edged sword.

Action:
1 Don't try to reassure yourself that there are plenty of people in the world who are worse off than you are. Of course there are: there always will be. This awareness will do nothing to relieve your own sense of bereavement. Each one of us loves in our own way and grieves in our own way.
2 Be aware that the timing of successive losses can knock the stuffing out of you, at least for a time.
3 Do not expect other people – even your family and others who know you well – to understand how you feel. They cannot. Your feelings are your own and they are just as real for you as other people's are for them. The same cause, or a similar one, can lead to very different emotional results in different people.
4 Deal with each loss as best you can. Hope that it will be the last of the series of losses but do not bank on it.
5 Equally, do not assume that life cannot suddenly take a turn for the better. Twists and turns of fate have their own direction and their own timetable.
6 Remember that your emotional reactions are always a choice, depending upon your values. Good values should be kept while the suffering is endured. Inadequate values should be changed.
7 Think about all the possible implications, to you and to others, before you sign any document.
8 Consider how fortunate you are if you have a close personal relationship. Ask yourself if that is reciprocal.

Reminder: If you run away, you may find yourself in some very strange places – and you may then want to come back.

Notes:

I am very familiar with displacement activities. These are the things that people do in order to try to escape from the reality of their lives. I have seen other people do them and I have done them myself.

When we are emotionally vulnerable, we look for comfort – sometimes in the arms of other people. This isn't clever and it can be very destructive.

In this recent crisis, I would do Su Doku puzzles for hours at night until I was fed up with them. I would bury myself in my daily work in my medical practice and in my counselling work and in training my staff in the treatment centre – all in order to try to disguise from myself the nature of my financial plight. I felt that I needed rewards of some kind. If nothing else, I felt that I deserved a few moments of respite from the constant grind.

In previous crises (we all have plenty in the course of our lifetimes but not quite as dramatic as the one I had recently gone through) I used to shop for England. (Men under pressure commonly buy computer equipment, or sports equipment or clean out the garden centre. Women tend to buy clothes or cosmetics.) On one occasion I ran a marathon. It's a long way and it didn't get me anywhere. In previous times, despite being a doctor and fully aware of all the dangers, I smoked or drank or ate too much. Most of all, I made plans. Almost always they were crazy: they had no basis in reality because my reality was changing so fast from day to day.

Yet still I would look for any and every way to escape from the reality that was grinding me down each day.

Eventually I had to stop running away and see my situation as it really was. I could make sensible plans only when my life settled down and when I was content where I was.

Principles:

1 Displacement activities are psychological escapes from reality. They do not succeed in this quest.

2 We make emotional relationships in accordance with our own emotional state. When we are vulnerable, we attract vulnerable people.

3 Changing our bodies, by taking excessive exercise or by having plastic surgery, is emotionally unhelpful. Gyms and cosmetic surgeons are dubious – and sometimes dangerous – luxuries.

Action:

1 Avoid compulsive behaviour, doing things such as drinking, eating, gambling, working, exercising and shopping or spending excessively. Don't smoke cigarettes or take drugs at all.

2 A general guide for people who have suffered any form of bereavement is that you should first buy a plant. If it is still alive at the end of one year, you should get a pet. If the pet is still alive at the end of the second year, you are then ready to have a relationship with a human being.

3 Be aware that the fashion industry is based upon trying to change external appearances in order to satisfy internal emotional needs. This cannot possibly work.

4 Be aware that newspapers and television programmes tend to create a culture of dissatisfaction with the present – and of satisfaction only if we change things in ourselves or in our environment. These can be perfectly healthy processes but they can also be distinctly unhelpful when nothing really needed changing in the first place. The consumer culture and the entitlement culture are closely allied to the dependency culture so that our wants very quickly become our needs and demands.

5 Be content, as far as possible, where you are each day, even while trying to change the distressing circumstances of your life. This will give you peace of mind.

Reminder: Grief reactions run their natural course through denial, anger, sadness, negotiation and, finally, acceptance. This process usually takes up to two years.

Notes:
I didn't shed a single tear while we were still fighting to retain something. I cried every day for three months when I realized that all was lost. I had thought that my natural stamina and resilience would carry me through. They didn't.

I was angry with myself more than with anyone else, although I have to say that some people behaved despicably towards us. But those experiences were balanced by the actions of other people who were exceptionally kind.

Gradually the loss sunk in. My treatment centre had gone. My medical career had come to an end. We were homeless. Our whole lives would inevitably change. I felt desolate.

I tried to maintain my counselling skills by doing some work but I realized that I was not in a fit state to look after other people when I couldn't look after myself. I had to allow myself to grieve.

In time, my heart and my head settled. I began to look at what I might possibly do with my life in the future. Other doctors very kindly offered to help me to start again in medical practice but I felt that the excessive regulations of various authorities would take away all pleasure and any opportunity for innovation. I looked at trying to re-create what I had done before in the counselling world but it seemed to me that I would be looking back rather than forward.

I recognised that my assets were not as dependable as I thought they were. I was not a registered doctor any more. I had dropped out of my clinical world and I became estranged from my professional surroundings and contacts.

It wasn't until the heavy year of my bankruptcy was complete that I began to write again and then to get some new ideas.

Principles:

1 Grief reactions run the same course irrespective of their cause.
2 Brain biochemistry has its own timescale. It cannot be hurried.
3 Stamina and resilience are powerless in countering grief.
4 There is evidence (in Attribution Theory) that people come through grief reactions more smoothly if they blame someone else for their predicament. However, the sense of blame must surely be resolved at some time because otherwise it will act as a spiritual dead weight. For those of us who have addictive natures, self-pity and blame are killers. They tend to drive us relentlessly back towards active addiction.
5 Ultimately one has no choice but to come to terms with the new reality, whatever it may be.
6 The only purpose of looking back is to treasure the good memories. It is very damaging to go on grieving indefinitely.
7 When the heart and head are well, new creativity blossoms.

Action:

1 Allow yourself to grieve and go through the natural course of a bereavement reaction.
2 There is a time to shed tears. There is no harm in that – and possibly a lot of good.
3 Do not work again (if you wish to at all) until you are mentally and emotionally ready to give your best. But keep your mind alive in any constructive way that you can.
4 Treasure all fond memories of people, places, possessions and events. Remember the good times with happy reflection.
5 Put down your resentments when you are ready to do so. Otherwise they will hinder new relationships and creativity.
6 Get out of your own way. Remember that you will have a beautiful future only if you give it a chance to be that.
7 Beware of making new close relationships until you are completely through the grief process.

Reminder: For every sorrowful loser, there is a satisfied winner.

Notes:
A lot of people lost a lot of money on the failure of our companies and the fall in value of our properties. Most of the banks lost money on mortgages we could not service and on loans we could not repay. Secondary lenders and hire purchase companies came out with nothing, even when they had charges over property, because the enforced sale of assets financially covered only the first mortgages, if that.

Bills from the local councils and the commodity companies, supplying electricity, gas, oil and telephone services, were left unpaid. Small traders got nothing. The butcher didn't get paid although our patients and staff had eaten his meat. The local garage didn't get paid although we had consumed the fuel. Individuals such as the NLP practitioner who supplied skilled services to us didn't get paid.

I felt deeply ashamed over all these losses. I had never anticipated not being able to pay a bill. At the time that I ceased trading, I had thought that the sale of our properties would more than cover all my debts. Even so, the ultimate responsibility for all the losses was mine.

I cannot criticize the money men who did well out of my financial demise. The successful bankers, lawyers and accountants, liquidators and trustees in bankruptcy were doing the work that they do. The people who bought our properties at knock-down prices did so in the open market.

I might wish that these various winners might sometimes do so with a better grace. Perhaps they might develop more awareness of the human suffering of the various losers, including my staff who lost their employment. However, I suppose that this is not the general way that these particular people function. Theirs is a weird trade.

I am highly competitive myself in my professional work. I want to be the best in my field – but not at the expense of other people.

Principles:

1 All financial trading is a gamble at some level.
2 Winners and losers balance out.
3 There is no such thing as a painless loss.
4 Small traders provide the vast majority of all employment and financial trade. They drive the economy of the country but they are always the ones who take the greatest hit when things go wrong: they very rarely have any security against their trading losses.
5 Businesses go bust on cash flow, not on their balance sheets.
6 People who work for the state have it cushy. They do not deserve the feather-bedded pensions and benefits that they get, sometimes on top of very hefty salaries. Their security is all funded by taxation on the private sector.
7 No one in the private sector has the right to a job at any level. The same should apply in the state sector.
8 Some winners in the private sector are extremely generous in their donations to charity, even in our welfare state.
9 The good times will come again – but so will the bad times. We need to be appropriately cautious at all times.

Action:

1 Don't work in the kitchen if you can't take the heat.
2 Take responsibility for due diligence (assessing all risks and benefits as far as possible), whether you are a lender or a borrower.
3 Keep short credit lines, if you can, if you are a small trader.
4 Admire rather than resent people who do well – but have some consideration for people whose lives are swept away in the tsunami of a financial crisis.
5 Lenders tend to be blamed when people cannot pay back their loans. This cannot be justified. If the loan had not been taken out, it could not be called in or defaulted upon.
6 Lenders often lose money. Then they get criticised for making bad loans. When they do make money, they get criticised just the same.

Reminder: Behind every statistic is a human face.

Notes:

I read that almost two per cent of all bankruptcies are in people of my wife's and my age. We were trying to earn our livings and provide employment for others at a time when most people have retired. We did so because we had the privilege of enjoying our work.

My parents were missionaries. There was no family money. I had to build everything for myself. My wife's family were teachers and they also had nothing. We built our first medical practice by putting up a sign that said 'Doctor' and we waited for the first patient. When I left the National Health Service, I had to start again pretty well from nothing. Very few patients came across from the state to the private sector. (I left the NHS in order to put my own ideas into practice, rather than follow the dictates of the Department of Health.)

The jobs of the people I employed were mine: I created them. The salaries that my staff earned were theirs because they worked for them. Eventually, we employed over one hundred and twenty staff. When I lost my employment, they all lost theirs (other than a few who went with my son, Robin, who bought one of our companies from the liquidator).

I was very fond of my staff. I recall a *Sunday Times* report on Sir Kenneth Cork, 'the master liquidator', who 'has amassed a fortune out of other people's mistakes'. He was quoted as saying 'Never get emotionally involved in what you are doing'. I understand what he meant – but I wouldn't want to live like that, professionally or personally.

I feel sad for my staff who became unemployed. Many told me that they would be glad to work for me again. I am very gratified by that but I am still saddened and ashamed that I let them down.

I tended not to think of my own human face. I was an employer, not a Civil Servant or an employee. The buck stopped with me.

Principles:

1 Some people work for money and then spend it on things they enjoy. Others enjoy their work. These people generally prefer to make a profit, rather than a loss, but their motivation tends not to be primarily financial.
2 Some people want the easy predictable life of working within a fixed framework. Others have the urge to create things.
3 There should be two distinct populations: those who work in state services and those who work in the private sector. People who compromise these boundaries may get themselves into difficult practical and ethical muddles.
4 Taxpayers are entitled to the benefits and services for which they pay. Employees are not entitled to anything that is not specified in their contracts, although their employers often give bonuses.
5 It is not possible to create anything original while working for the state. It is a top-down directed management system. In the private sector new ideas can take root only through the willing and enthusiastic co-operation of all the staff.
6 A life without passion is not worth living.
7 A loyal relationship between employer and staff is mutual.

Action:

1 Do work that you enjoy (if you can).
2 Keep on working: it will keep you young.
3 People who are born into riches often lose them – because they do not respect what it took to create them. Pity them.
4 Do not compromise your professional and ethical standards by working in both the state and private sectors at the same time.
5 Never forget that creating an enterprise – and taking all the responsibility – gives you the right to determine how it is run.
6 Stay passionately committed to your work and to the people with whom you work. Any alternative is unworthy.
7 Stay human.

Reminder: Everyone in a family suffers when the head goes down.

Notes:

Our elder son, Robin, worked with us and we had hoped in due course to hand on the business to him. It was already his in practice. He had put a lot into it, financially and managerially, but we were still the dominant influences. Our wills said that we wanted one-third of the value of the properties to go to each of our other two children. After our bankruptcy, we had nothing to hand on. Our wills, with their various bequests, looked pathetic.

Robin took on the rump of the business, apart from the medical practice, and did what he could with it. Our daughter, Nicola, was tremendously helpful in trying to keep us afloat and, subsequently, in helping to dispose of our properties and helping us to move. Our younger son, Henry, twice came over from Australia to do what he could in trying to negotiate with creditors. This was a fruitless exercise, as it turned out, with two of the creditors saying that it was their absolute policy to bankrupt people who did not pay up in full – and one of them did exactly that to us.

Just as we might have hoped to have had something to show for our life's work, our children might reasonably have expected some form of inheritance. Now we and they had nothing.

My brother was helpful to us in various ways. My wife's sister, Hilary, was a tower of strength.

Our children's children (I never refer to myself as a grandparent because I do not wish to muscle in on parental authority) missed out on the various things we had previously done together.

It would be easy to present our bankruptcies as an individual crisis for my wife and me. It was far more than that. It was a disaster for our whole family and also for many other people as well.

People who imagine that bankruptcy is simply a temporary glitch have no idea how traumatic the whole process can be.

Principles:

1 Entrepreneurship rarely survives for longer than one generation (the next generation does not have the initial stimulus of hunger) and, through bankruptcy, it may not survive at all.

2 Expectation of inheritance might even possibly inhibit creativity.

3 Just as a business cannot be run without proper financial management, there is much more to a business than mere financial management.

4 Some lenders are vicious. That is the way they choose to run their businesses and that is their right: it is their money.

5 All family relationships are challenging at any time and most of all in times of crisis.

6 As Victor Borge, the comedian, said 'Your parents get on with your children because they have a common enemy – you'.

Action:

1 Beware of trying to establish a dynasty. It may be a curse rather than a blessing.

2 Remember that 'something for nothing' is as damaging in family inheritance as it is in state handouts.

3 Be aware that nowadays many of the major banks have taken on the attitudes and behaviour of backstreet lenders – because they believe that they should also have rich pickings. Borrowing is always dangerous.

4 Appreciate family members for the help that they give. But don't rely on it or expect it.

5 Be aware that making a special relationship with grand-children can be very undermining of their parents and hence cause significant disruption in the family. Enjoy your children's children as they are.

6 Especially at a time of general economic collapse, when large numbers of people are being made bankrupt, spare a thought for the stress that this creates for families and for employees.

Reminder: Nobody owes a living to anyone else.

Notes:
As a doctor, I tried over the years to help people who, for one reason or another, were unable to help themselves. In the UK we live in a remarkably compassionate society. 75% of the income of many charities comes from the government, in order to disguise the full extent of state incursion into our lives. Many billions of pounds are given to charities by government and by individuals, despite our having a 'free and comprehensive' welfare state.

I believe that a minimal state (covering only the upholding of contract law and the employment of police and armed forces so that we ourselves do not have to carry weapons) would be preferable to the present situation in which the government squanders vast sums of taxpayers money and individual donations on pet projects that may achieve little.

I paid my tax and I created employment through which my staff paid their tax. Since leaving the NHS thirty years ago I took no income from the state until my wife and I took our old age pensions (which for the two of us came to less than the minimum wage for a forty hour week for a single person). I make no complaint other than to say that I believe that many entrepreneurs could have done more creative things with this tax money than the government did with it.

I chose to work again as soon as I was fit enough to do so. It may seem odd to say that I wanted to become a taxpayer again but I disliked my dependence on the state. I wanted my dignity.

An aunt of mine died while I was bankrupt. Her legacy to me, quite rightly, went into the creditors' pot. I expect nothing from anybody. I have had a very privileged life and I want to put something into society, in my own way, rather than take from it. I want to create something again. At the very least, in future, I should like to be able to provide for my wife and myself.

Principles:
1 If we wish to belong to a compassionate society we have to do whatever we can to contribute to it.
2 Perceived needs and demands will always exceed any capacity to provide.
3 Governments tend to demand appreciation for themselves when they give away other people's hard-earned money.
4 Defaulting borrowers should pay a price. Otherwise we would get away with theft.
5 Providing for oneself and for one's family should be a universal expectation for people who have the mental and physical capacity to do so.

Action:
1 Contribute something – money or time or skill – to some form of charitable work, not necessarily to a registered charity. Understand that the state very commonly does not provide for those most in need but some charities, such as The Salvation Army, do and so do many individuals. Self-serving though some charities may be, they remain a more focussed option than universal provision by the state, when considering giving help to those most in need.
2 Acknowledge Benjamin Franklin's saying that 'In this world nothing can be said to be certain, except death and taxes'. Pay the tax but oppose the concept and look for better ideas.
3 Pay your bills or take the consequences.
4 Whatever happens, do not be discouraged. Start again and provide as well as you can for yourself and for your family.
5 Do not buy into the emotional blackmail that other people have a right to the money you worked hard to earn, the possessions that you purchased and the enterprises that you created.
6 When people expect you to do something without charge, offer them the opportunity to contribute to the costs of doing so.
7 Whatever your circumstances, count your blessings.

Reminder: Settling old scores hurts everybody.

Notes:
Addicts tend to resent the very people who are trying to guide them towards abstinence from mood-altering substances, behaviours or relationships. As a GP I did upset some patients but I had no formal complaint against me from over a quarter of a million consultations. In my treatment centre, I would get formal complaints to the health authorities or to the General Medical Council – or both – several times a year. There are abusive statements about me on the Internet. My website has been attacked with malicious software (although this can happen to anyone) and I still receive abusive letters occasionally from people who believe that I misdiagnosed or mistreated them or a member of their family.

Addicts want to learn how to use their chosen behaviour 'sensibly'. They want to get out of trouble. They want someone else to fix them rather than take responsibility for themselves on a continuing daily basis. They resent anything that gets in their way and they attack – in one way or another – anybody who sees things differently from their determined way of seeing things. I understand and accept all of this: it is in the nature of the work that I do.

When my cottage was burnt to the ground, the arsonist was a complete stranger who had 'a message from God'. I would have preferred him to have been on the Blues Brothers' mission from God. When my treatment centre was burnt to the ground, I suspect it was simply vandalism. Not everything that happens to me is caused by addicts. My medical practice was totally stripped by a creditor and the contents advertised in a bankruptcy sale mentioning my name, which was a deliberate act of (illegal) vengeance.

What matters to me is that I myself should never be resentful nor at any time retaliate in any way. If I were to point a finger at someone else, there would be three fingers pointing back at me.

Principles:
1 Life is difficult.
2 Addicts (probably ten to fifteen per cent of the population) make life even more difficult for themselves and others.
3 We are totally responsible for our reactions. When other people are abusive to us, it does not follow that we should be abusive to them. This would give them the power to determine our behaviour.
4 Addicts are not alone in biting the hands that feed them but they get a lot of practice in doing so.
5 The Mental Health Act exists to care for people who do not have the mental competence to be responsible for their actions.
6 When anger – through repeated self-justification – is fuelled into becoming a continuing resentment, a normal healthy emotion becomes a poison.
7 The Blues Brothers' mission to recreate a jazz band was on the right lines for the creation of a happy life.

Action:
1 Listen to complaints: they might be justified.
2 Be as understanding as is reasonable over other people's behaviour.
3 Give addicts good or bad consequences for their behaviour.
4 Respond to abusive letters by being polite and respectful but do not expect the complainant to accept your explanation. Head your letter 'Without prejudice', in order to avoid getting into a legal minefield.
5 Remember that there are a lot of unhappy people in the world and that there is no need to add to them.
6 Watch the film The Blues Brothers and be at peace.
7 Avoid getting into a fixed state of mind, believing that you have been singled out for traumatic experiences. Sometimes the dice, in life's continuing game of chance, appear to be loaded. But they are not. Usually, good and bad luck even out eventually.

Reminder: Long-term patterns of behaviour are likely to continue.

Notes:

George Santayana said that those who cannot remember the past are condemned to repeat it. I failed to learn from the previous systematic thefts by a long-term member of staff in my medical practice. Through my compulsive helping, I was too trusting – and that persisted. I didn't want to believe that close colleagues could steal so determinedly. As with government social services, I went beyond caring into care-taking. I took too much responsibility – and I thereby belittled the capacity of my staff and patients to care for themselves and change their own behaviour. I harmed myself and also everyone else in the process.

I am capable of standing up for myself, as I did when a Professor of Sociology attacked me in print, despite never having met me and, quite clearly, not having read my books. I attended a conference in which he was the principal speaker and I spoke back to him in public. I know how to defend myself when I finally get round to doing so.

For the last twenty-five years I have been trying to counter the arrogance and inconsiderate behaviour of my own earlier life. I do not like what various mood-altering substances and behaviours do to me and, through my behaviour, to those around me. Through working a daily therapeutic programme, this pattern has changed. I now need to ensure that I focus more carefully on my compulsive helping.

I work in the field of addictive behaviour, primarily with patients suffering from alcoholism, drug addiction or eating disorders (but also any other compulsion) and I do what I can to help them to change the long-term patterns of their behaviour.

I cannot be much use to them, or to their families, if I still have active compulsive behaviour of my own. I need to follow the advice that I give to them: total abstinence is the only effective way forward.

Principles:
1 Learn from experience.
2 Compulsive helping is not a virtue: it is a highly destructive behaviour. People working in the helping professions become very damaging when their natural or professional helping becomes compulsive helping (with a need to be needed and a determination to persist with a behaviour regardless of the fact that it is ineffective and also damaging to self and others).
3 When compulsive helpers are involved in government at any level, the financial costs are considerable. The human suffering when people do not take personal responsibility to change their own behaviour is also huge.
4 A possibly genetically inherited compulsive behavioural pattern can be modified on a day-to-day basis by taking it into account rather than hoping we do not have it.
5 Addiction is an illness which can be treated appropriately, rather than a weakness of willpower or a consequence of being brought up badly or led into bad ways.
6 Addicts can learn to be highly responsible when they are totally abstinent from damaging mood-altering substances or behaviours and when they maintain their therapeutic programme on a day to day basis.

Action:
1 Learn from experience. Learn from experience. Learn from experience.
2 Observe and understand how damaging compulsive helping can be, particularly in the helping professions and in government but also at an individual level in families and at work.
3 Accept responsibility for your own behaviour and see whether some aspects need to be changed on a continuing basis.
4 Those of us who work in the field of addiction treatment, need to ensure that we are squeaky clean ourselves.

Reminder: Being responsible to people differs from being responsible for them.

Notes:
When our children were young, my wife and I were responsible for them in providing love, food, clothing, housing, schooling, and many other things. We were responsible to them in giving them a good example and helping them to establish their own system of values. When they grew up, we were no longer responsible for them but we were still responsible to them. When our parents were elderly, our earlier roles were reversed and we became responsible for them.

I had a responsibility to my staff to educate, train, inspire, encourage and pay them and to challenge those who were unreliable. Occasionally, one of them would ask for a pay rise because of difficulty in paying off prior debts. I had no responsibility for that.

I have a responsibility to my wife to behave myself and to be considerate to her and I am responsible for her if she is unwell.

I take on whatever responsibility I want. I do not take on any responsibility that I do not want: I owe my life to no one. I do not believe that I had an obligation to work in the NHS even though I was trained in it, rather inadequately at times. I contributed (for no fee) to the training of a great many medical students even when I was working in the fully private sector. These students owe me nothing.

I have chosen to work far harder than many other doctors, doing a seven-day week for twenty-three years, and I looked after a particularly challenging group of patients, Yet I did not burn out. I enjoyed the work. By contrast, many medical and nursing staff complain of burn-out. This may be because of unrecognized compulsive helping or it may be because they do not have the talent or appropriate training and helpful supervision for their particular job.

I am still responsible *to* my family and patients but not *for* any of them. I am responsible only for myself.

148

Principles:

1 We have a responsibility for children and the elderly and others who are incapable of looking after themselves. We have no responsibility for anyone else.

2 We have a responsibility to our children in setting them a good example. Terrible damage is done to children by irresponsible parents failing to give an example of a decent set of values.

3 Failure to challenge unreliable staff betrays the reliable staff.

4 There are many responsibilities within a marriage or within any other long-term relationship.

5 Guilt trips need to be firmly rejected.

6 Being trained in either the state or private sector does not lead to a life-long obligation to that sector.

7 The cause of professional burnout is usually in the individual.

Action:

1 Take responsibility for the children you created. You had a choice: they did not.

2 Be responsible to yourself and to other people in the example that you set through your own behaviour.

3 Accept responsibility for contributing to the care of those who cannot care for themselves. Do not assume that the state or other people will necessarily do so. Practical action, rather than simple financial contribution, makes the real difference.

4 Challenge unreliable staff. Failure to do so devalues the work done by all the others.

5 Ask those who criticize you to say what they themselves have ever done to contribute to the care of others or to put something into a wider community than their own backyard.

6 Look after your staff appropriately and do not unthinkingly accept responsibility for their burnout.

7 Become more familiar with the concept of compulsive helping and see how destructive this process can be.

Reminder: 'Thank you for not sharing your feelings.'(Seen on a T-shirt in San Francisco.)

Notes:
I felt a need to talk to people about my predicament. People often asked me what had happened – and I told them my version of events. I wanted their understanding but, quite rightly, this was not always the response that I received. I remember my politician uncle quoting to me 'Never tell people your troubles: half don't want to know and the other half are delighted'. I sensed that I was more likely to lose friends than to gain them by rabbiting on about my difficulties. However, I still felt a need to tell my story to someone.

My family were quick to point out that I myself contributed significantly to my undoing. I came to recognize that my own compulsive helping and risk-taking were the prime underlying cause, just as my addictive nature was the antecedent cause of many of the difficulties in my earlier life.

The behaviour of other people and of the Government were contributory causes. A dramatic fall in patient numbers, due to the credit crunch, was the immediate precipitant cause.

I came to these realizations as a result of talks with my mentor (another private GP), who shared the same exasperation over state regulation, my supervisor, a clinical psychologist who understood all the challenges of counselling work, and my (personal but non-financial) sponsor who understood my addictive nature because he has the same basic defect even though it comes out in other ways that are personal to him.

I recognized that, rather than needing to tell, I really needed to listen and then I needed to act in new ways. If I persisted with my previous ideas and behaviour, I would get the same results all over again. I therefore had to look at where my former concepts and actions had got me into trouble. I needed help with seeing that.

Principles:

1 Governments and the security services share information on a 'need to know' basis. There is also a human need to tell.
2 Emotional incontinence can be very tiresome to other people.
3 The prime focus of lasting friendship is to enjoy discussions and share activities, rather than for a mutual non-professional therapy.
4 Family members often feel an obligation to tell home truths.
5 The antecedent underlying cause of any event is the most significant because it will lead to further damage unless it is tackled. Contributory causes are often given as the prime reasons for an event by people who have no insight into their own behaviour. Precipitant causes are usually simply the final straws that broke the camel's back.
6 The more challenging the situation, the more care needs to be given to finding sensible people (with no axes to grind) with whom to discuss the difficulties.
7 Ultimately, we need to listen rather than talk if we are to make the necessary changes to our ideas and behaviour.

Action:

1 Self-indulgent feelings are most appropriately shared on stage rather than landed on long-suffering friends, family members or even strangers.
2 Look for the antecedent cause of your current distress and recognize that it is most probably in yourself.
3 Beware of seeking help from people who have little in common with you and who may, despite impressive-sounding professional titles, have little talent for the task in hand.
4 Listen rather than talk, if you really want to change your thoughts, feelings and behaviour for the future.
5 Look towards developing new ideas and behaviours with a sense of spontaneity, creativity and enthusiasm.
6 Maintain your sense of humour.

Reminder: All growth is a leap in the dark.

Notes:
I had to consider some of the most difficult decisions of my life at a time when I really wasn't in a fit state to take them. Where would we live? Should we apply for council housing or approach a charity? Should I stay working as a doctor? If I were to do so, how would I pay for professional registration and insurance? What would be my alternatives? Should I try to work on my own as a counsellor? Should I work towards setting up another treatment centre? Should I work for someone else? Could I work as a trainer in some way? Would it be possible for me to earn some sort of living as a writer? How would I get the money to start anything at all?

Clearly I could not go back to what I had before because there was nothing left of it: the properties and the staff had gone. I had well-wishers but these were hard times and I did not imagine that people would be benefactors to me. Why should they? Whatever I was going to do in the future would have to be based on my own wits.

I was not frightened of starting something new. I simply couldn't see how it could be done. People who knew me well said that they had every confidence that I would create something new. Others who hardly knew me at all suggested that I should enjoy a well-earned retirement. That had no attraction for me.

I had to remember (heaven help me if I ever forget) that I have a wife and that she would have views of her own on our future. She made it quite clear that she did not want to live in constant fear, nor to have the telephone ringing in the middle of almost every night. I very much needed to discuss things with her, rather than impose decisions upon her.

As it was, I had no idea how I could begin a new professional life. I couldn't go back to any aspect of my previous one but I could not see any clear way ahead.

Principles:

1 Easy decisions are taken in easy times. Difficult decisions tend to be required in difficult times.
2 There is no shortage of people who are absolutely sure what should be done in any circumstance.
3 The realities of life can be harsh.
4 There are people who look forward to retirement. Interestingly, doctors who choose to retire early, for reasons other than ill health, tend to die at a younger age than those who continue working.
5 In a long-term relationship, or in any at all, it is wise to discuss options rather than impose decisions.
6 Gestalt therapists refer to 'a fertile void' between one completed cycle of life events and another one beginning.

Action:

1 Take only those decisions that you have to take: the others can wait until your head is in better shape.
2 By all means look at options for the future but keep your mind as open as possible and make as few irrevocable decisions as possible.
3 New ideas and opportunities may occur out of the blue.
4 Retire if you want to but be wary of stagnating so that your mind and your arteries silt up.
5 Start with two clean sheets: one for yourself and one for the other significant person in your life (if there is one). Write down what each of you would like to do in life and how you would suggest moving towards that goal. Then compare the two and see where ideas and prospects agree or disagree. Make no compromises: try to find a win/win solution that gives each person the chance to do something that he or she most values while, at the same time, living happily alongside the other.
6 Remember that one person's excitement may be another person's worst fear.
7 Read up on Gestalt therapy, if you so wish.

Reminder: What goes up may come crashing down again.

Notes:
Ten months into my bankruptcy, my head still wasn't settled. If I had a really good day, feeling bright and positive, I could almost guarantee that the following day I would feel wretched. I wasn't trying to talk myself into negativity; quite the opposite. I wanted a sense of enthusiasm to break through but my head wasn't ready for it. It seemed to have a life of its own. Like it or not, I had to come to terms with these day-to-day variations in mental capacity.

This was very hard on my wife who had no escape from listening to me. It was also hard on people who wanted me to become more predictable. I was not prepared to be ruled but I did not want to be a risk to other people. I needed to protect myself but also to be sensitive to others. In particular, I had to be aware of my capacity for making impetuous decisions and note that they would simply cause me further trouble. I suppose I was still grieving and that I was in the negotiation phase of the standard bereavement reaction.

Gradually I developed a sense of bonding with my new familiars – our small flat and the few possessions that we had been allowed to keep and our new way of life. Gradually I moved through the stage of negotiation towards acceptance.

I still wasn't ready to make any plans for the future but at least I was getting to the stage where I was stuck in the present rather than in the past.

I spent most of my time working with my sponsor on looking at how I could clear the emotional wreckage out of my head and move forward into some form of stability. It helped me to reflect not only on my primary addictive behaviour, in the use of mood-altering substances and behaviours, but also on my compulsive helping. This was the most damaging of all my addictive behaviours. I had to come to terms with that before I could move on in my life.

Principles:
1 False dawns can be very dispiriting unless one sees them as part of the natural healing process.
2 A head that has been through the wringer will inevitably have day-to-day variations as it gradually learns to function properly again. This is not something that can be controlled: a head takes its own time to go through the healing process in its own way. Taking antidepressants or other mood-altering drugs prevents a head from going through the natural healing process.
3 Telling other people about the ups and downs in our own feelings can be very tiresome for them.
4 Being advised and helped by other people may be necessary, to some extent, if there is a risk of an unsettled head leading towards making damaging impetuous decisions.
5 In the negotiation stage of the standard grief reaction, we try things out, discovering what works and what doesn't, but mostly we just allow ourselves to go through it.
6 In time we make new bonds and establish new emotional and behavioural anchors.
7 Being stuck in the present is at least better than still drowning in grief over the past.
8 Giving time to working on oneself is beneficial.

Action:
1 Accept that the clarity of your thoughts and the stability of your feelings will vary from day to day when you are in the negotiation phase of the standard bereavement reaction.
2 Be wary of making impetuous decisions.
3 Listen to advice but do not surrender all your autonomy by letting yourself be ruled by other people.
4 Create new bonds and anchors with your new familiars.
5 Take time to work on yourself in whatever therapeutic programme suits you best.

Reminder: We each make progress at our own pace.

Notes:
I would have liked to shrug my shoulders and move on but it didn't work that way. I knew, from my work with patients going through their grief reactions, that the same stimulus (stressor) can have very different reactions (stress) in different people. Some get stuck for quite some time in one or another phase of the grief reaction.

In any process (Gestalt) there is a cycle from sensation of perceived needs to awareness of social or biological needs, motivation and excitation, action, making final contact, having satisfaction and then returning to start with new sensations. Gestalt therapy aims to help people who get stuck in any one of these phases. I have used this with other people. This helped me to begin to understand and accept what was happening to me.

Similarly, my experience in Transactional Analysis of the discussions patients have with an internal 'parent', 'adult' or 'child', and of psychological games that people play, made me aware of these same processes in myself.

I was too young in heart and mind to consider putting my feet up. I was very much still alive and keen to do something positive with my life. – But what?

I recognized that I would need every facet of my own creativity if I were to come through the challenges that I would face after being discharged from bankruptcy. I was becoming ready to move on but I did not know how to do so. Nor did I have any idea of where I was going in the next phase of my life.

I continued to work on myself, not making plans for the future but, through reading and talking and generally getting involved with the outside world, I was able to help my own internal world to settle down and be ready for whatever my future might be. I could only hope that it would be as stimulating as what had gone before.

Principles:

1 Shrugging shoulders is fine – but it doesn't help us to move on.

2 Nothing and nobody can make us stressed. The external stressor (such as a bereavement of some kind) may be the same for many people but stress reactions are individual.

3 Gestalt therapy helps people to become unstuck in their thoughts, feelings and behavioural processes.

4 Transactional Analysis helps people to become aware of their internalized 'parent', 'adult' or 'child' voices and recognise the psychological games that they play.

5 Being discharged from bankruptcy – or creating a new relationship – is not simply the end of previous difficulties. It is the beginning of a new challenge.

6 It is helpful to try to break the deadlock of a head going round and round in circles. Getting involved with the outside world is the best way to become ready for any possible future.

Action:

1 Shrug your shoulders only if you have an itch on your back.

2 Understand that you may not be able to influence an external stressor but you do have the power to influence the internal stress that you experience.

3 Ask for help through Gestalt therapy if you get stuck.

4 Ask for help through Transactional Analysis if your internalized 'parent', 'adult' or 'child' voices are still taunting you.

5 Know from Rational Emotive Behaviour Therapy that you can talk back to your internal voices and challenge them.

6 Read Eric Berne's book *Games People Play*.

7 Know that we grow through challenge and change and that life would be indescribably boring if we have no challenge or change at all in any way.

8 Get involved in the outside world in any way that you can, provided that it gives you a sense of privilege and vitality.

Reminder: The brain looks after itself very well.

Notes:
As a medical student, I was taught the basics of brain biochemistry – how various chemicals influenced the function of the brain. I was taught pharmacology (the study of drugs), and therapeutics (the study of how they could be used for treatment). The diagrams used in lectures, and in pharmaceutical company circulars to doctors, were incredibly complex. I was meant to be baffled by science and I was. Over the years, the diagrams became progressively more complicated. A whole series of new drugs – particularly those acting on the mind – was introduced, one after another. When one was found in clinical practice with patients to be ineffective or dangerous or addictive, it was straightforwardly replaced by another. There was always a magic bullet for us to prescribe and, if the first one didn't work, there were plenty of others we could try, either on their own or in combination.

I did not believe what I was told. I believed what I saw in many patients: they became zombies or hyper-excitable or addicted. I remember a Professor of Psychiatry in a London teaching hospital telling me that he prescribed barbiturates to help people to get to sleep and amphetamines to brighten them up in the morning. He said that the great advantage of these drugs was that neither was addictive. Time showed him to be absolutely wrong. It should be obvious that any drug that has an effect on the mind is bound to be addictive to people who have addictive natures.

My own prescribing costs were only forty per cent of those of other doctors working in my area in London – primarily because I did not prescribe mood-altering drugs, such as tranquillisers, sleeping tablets or antidepressants. While delegating the clinical monitoring of hypertension, diabetes and other chronic illnesses to nurses, I gave patients my time. They did very well. Their brains looked after themselves.

Principles:

1 Pharmaceutical companies occupy many of the top places in the league of financial markets. Their profits come largely from psycho-tropic drugs that act on the mind.

2 Published controlled trials of drugs such as the 'antidepressant' Prozac show only twenty per cent more effectiveness than placebo (tablets that have no pharmacological content). Tragically, even so, these drugs are sometimes used in attempts to commit suicide.

3 When 'tranquillizers' such as Valium/Diazepam were discouraged, because of the risk that they were habit forming, the pharmaceutical companies responded by saying that some antidepressants could also be used as tranquillizers.

4 Cocaine would treat toothache but, hopefully, no one would prescribe it for that. Correspondingly, tranquillizers, antidepressants and sleeping tablets should perhaps not be prescribed even – and maybe especially – if they are clinically effective. There are many non-pharmacological ways of helping people to alter their mood. It is not healthy for either doctors or patients to believe that there should be a pill for every emotional ill.

5 There is plenty of time in general medical practice (I myself had 3,500 NHS patients) provided that the doctor is well organized and knows how to delegate to nurse practitioners and to practice managers.

6 The time of a doctor is valuably spent in helping people with emotional problems by listening to them and supporting them.

7 Patients often ask doctors for mood-altering drugs because they believe that they need them and because they want to avoid all feelings of being uncomfortable. This is unrealistic and unsafe.

Action:

1 Follow the advice of your own doctor but, if you have the opportunity, choose him or her with care.

Reminder: The brain constantly remakes itself.

Notes:

I had been taught that the brain and nerve cells could die but never regenerate. Recent research shows that this is not true. Magnetic resonance imaging (MRI) scans of the brains of London taxi drivers show that their posterior hippocampi (the part of the brain concerned with orienteering) are particularly enlarged. After they retire, their hippocampi go back to being the same size as anyone else's. This finding of 'neuroplasticity' means that we get progressively better at doing things that we practice – because we change the physical structure of the part of our brain that governs that activity.

I worked as a doctor all my adult life. Being a doctor is in my ears and eyes and hands as well as in the way I think. Now the part of my brain that I used for that purpose will shrink. The counselling part of my brain has always been present and fairly well developed but it will now become even more so. I have reassessed what I want to do with my life and this is it. Addicts are my people. In tackling their multiple problems, I develop progressively more skills at helping them with the emotional challenges in their lives – and that part of my brain becomes more developed.

The ending of my year of bankruptcy was not marked with a certificate or an interview. It was a damp squib. It just happened. My thoughts and feelings were mostly settled already. I noticed very little difference in my day-to-day life. New work did not suddenly appear. I had to create my own future. It was encouraging to know that my brain did not need to stay stuck in the past, either physically or mentally. It can grow in any way I want in response to whatever practice I give it.

I look to the future with a fresh mind, not a damaged one. I learn from my experience and I move forward. I have no idea what my precise future will be. That uncertainty is what I love most about it.

Principles:

1 Science progresses. The things that we were taught in our student days may no longer be true. Entirely new concepts and ways of looking at things may come to the fore.
2 It is not true that our childhood marks us forever. It certainly will do so if, through Analytical Psychotherapy or Cognitive Analytical Therapy, we go on digging it over. It is better simply to accept it as part of our history – and let it go.
3 Practice may not make us perfect – but it certainly helps us to improve and we can't get better without it.
4 When we get out of practice we quickly lose our skills.
5 By practising something new, we develop new skills and we enlarge the parts of our brain associated with them.
6 Things do not suddenly change overnight with any rite of passage.
7 When we work out what we really want to do in our lives, we can achieve whatever we wish – provided that we look to the future rather than the past.

Action:

1 Remember the centipede that developed an analysis paralysis when asked which of its legs it moved first.
2 Keep up to date with changes in scientific understanding, whether or not you are a trained scientist.
3 Maintain your skills with regular practice if you want to retain and enhance them.
4 Let go of the past. See it simply as training for the future.
5 As in Dustin Hoffman's film *Tootsie*, do not anticipate needing an agent to field all your future professional offers or personal opportunities. There may not be any. But life is still for living – just for today as it is.
6 As *Bugsy Malone* said, you can be anything that you want to be.
7 Relish uncertainty. See it as having the potential to give you even greater rewards than you ever imagined possible.

Reminder: Physical fitness is less significant than mental, emotional or spiritual fitness.

Notes:

I hated team sports at school because I am short-sighted and couldn't see the ball. I was an embarrassment rather than an asset to any team. Fifty years later I am fit but some of my more athletic contemporaries have gone off.

I value physical fitness as a way of keeping my heart healthy and my joints supple. I respect my body and I am careful not to damage it but I do not believe that rippling muscles are either attractive or a sign of supreme health.

I am more concerned to be mentally healthy, keeping myself sharp by reading and writing and doing puzzles and not filling my mind with a load of rubbish.

I keep myself emotionally healthy by making a list of the good and bad things I have done each day and the people affected by my actions. I do things that I enjoy and, where I can, I avoid activities that I dislike.

My spiritual health matters to me most of all. I try to be kind, honest, open-minded and willing, sensible and considerate, accepting and grateful, enthusiastic and creative. All these abstract qualities make a huge difference in my life when I come close to attaining any of them.

Emerging from bankruptcy, I had to be aware that my creditors would still be watching me. They would look in vain for undeclared property or a stash of some kind – there were none – but I felt that I needed them to be aware that I really was starting from nothing. Further, I needed to be sensitive to them and not be flamboyant in any way. Also, I needed to be appropriately cautious so as not to repeat the whole sorry process. My grief reaction lasted more than a year from the time that our companies went into liquidation. Then I was ready to see how my experience could be of some benefit to others.

Principles:

1 Encouraging children to get involved in sporting activities does not necessarily lead to them being physically fit as adults.

2 Physical fitness, and maintaining a healthy diet and body weight, improves the chances of living a long and happy life.

3 Mental fitness can be very rewarding irrespective of actual intelligence. The alternative, in William Blake's imagery, is to breed reptiles of the mind.

4 Emotional fitness comes from an awareness of the effects of our behaviour. When we do good things, we feel good. When we do bad things, we feel bad. Living a 'selfish' (not self-centred) life – doing what we really enjoy – is therefore very beneficial to us and to those who are close to us. Doing things out of resentful duty or merciless shame is very destructive.

5 Spiritual health is fundamental to individual happiness and rewarding personal relationships.

6 Sensitivity towards other people, irrespective of who they are or what they do to us, is an important human value.

7 Being kind and understanding often leads to other people behaving in the same way. It doesn't really matter if they don't. These are rewarding behaviours in their own right.

Action:

1 Get physically fit for its own sake, not because you believe that athletic prowess says something about you as a person.

2 Maintain a sensible body weight and a healthy diet.

3 Be careful what you put into your mind: it may shrivel it.

4 Be truly 'selfish' through being kind and considerate to others.

5 Establish your own list of spiritual values.

6 Be cautious so as not to go down into the depths again.

7 Be sensitive to other people, not flaunting success of any kind.

8 Allow your own grief reaction to take its time.

9 Use all your experience beneficially for others, if you so wish.

Reminder: There are almost as many therapies as there are therapists.

Notes:
I studied Freudian Analytical Psychotherapy for eighteen months, half a day each week. Then I attended an analytical therapy group for a further six months. Receiving analysis trains people to become analysts. I don't think it achieves much else, other than self-obsession. I studied Behaviour Therapy, which gives patients increasing exposure to things that frighten them. It is an unpleasant treatment, whereas skilful use of Neuro-Linguistic Programming (NLP) can gently dispel a phobia in minutes and do many other wonderful things. Cognitive Behavioural Therapy is much revered by doctors because it is rational. I work with people whose resistance to change is often irrational. Reason doesn't work for them initially. It is useful only when they are emotionally stable and completely free from mood-altering drugs of any kind.

Gestalt therapy and Transactional Analysis are fun and they present a human face to human beings in difficulty. Choice Theory helps people to recognize their own capacity to help themselves, as does Cognitive Dialectical Therapy. Mindfulness encourages people to take time to ponder and reflect. Psychodrama works on thoughts, feelings and behaviour all at the same time and can be immensely helpful (but destructive in the hands of an insensitive director). Eye Movement Desensitization and Reprocessing (EMDR) sounds – and looks – weird but is in fact extremely helpful, particularly in the treatment of Post Traumatic Stress Disorder. The Twelve Step programme helps co-participants to gain external power over their progressively more destructive and unmanageable behaviour when they find that they are powerless to influence it by themselves. I have observed skilled therapists or participants in all these disciplines and I have had considerable privileged experience in some of them. Psychosynthesis, combining a bit of everything, is nuts.

Principles:

1 The difference between a counsellor, a therapist and a psychotherapist is primarily in the size of the fee.
2 A really skilled therapist would probably be equally successful whichever approach he or she used. Incompetent therapists would probably be unsuccessful in all of them.
3 Anything is preferable to prescribed drugs or Electro-Convulsive Therapy (ECT), stereo-tactic surgery on the brain or a frontal lobotomy. Drugs diminish the capacity of patients to think and feel and act for themselves, even though they may initially feel much brighter and say that they are more functional. The sting comes in the tail when they try to withdraw from them. Invasive therapies, such as ECT or surgery, are destructive. Their ethics are questionable, particularly when non-invasive therapies are available. Tom Lehrer said, blearily, 'I'd rather have a bottle in front of me than a frontal lobotomy'.
4 In the UK there are more counsellors than doctors. Talent is not universally equally distributed in either profession. Some counsellors have very little training but this does not appear to discourage them from providing their form of care for other people. Even those counsellors who do have training and certification do not necessarily have great therapeutic skill.
5 The world is in a mess but this does not imply that everyone in the world needs therapy.

Action:

1 Try the therapeutic approach (if you need one at all) that suits you.
2 Be aware that terrible damage can be done by some well-meaning doctors or therapists. A good rule of thumb is to ask friends what and whom they would recommend.
3 Read up on the history of psychiatry. It is a horror story.
4 Become aware of a range of effective therapeutic approaches that are not based upon medical or surgical methods.

Reminder: True resources are within.

Notes:
My treatment centre and my medical practice have gone but my experience and, hopefully, my intelligence, creativity and enthusiasm can remain. I seem to have been born with energy and stamina. I doubted that they would desert me. My commitment to doing something positive and exciting is definitely still there.

I am not frightened of expressing my own viewpoints and I am happy to be challenged on them. I learn nothing from yes-men: I learn from people who have ideas of their own.

I have visited the USA thirty-one times, attending conferences and speaking at them and visiting treatment centres and learning from their experience. In the field of treating addiction problems, the USA is at least thirty years ahead of the UK. As Sir Winston Churchill said, 'Our two countries are divided by a common language'.

Nowadays, we tend to blame American bankers for the credit crunch and for the unpopular and expensive wars in Iraq and Afghanistan. We scorn the USA health care system while sanctifying our NHS. We pride ourselves on our history, even though our state schools are determinedly rewriting it.

Our concept of tolerance is now governed more by political correctness than by a concern to listen to the opinions of others.

With these stark opinions of my own, I make no attempt to appeal to friends I already have. I want to learn from people who disagree with me. That is what I call making progress. I want to be challenged so that I can see where my ideas – particularly those I cling to most fervently – can be improved or even replaced.

I do not look to the government or to medical authorities to guide me in my quest for new knowledge and understanding. Progress in ideas tends to come from the periphery, from the iconoclasts, rather than from the centre.

Principles:

1 Whatever we may have lost, our internal resources persist.

2 A bereavement of any kind is a dreadful thing to go through – but we do go through it and, hopefully, come out with all our natural talents still in place.

3 People who are frightened of being challenged on their opinions are unlikely to have had any opinions worth having. Their views will tend to have been second-hand from parents, teachers, the media or downloaded from websites. They lack the authority of truly original thinkers.

4 The UK is a small island. The USA is one third of a continent. We would do well to forget our imperial past.

5 Tolerance and open-mindedness involve looking for where we might be wrong and then ferreting out new ideas.

6 Curiosity and eagerness to learn are the hallmarks of active minds and the passport to a happy and rewarding future.

Action:

1 Whatever you have lost, focus your attention now on the true inner resources that you have retained.

2 Make friends with people who disagree with you. They may have a great deal to teach you, either by showing you exciting new ideas, a fresh understanding and a better way of doing something or by showing you concepts with which you profoundly disagree and have no intention of copying.

3 Get rid of insular viewpoints by travelling widely and seeing other ways of implementing philosophical and political ideas. An armchair in front of the TV gives a very restricted view of life.

4 Discard political correctness. It is a force for stagnation.

5 Nurture your own child-like curiosity and eagerness to learn.

6 Take life as it comes and grasp it with both hands, making whatever you can with it.

7 Rebel.

Reminder: You tell a man by his enemies.

Notes:
I hope I shall always be polite and respectful to other people but I have no hesitation in expressing disagreement with ideas. I have twice been called 'a dangerous man' simply because I do have original ideas and speak up in support of them. I have learned to be appropriately frightened of people who shoot the messenger.

Courage is not the absence of fear. It is the persistence with an idea or an action that we believe to be correct, despite knowing that the opposition given by some people could extend beyond simple verbal disagreement.

I am proud to say that at school I was once knocked unconscious for my Socialist political ideas but I retained my viewpoint unchanged.

Later I learned that fear may indicate False Evidence Appearing Real. I looked at my own fears and I saw that they were often paper tigers. I looked at other people's fears and I understood them from their perspective. I learned not to make assumptions based solely upon the way that I see and do things. I recognized that my responses to my own fear or anger, or to the fear or anger of other people, might be very different from the responses that other people might make.

I learned that all feelings can be normal and healthy or otherwise. For example, we teach young children to be fearful of walking out into the road or of trusting strangers. In adult life I believe we should be fearful of democratic, as well as totalitarian, governments. The one may lead to another.

In adult life I learned how to combat my fears. At times this went too far and I did some things without sufficient thought for the security of my wife and myself. I have vowed not to make that mistake again. I look to the future with excitement but also with a reasonable measure of caution.

Principles:

1 People who have no enemies have never said or done anything of significance.
2 Dictators, and even politicians and bureaucrats in a democracy, may call people 'dangerous' when these people don't toe the party line or say and do what they 'should' say and do.
3 It takes courage to attack ideas that other people in our society might take for granted.
4 Sometimes we have nothing to fear but fear itself.
5 We are not all the same in our reactions to our own or other people's fear and anger.
6 Feelings can be healthy or unhealthy according to context.
7 Courage can go too far and become foolhardiness.

Action:

1 Stay polite and respectful (for the good of your own peace of mind), rather than take your lead from behaviour in parliament or in television interviews or 'discussions'.
2 Don't have original ideas if you want a quiet life. Do have original ideas if you want life to be fun.
3 Recognise that new ideas are often seen as a threat to other people, particularly to those in authority.
4 Examine your fears to see whether or not they are based in reality.
5 Accept that other people are different from you. They have a right to be respected as individuals.
6 Examine your own and other people's reactions to fear and anger. You may get some surprises in discovering how different people have very different reactions to their own or other people's fear or anger.
7 Teach children and adults to have appropriate fears over potentially dangerous situations.
8 Understand that feelings have no power in themselves but only when they lead to actions.
9 Don't take too many risks in the pursuit of an exciting life.

Reminder: 'Ain't it awful' is a self-fulfilling prophecy.

Notes:
Shock/horror stories sell newspapers. I once looked at a news-paper that focuses only upon good news. It was unreadable.

We seem to enjoy worrying ourselves to death but, as a Louisa M Alcott character said 'It ain't worth worrying a day until it's all worn out, on account of one thing always leading to another'.

At the beginning of my year in bankruptcy, I could foresee nothing good in my future. An NLP trainer challenged me by asking four questions:

> Am I sure that my anticipation is correct?
> Am I absolutely sure that there are no other possibilities?
> What happens (how do I react) when I believe another thought?
> Who would I be (with what capabilities) with that thought?

I took much heart from that. Now, the future was altogether much more positive in my mind. Life was not going to be awful: it was going to be very exciting, regardless of what might be happening in the wider political, financial or clinical world – because I had decided that it would be.

I recognized that only negative people really want to talk about negative things. I want to be positive. I have a sense of responsibility to myself, alongside my sense of responsibility to my wife and family. I knew that if I were to go down again I would be likely to drag my wife down. But if I were to be posi-tive, she would inevitably benefit and she would be able to be much more creative in her own life in the ways that she wished.

I don't go along with the fatuous positivity of Pollyanna. She met all troubles with a smiling face and a 'could be worse' attitude. Life is serious and it has to be taken seriously – with a light touch.

Principles:

1 Being negative or positive is a choice.
2 When we look into the future, we see what we want to see.
3 The world of politics and finance and particular features of our own professional or personal world might well be awful – but that doesn't mean that we ourselves have to feel dreadful.
4 If we go down, we take other close people down with us. If we are positive and creative, we enable and encourage others.
5 We can be realistic without being heavy-handed.

Action:

1 Read the newspapers, listen to the radio and watch television in order to stay in touch with the outside world – but do not be discouraged. Remember that there are a lot of lovely things happening in the world, even if they don't make news.
2 In considering any fixed belief, ask yourself the four questions that my NLP trainer asked me. They are based on the work of Byron Katie. Look her up on YouTube.
3 Reframe your projections – and realities – so that you see them as encouraging opportunities beyond the crises.
4 Avoid the insufferable banality of Pollyanna, the young girl American heroine, who was always grateful despite whatever happened to her. She was a pain.
5 Remember *Monty Python's Life of Brian* and the song 'Always Look on the Bright Side of Life', that is nowadays often sung (and whistled) more in genuine encouragement than irony.
6 Remember the proverb 'Laugh and the world laughs with you; weep and you weep alone'.
7 Remember that your nearest and dearest did not form a relationship with you in order to be miserable. Being positive in your own thoughts and behaviour will help you especially – but also everyone else around you.
8 Be serious – with a light touch.

Reminder: There are a great many 'one true' faiths.

Notes:
It is said that one cannot discuss religion with a Catholic, politics with a Marxist or psychology with a Freudian. Their firm belief in the correctness of their viewpoints is so secure that they believe the rest of us to be just plain wrong.

'Can't you see?' said my Socialist aunt. I could see her political views perfectly clearly but I didn't agree with them. She couldn't understand that at all. My parents were Christian missionaries in India. I thought the resident Muslims and Hindus were doing all right as they were – even though they fought each other.

My great concern over True Believers is that they may come to believe that they have the right – and even the duty – to kill non-believers. An alliance between church and state, a theocracy, has historically been amongst the most barbaric of all power bases; the wars between opposing religious believers among the most vicious.

Politically I am a Libertarian. I believe that the state – even the welfare state or the nanny state – is more commonly a force for destruction than for creativity. Wars and pogroms are imposed by governments, not just by deranged individuals.

I would hope that psychologists would know better than political dictators, bearing in mind that the reason for their existence is to try to understand human nature and guide it. That hope is forlorn; psychologists can fight each other as ferociously as any clans.

I prefer to accept people's differences. I am interested by them and I like to see where I can learn from them. For this tolerance – my agnosticism in religious terms, and my open-mindedness to psychological ideas – I risk being ostracized or worse. So be it.

I am aware that my former medical colleagues often refer to me as a maverick. I take that as a compliment, illustrating that I think for myself, rather than follow the herd.

Principles:

1 When we are in a vulnerable state we are easy meat for God-botherers, political zealots and psychological crazies. We need to be careful to consider religious, political and psychological beliefs with the same healthy open-minded scepticism that we would bring to scientific claims.

2 A scientific idea has to be disprovable; otherwise it is a faith. To say 'The moon is made of Wensleydale cheese' is nowadays disprovable by going there. Therefore, however bizarre or entertaining it may be, this statement is scientific. To say that a particular political or psychological belief is absolutely true is no more provable than saying the same of a religious belief.

3 We should be appropriately frightened of the power of the church or the state and particularly when they combine.

4 Ayn Rand's view was that the difference between a welfare state and a totalitarian state is merely a matter of time. One compromise and loss of liberty would lead to another.

5 Psychologists can be just as misguided and dangerous as anyone else if they come to believe in absolute truths.

Action:

1 Be aware that keeping a genuinely open mind can bring the forces of wrath and damnation down upon your head.

2 Remember Sir Winston Churchill's insight that democracy is a poor form of government until one considers the alternatives.

3 Remember that the forces for good and evil are not external. They are inside each one of us.

4 Beware of blindly following religious, political or psychological charismatic leaders.

5 Take the risk of having ideas of your own. The alternative, of always believing what other people tell you, is death by degrees.

6 Learn from your critics.

7 Celebrate differences.

Reminder: A clear destination will determine the route.

Notes:
I ask trainees 'How would you get from here to Kodaikanal?' Usually they don't know. I then give them a piece of useless information: it is the place of my birth. Only after further blank stares do I tell them that it is in South India. They didn't know how to get there until I gave them crucial helpful information.

Correspondingly, unless they have a clear goal in mind for the next stage of their own professional career and what they want to achieve for individual patients, they will have no idea how to begin. A medical professor once asked me 'Do you try to unsettle your students?' I replied that of course I do: I want to train them to think for themselves. My mother once told me that she wished I would have the same ideas two years in a row. I replied that I hope I never shall. I want to continue to learn.

Patients often say that they want to find out who they are. I know who I am. My identity and my ideas are reflected in my actions as they affect other people. If they all say I am kind or stupid then that is what and who I am.

I know what I want in life. My dream is to help addicts and their families. I want to bring a deeper understanding to the subjects of depression and addictive disease and to the processes of recovery.

It has taken time for me to come to these realizations. I had to throw out many of my childhood beliefs and many of the insights and indoctrinations that came from my medical training. I retained my Cambridge University eagerness to learn and to change my beliefs and goals when I find new ones that appeal to me more.

But change is difficult, exciting though it may be. I remember that when I resigned from the NHS practice I had created, I had no idea what I would do next – but I did know that I could not grow if I stayed where I was. I wanted my life to mean more than that.

Principles:

1 We need to find out who we are by getting a clear assessment of the impact of our behaviour on the people around us.

2 Establishing a precise goal is necessary before starting any new project.

3 The minds of students should be unsettled if they are ever to think for themselves rather than be robots.

4 Changing ideas is a sign of intellectual health.

5 Without a dream, life has little point or direction.

6 As Dr William Glasser points out, 'Universities sometimes exist to prevent the spread of human knowledge'.

7 It is a good idea to go out into the blue when ending one phase of life. That way our minds are open to all possibilities.

Action:

1 Monty Python's *Brian* encouraged the multitude to think for themselves. He said 'You are individuals'. A solitary voice from the back said 'I'm not'. That was true individuality! This is the example that we should follow if we want a stimulating and creative life.

2 Remember that Dr Mengele did what Adolf Hitler told him to do and that totalitarian regimes throughout history have used obedient doctors to commit truly terrible acts.

3 Always be on the lookout for better ideas.

4 Challenge the beliefs of your childhood. You may keep them or you may not.

5 Reject all indoctrination. Retain an eagerness to learn and a commitment to the process of learning.

6 Read Dr William Glasser's book *Choice Theory*.

7 Have the courage to recognize that a new phase of life can be much more exciting and rewarding when it is not contaminated by leftover ideas and activities from the previous phase – unless these are truly valuable for the future.

Reminder: It always ends in tears – but it hasn't ended yet.

Notes:
I remember learning that single-cell organisms are immortal. They reproduce by simply dividing into two cells. An individual cell may die but its clone lives on. Complex organisms hand on, to the next generation, genetic material governing behavioural and social patterns as well as physical characteristics. Mankind bequeaths not only its genetic material but also its creations and its constructive or destructive ideas and values

I remember the fall of Lady Thatcher, one of the most influential politicians of our time. At an upstairs window in Downing Street, there were tears in her eyes. My own medical career ended in tears. My elderly parents' lives ended perhaps with more sadness for me than for them. I hope that my own departure is more tranquil and dignified than theirs.

I see sadness as the reaction to an unfortunate event. I see depression as a sense of inner emptiness that has no external cause. To judge from the sheer number of prescriptions for so-called 'anti-depressants', doctors are often attempting to treat sadness with tablets.

I see true depression as a dis-ease of the human spirit. The sufferer often discovers the mood-altering effects of some substances, behaviours and relationships and then becomes addicted to using them through fear of returning to the former crushing void.

I work to provide a creative alternative and give people a sense of optimism, based upon positive values and attained through simple behavioural changes: taking responsibility for themselves, handing over their lives to a higher power than self when problems are outside their capacity to solve, and taking their minds off themselves by reaching out to help others anonymously on a continuing daily basis.

Eventually we die but – we don't need to waste time worrying about that when there are so many creative opportunities right now.

Principles:

1 Mankind usually has the privilege of living beyond the time of reproduction and witnessing its own genetic and cultural bequest.

2 Death is ultimately inevitable. There may be questionable ethics in doctors determinedly preserving physical life – often at great cost to dignity as well as to individual or state or other resources.

3 Spiritual, mental, emotional and social competence is as significant as full physical function in assessing our own quality of life. Judging the quality of life of other people is not straightforward. They have a right to their own concepts.

4 Sadness is best treated with understanding, support and time.

5 True depression and addiction are the same thing – before and after the discovery of mood-altering substances, behaviours and relationships that fill up the sense of inner emptiness.

6 Depression/addiction is totally treatable: a devastating clinical condition, with multiple disastrous consequences spread across the whole experience of life, can resolve with no trace – provided that simple daily activities are undertaken on a continuing basis.

Action:

1 Enjoy, if you have that privilege, seeing the next generation carry on your genetic material.

2 If you are not so fortunate, enjoy – alongside everyone else – seeing the fruits of your ideas, values and creations.

3 Value the quality of your life rather than merely its extent. Allow the elderly and infirm to die in peace at their allotted time (not against their will). Discourage doctors and nurses from struggling officiously to maintain a patient's degenerated physical and mental life irrespective of the wishes of the individual or family.

4 Do not confuse sadness and depression. Take time to identify depression/addiction through the questionnaire found on my website: www.doctor-robert.com.

Reminder: People who know all the answers don't understand the question.

Notes:

In *The Hitchhiker's Guide to the Galaxy* by Douglas Adams, I learned that the answer to the ultimate question is 42. Douglas Adams is mocking convergent thinkers, who are always looking for answers, in comparison with divergent thinkers, who are always looking for the next question. It is the journey itself, not arriving at the destination, that is so exciting.

Acknowledging that I could be wrong is a particularly stimulating process because it can lead me to follow an entirely new direction. At school I did Mathematics. I went up to university with the intention of studying Music but finished up, almost accidentally, with a degree in Medicine.

At the time of my graduation, my mother said to me 'I wish you had been a musician'. I may have been one of very few graduating doctors in history to have disappointed his or her mother!

My broad interest in the arts and the sciences has continued. In many ways the counselling work that I do now is a combination of both, having the imagery of the arts alongside the discipline of the sciences. I have retained the curiosity of my early childhood.

I am much influenced by Robert Thouless' book *Straight and Crooked Thinking* and by Jamie Whyte's book *Bad Thoughts: a Guide to Clear Thinking* and also by Karl Popper's ideas on the philosophy of science. This makes me sound like an egghead, which I am absolutely not: I am no academic. But I am interested in ideas. They keep me young. They are fun to explore, although this has to be done with a light touch: I enjoy Monty Python's humorous over-emphasis on 'the Meaning of life'.

I know many people – doctors mostly – who believe they have the answers to all life's challenges for themselves and for others.

Principles:

1 If we want to be totally secure in our knowledge, we will never create anything of any value. It is the questions, rather than the answers, that are most stimulating.

2 Acknowledging that we could be wrong is the starting position for any journey in a new direction.

3 Education is a continuing process: it does not stop when we leave school or university. Compulsory post-graduate lectures may, as has been said before, merely transfer the notes of the lecturer to the notes of the listener without passing through the minds of either.

4 Broad interests give us something in common with many people. They stimulate us to broaden our understanding even further when we hear experts talking on their own subjects.

5 The dusty world of academia is not so dusty after all when we come to know it – but the 'real' world for all of us is where ideas have to be put into practice.

6 We can be fearfully boring if we take ourselves too seriously.

7 Doctors have the power to prescribe or operate. These can be very dangerous processes when unaccompanied by thoughtful reflection on what really matters in life.

Action:

1 In contemplating your future after an acute crisis, enjoy the journey itself, rather than be forever looking towards the destination.

2 Consider that you could be wrong, particularly in your most fundamental beliefs. That way lies a sense of excitement that can last for the rest of your life.

3 Learn from anybody. See what really excites each person.

4 Recapture the curiosity of early childhood.

5 Remember that really clear thinkers express their ideas simply and understandably.

6 Have fun in exploring new ideas.

Reminder: Enthusiasm is infectious.

Notes:

I like knowing that the word enthusiasm comes from Greek words meaning 'God within'. When I am enthusiastic, I come alive. I get carried away sometimes and go too far but, looking back over my life, I can say that I have really lived.

I conducted Puccini's opera *La Bohème.* I gave a solo recital in the Purcell Room on the South Bank. I stood for Parliament. I farmed. I created an NHS group medical practice, a private diagnostic centre and a private rehabilitation clinic. I have learned and lectured all over the world. Now I can add a further experience: I have been totally wiped out. My enthusiasm is undimmed. My inner journey is still work in process. Hopefully, my outer journey will soon catch up.

Jean Houston's book *A Mythic Life* is a festival of enthusiasm from start to finish. She tells us the myths of widely differing cultures and helps us to explore our own full potential, following her example.

Deepak Chopra notes that the retina of the eye is sensitive to photons of light and the brain then converts electrical messages into images. He then asks 'Who is doing the looking?' His answer is that each one of us is a part of the Universal Spirit. Thus we are all part of each other already, not simply supposedly after the time of our death. In any case, at the sub-atomic level, the whole concept of existence is questionable: we flash in and out of existence at the speed of light all the time.

I find these ideas fascinating and I am stimulated by Deepak Chopra's enthusiasm. Rather than take on narrow religious concepts of life after death, I am delighted to learn that I am both alive and dead at the same time already. The next transition, when I shall have no physical body, will change nothing else. What fun!

I like to surround myself with enthusiastic people, irrespective of the subjects of their passion. They have a sense of life.

Principles:

1 We see the God within each other when we share our enthusiasm.
2 Life is for living – not simply for going through.
3 Our outer journey is of no great significance in comparison with our inner journey.
4 Our current civilization has a great deal to learn from others, past and present.
5 Our own full human potential is vastly greater than we might previously have imagined.
6 Material existence is a conventional concept but it is questionable in ultimate reality. We live in the 'real' world – but it isn't the only one, physically or spiritually.
7 Each one of us has our own concepts (or not) of life after death. It does us no harm to broaden our minds to wider possibilities than those we may previously have considered.

Action:

1 Seek out enthusiastic people – particularly teachers.
2 Get in touch with your own 'God within' and take your enthusiasm into everything you do.
3 Read Jean Houston's book *A Mythic Life*.
4 Consider Deepak Chopra's ideas.
5 Live in the real world, being productive and kind.
6 Worship life rather than death.
7 Be respectful to those whose ideas differ from yours.
8 Think about how your human spirit can achieve its full potential in this world.
9 Look forward enthusiastically, and without any fear, to the next transition. The miracle of our existence, moving from where we were before we were conceived to where we are now, has already occurred. Why should the next transition, to whatever happens after death, be any less miraculous? We may simply cease to exist but that seems unlikely in view of the fact of our present existence.

Reminder: When one door opens, another door opens.

Notes:
I find that doing things spontaneously is enormously pleasurable. Instead of asking myself why I should do something, I am more inclined to ask 'Why ever not?' I like the question: Two birds were sitting on a branch. One decided to fly away. How many were left? The answer is two – because the decision wasn't followed by action.

For me, predictability would be death. I enjoy not knowing what will happen. In this way, I had twenty-three years of running my treatment centre, not one year's experience repeated twenty-three times. Each year, each month, each week and even each day was different.

The lectures I gave were all unscripted. The patients or visitors chose the subjects at the time. In this way, I kept myself fresh. I myself learned from the process. Eventually I wrote a book based on those lectures: I had not written it in advance.

I would go into a group therapy or psychodrama session without any advance thought of what I would do. I responded to what I sensed in the room. Had I done otherwise, these sessions would have been mine rather than the patients'.

I learned from the work of Jacob Levy Moreno, the originator of psychodrama, how to direct a therapeutic interchange spontaneously, modifying it in response to the patients' contributions as it went along. I also learned from his widow and collaborator, Zerka, and from his pupil, Marsha Karp, and other skilled psychodramatists.

I learned directly from Richard Bandler, the co-originator of Neuro Linguistic Programming (NLP), how to observe patients' eye movements, as well as their body language, in order to understand how they were thinking and feeling.

Through being spontaneous, my whole therapeutic world was refreshing and stimulating, rather than mundane and repetitive. I looked forward to each of the eleven group sessions I ran each week.

Principles:

1 Amazing things happen when we are on a roll.
2 Doing things spontaneously brings unanticipated results. Our reach can exceed our grasp.
3 To think and plan, or even decide, is still a long way short of doing something.
4 Predictability inevitably leads to stagnation.
5 We gain experience through continually changing what we do, not by simply repeating it.
6 Doing a lecture, or a radio or TV programme, 'live' sharpens up the presenter.
7 If we have no preconceptions, we become sensitive to the feelings and wishes of other people. Also we hear what they really said, rather than what we thought or hoped they said.
8 We can learn from genius, rather than simply sit in admiration.
9 Psychodrama and NLP (unlike therapeutic processes that merely follow established routines) require the possession of spontaneous creative talent in the practitioner.

Action:

1 Take your chance when it comes. Otherwise create chances.
2 Capitalize on your good fortune when things go well.
3 Remember that 'action' is the magic word.
4 Create your own experience, by actively looking for it as you go along, and continually learn from it.
5 Make no presumptions. Keep all your senses alert.
6 Learn from the work of genius. Go out of your way to find it.
7 Remember that all creative work is estimated to be only one per cent inspiration but ninety-nine per cent perspiration. There are no short cuts that avoid sheer hard work.
8 Be dissatisfied with the ordinary. Look for the exceptional.
9 Treasure spontaneity. That way you will never get tired, let alone suffer from burnout.

Reminder: The gods laugh at plans.

Notes:
I wanted to make plans for my future but it was difficult to know how to begin. How would I find the down-payment even for renting a property? How would I take on staff that I could not guarantee to pay? At what level should I attempt to begin again – something very small or something likely to earn more money? I decided to leave all these questions unanswered and not make formal business plans (which are all make-believe anyway). I would simply take each day as it comes.

My security comes primarily from within. I feel that my principles are self-sustaining and that, to an appropriate degree, I am self-reliant. I have the privilege of living in a country where there is reasonable political freedom. I have supportive friends and a loving family. I am very privileged.

I found, however, that I had less time rather than more – because there is so much that I want to do. Parkinson's Law (stating that work expands to fill the time available and implying that we do not necessarily achieve more when we have more time) could be re-interpreted in the opposite way from its original implication, by saying that I could achieve more within each unit of time.

Ever one for the big idea, I looked for what might drive the next phase of my life. I knew that inside each one of us there are high valency atoms that were originally constructed within super-novae (exploding stars). This shows me my place in the wider universe. I knew from Thomas Gold's book *The Deep Hot Biosphere* that coal is more likely to be solidified oil, rather than a fossil fuel, and also that life is being created even today in vents in the floors of the oceans and that water, carbon dioxide, ammonia and hydrocarbons exist in vast quantities in space and can be the building bricks of further new life. Why should I not also produce ideas as original as these? They come from daring to think that each and every one of us has that potential.

Principles:

1 Starting again from nothing is a stimulating challenge in itself.
2 All business plans are suspended from sky hooks.
3 Taking each day as it comes leaves us open to wide possibilities.
4 Security is mainly an inside job.
5 Time is fluid: we can do as little or as much as we want in it.
6 We can think as big – or as little – as we want.
7 We have to take other people, such as wives or partners, into consideration because otherwise we can be in Big Trouble.

Action:

1 Be realistic in assessing your starting position. The last thing you want to do is to repeat any disastrous experience.
2 Keep your mind open as long as possible. It would be a shame to miss an important chance, or go down the wrong route altogether, simply as a result of making a hasty decision.
3 Build firm values and principles that are self-sustaining, rather than shallow and fragile.
4 Be as self-reliant as is appropriate, while remembering your previous difficulties and acknowledging that you have to take other people into consideration.
5 Do as much or as little as you want to do. Never complain that you have too little time – use it wisely and imaginatively.
6 Recognize your own place in the wider universe, rather than see yourself as merely a unit in your family or workplace.
7 Read Thomas Gold's book *The Deep Hot Biosphere* and dare to acknowledge that he might be right, while other conventional viewpoints could be wrong in this and also in other subjects.
8 Think as big or as small as you wish. Be as original as you can be because that distinguishes you from other people and gives you the opportunity to create something special.
9 Surprise yourself by doing something that you have never done before. This helps towards realising your full potential.

Reminder: Peace of mind comes primarily from living within one's financial means.

Notes:
Our new two-roomed flat in the almshouse would fit comfortably inside the living room of our previous flat in London. Thinking about this, I realize that I have almost always lived in two rooms. I very rarely made full use of all the space I did have. Writing, eating and sleeping do not take up a lot of space. They can be done even in a hammock in the garden. I can still function very well. I haven't really lost anything that is vital to creative existence.

I was never a big spender on personal things. We had few foreign holidays. We bought second-hand cars. My only indulgence was that I ran out of space for books. Downsizing was not the worst thing that could have happened. Living frugally is not an insuperable challenge.

When I emerged from bankruptcy, I had no assets but I also had no debts. I had no borrowings and I no longer had any fear that my possessions would be taken away from me. There are advantages in having so few. I recognised that we had no need ever to move again from our accommodation, tiny though it was. Our true needs were being met perfectly adequately.

On a personal basis, I do not need public acclaim – or even notoriety – and I am happy with the professional acknowledgement of a few friends and colleagues. I do not need to build another empire (such as it was). I have no intention whatever of putting myself again into the claws, beaks and talons of government regulation, dedicating my life to the furtherance of other people's ideas.

Far from being dispirited, I am simply more determined to do the creative things that I enjoy and to protect my wife and myself. I have very few personal possessions but they are not important to me. What matters to me is opportunity – and I can create that.

Principles:
1 We do not need a lot of space to be comfortable, either emotionally or physically.
2 When catastrophe occurs, it is helpful never to have been over-indulgent on ourselves – because we have less to lose, not only in terms of possessions but also in self-perception of status.
3 Trinkets and toys can be incredibly expensive in immature self-doubting hands.
4 True needs are remarkably few.
5 Public acclaim is fickle at the best of times.
6 Governments and trade unions (including the British Medical Association) may see us all merely as units of production – but we can be much more than that when we claim the right to manage our own professional and personal lives (if we can).

Action:
1 Work out what you really need. It may be much less than you think you need.
2 Avoid extravagant self-indulgence.
3 Live frugally, whether or not you need to do so. This is almost certainly healthier but it will also make it much easier to survive whatever difficult times might happen in future. None of us is for ever protected from the hand of fate or the stupidity of government.
4 Be comforted that you may not have lost anything that really matters to you.
5 Rise to the challenge of your new situation.
6 Look for the advantages in being as you are.
7 Reconsider whether you really want to build an empire or a dynasty. There are considerable advantages in staying small.
8 Be aware that government regulation is nowadays as intrusive in the private sector as it is in the state sector.
9 Generate new ideas to the best of your creative ability. Make new opportunities, rather than wait for them to happen.

Reminder: Friendships have to be actively maintained.

Notes:
I have made some enemies in my time. People who have addiction problems usually want to find ways of continuing with their behaviour but avoiding the damaging consequences. They would sometimes get angry with me when I said that this cannot be done.

I left people to make their own diagnosis through filling in my questionnaires but still some would say 'I know someone who . . .', using that limited personal encounter to contradict my professional insights. I can learn something from anyone but it is remarkable how many people try to teach me my own subject.

I recommended abstinence from all addictive substances and processes but this was sometimes rejected, despite the patients' previous attempts at 'sensible' use resulting in failure. Also, when patients relapsed, the disturbed attitudes and moods returned and I was seen as an enemy rather than as a friend. Often they said that the treatment hadn't worked and therefore they demanded their money back. Doctors who believe in prescribing drugs and in simply telling people to stop doing silly things, sometimes forcibly reject my ideas.

This is the heat of my particular kitchen. It is counterbalanced by some very appreciative doctors and by thousands of patients whom I was able to help – through their own efforts – to make radical changes in their lives.

In my medical practice, as well as in the treatment centre, I made a lot of long-term friends among my patients and staff. I also had many other friends outside my work environments. Most of my personal friends are highly creative people, coming from a wide range of professions. My wife and I had a very exciting social life. Leaving all that was a great sadness to us – but our friends didn't leave us: we stayed in touch. And, of course, we continue to make new friends when we meet people with whom we share values and interests.

Principles:
1 If we take friends for granted, they will go away.
2 Positive people are bound to make enemies of negative people.
3 Addicts are very good at making enemies; they have a lot of experience of it. When they are in recovery, being totally abstinent and working an appropriate continuing self-help programme, they can make close friendships – not only with each other but also with their families and other people in the outside world.
4 Personal experience (a study of just one or two friends) is not sufficient to counter the experience of professionals.
5 The attitudes and feelings of people towards an abstinent therapeutic programme will be determined very commonly by their own use (or not) of addictive substances and processes.
6 Doctors tend to do what they are trained to do. They may have little or no training in the understanding of the nature of addictive disease and recovery. They may reject these concepts, sometimes vehemently. They will usually be good at treating the medical consequences of addiction but may see addicts as a waste of time – unless they are paid by the government (or by the patients themselves) to prescribe pharmaceutical drugs that are merely a substitute addiction.

Action:
1 Stay in regular contact with your friends. You may need them.
2 It is probably best not to get involved in the treatment of addicts unless you yourself have experienced addiction problems in yourself and are now long-term abstinent and working a continuing recovery programme in Alcoholics Anonymous or similar Twelve Step programmes.
3 You may be interested in reading my book *Break Free From Addiction.*
4 Make friends outside your professional environment so that you have broad experience of life.

Reminder: We will never fully understand each other.

Notes:
My wife and I have known each other for fifty years but probably still understand very little about each other. It is known that couples tend to bicker over the same issues throughout all their lives. Instead of recognising that we have some fixed views, but are often prepared to change others, we all tend to focus on trying to change the fixed views of the other person.

We each have filters from our childhood and other experiences, through which we will tend to sieve – and alter – what people say to us. We may not be aware of our own filters. With thoughts and feelings and actions we each have open doors (through which we can be influenced), target doors (towards which we would like to influence the other person) and trap doors (through which we can tie the other person in knots). My open door is my feelings and my target door is my actions. My wife's open door is her thoughts and her target door is comfortable expression of her feelings. My trap door is my incessant capacity to intellectualize. My wife's trap door is her capacity to be forever busy. We communicate well because we understand our differences in these respects.

We also understand the archetypal roles (even if we ourselves do not follow them precisely) that men tend to want sex and risk (as well as food and laundry) whereas women tend to want love and security (and to go shopping). Universally, we need to feel special to at least one other person.

A good exercise is to change physical places and change roles with the other person and then speak from that other person's perspective. This can produce surprising insights and enable couples to grow closer together in time.

Even then, we can never know sufficient about another person to be sure of his or her perceptions.

Principles:

1 It is difficult enough trying to understand ourselves, let alone trying to understand someone else.

2 We waste a lot of time and effort trying to change other people's core viewpoints, rather than give up the unequal struggle and settle for the changes that we can get.

3 Self-assessment improves relationships. We need to be aware of our own filters so that we hear precisely what other people do say, rather than what we thought or hoped they said.

4 In close relationships we need to become aware of our own and other peoples' open and target and trap doors in their thoughts and feelings and actions. In this way we can communicate successfully with other people even though we may be very different from each other.

5 We need to be aware of archetypal roles (and where we might differ from them) so that we can get closer to giving other people what they most seek in our relationship, if we so wish.

6 Role-reversal with another person can be very illuminating.

Action:

1 Recognize that you never can fully understand someone else, however long you may have known that person.

2 When trying to influence other people, go for what you can get.

3 Be aware of your own filters and those of other people.

4 Become aware of your own open and target and trap doors as well as those of other people.

5 Understand archetypal roles or their personal modifications.

6 Recognize the need to feel special to at least one other person.

7 Try role-reversal exercises to improve your awareness of another person's perspective.

8 Remember that our perceptions are the reality that each of us lives in each day. Ours may differ significantly from those of other people, even when we have shared the same experience.

Reminder: Giving personal, rather than general, advice is patronising.

Notes:

Dr William Glasser says that when people tell you that they know what is good for you, you should run for your life. President Ronald Reagan said that the most frightening statement in the English language is 'I'm from the Government: I'm here to help'.

I have worked all my life in a helping profession. My experience is that it is not helpful to give specific, rather than general, advice. I do not tell people what to do in their own personal or professional lives but, as this book shows, I do think it is helpful to establish general principles and to make some general recommendations based upon them.

In the course of my lifetime, the breakdown of families has been very noticeable. Increasing divorce rates and numbers of single-parent families are frightening indicators of the disintegration of our society. Violent crime, with guns and knives, is on the increase. It often seems that governments penalize victims and pander to perpetrators. Social service provision fosters social collapse. As a general medical practitioner I have seen all of this at first hand. If I am ever a grumpy old man, it is for very good reason, based on practical experience.

Each new phase of life requires adjustments by everyone involved. New relationships, or changes in existing ones, may turn out to be more challenging than what went before.

Within my own family, I should like to individuate from my adult children, being my own person again. After all, during their adolescence, my children individuated from me. It's my turn now. I see myself as one of what I call 'the unencumbered generation'. I do not wish to be a boorish burden or a patronized pet: I do not want to be categorised in any way. I wish to be treated as an individual, just as I would hope I treat others.

Principles:

1 Giving specific personal advice is a dangerous conceit.

2 Human compassion is an individual attribute: it cannot be given through the state as such but only through the choice (or not) of individuals working for it (or not).

3 General principles and general recommendations should be based upon personal experience. Professors and politicians do not have credibility unless they have worked in the front line.

4 The 'underclass', as described in Charles Murray's social commentary, is a product of the state taking over responsibility from the individual. It should not be possible for long-term unemployment to be a lifestyle choice. Also, children need to learn that they do not become adults merely by having children of their own, least of all by then expecting state taxpayers to provide for them. Adulthood has to be earned.

5 Working through the difficulties in a relationship may, in the end, be much less demanding than starting another.

6 With increased expectation of life, the grey generation can come into its own again. A whole new phase of life can open up for people who might otherwise be considered to be past it.

7 We should expect to treat other people as (neither better than nor worse than) we would wish to be treated ourselves,

Action:

1 Avoid giving personal advice. It is more likely to be irritating than comforting. It is rarely positively productive.

2 Do not allow professors, politicians and bureaucrats to get away with believing that they, rather than front line workers, are the instruments of human compassion.

3 Make appropriate adjustments in your own reaction to new situations, particularly if you expect other people to do the same for you.

4 Make your own choice in your family relationships.

Reminder: Nurture the inner adult rather than the inner child.

Notes:
I like the Transactional Analysis concept of the free, creative, inner child. I believe that life really should be fun. I have a teddy bear – he sits on my bed. I do not carry him into therapy sessions. I am grown up now. My inner child is lively and imaginative – not a sad, pathetic creature demanding self-centred attention.

I have no sense of self-pity over my recent challenging experiences. I got myself into the mess and, with help from some very kind people, I had to find a way of getting myself out of it. I took no antidepressants or other medications and I had no formal psychotherapy. I believe that these would have hindered my progress towards taking full responsibility for myself again.

I have no sense of blame towards other people. It wouldn't help me if I did. To be sure, there were other factors – over and above my own blindness and stupidity – that contributed to the cascade of events that brought me down. However, they were only partial contributions rather than prime causes. I now want to move on from all that, just as I moved on from the abuse and abandonment in my childhood. My inner adult is now my constant companion.

The Scientologists produce excellent documentaries on the failings of psychiatry but I don't want what they put in its place.

I have been much impressed by Richard Bentall's thoughtful book *Doctoring the Mind*, in which he examines why psychiatric treatments fail. Far from being a negative book, it is exceedingly encouraging, with section headings such as 'What kind of psychiatry do you want?' and 'The virtue of kindness'. I like his style.

I am also much impressed by the diagrams in William Glasser's book *Choice Theory*, in which he shows the dramatic increase in scientific understanding over the last century but no improvement in human relationships, despite vast amounts of psychobabble.

Principles:

1 An inner child should be given free rein to be imaginative and creative. A self-centred inner child is a brat.

2 Self-pity and blame are the characteristics of active addictive behaviour. They have no place in responsible mature life.

3 Pills don't always help. They may hinder.

4 Our enemy's enemy is not necessarily our friend – in psychology as well as in politics.

5 We should consider alternatives before committing ourselves to any particular course of therapy.

6 'First do no harm' should guide all doctors and psychotherapists today, as it did Edith Cavell's nurses in the Crimean War.

7 The virtue of kindness cannot be excelled.

Action:

1 Leave your teddy bear on your bed.

2 Be lively and imaginative when you are in a fit state again.

3 Resist the curse of self-centredness, which seems almost to be encouraged by some psychotherapeutic approaches. Beating cushions and screaming helps people to become good at beating cushions and screaming. It does nothing whatever towards healing relationships. More probably it damages them.

4 Get rid of self-pity and blame. They will be no help to you. They will cause considerable damage.

5 Beware of antidepressants and other medications, even – and perhaps especially – when you feel you most need them.

6 Follow the advice of your own doctor but be aware that the diagnosis 'clinical depression' means 'Whatever anybody else may say, I am going to prescribe an antidepressant'. (The diagnosis of 'clinical depression' has no specific objective validity.)

7 Look at the Scientologists' evidence of psychiatric abuse.

8 Read Richard Bentall's book and also Willam Glasser's book.

9 Be kind.

Reminder: We are as old or as young as we want to be.

Notes:
Unlike many children in state schools today, I had the privilege (paid for by a Council grant) of being taught basic numeracy and literacy. However, I was still not taught things that I believe would be helpful in all schools: how to make a profit in business, how to create and maintain a long-term relationship and how to bring up children to be happy and self-motivating.

Maintaining a positive attitude and keeping my mind active has been vital throughout my life but particularly in the last two years. My physical appearance deteriorated last year but, as before, I now look younger than my years. My brain age, estimated on reaction times in a Nintendo game, is usually in my forties and sometimes thirties. I keep young company. I am keen to bring myself at least into the twentieth century as computer hardware and software develop.

I have been particularly impressed by the Harvard University study in which they took a large group of undergraduates, matched them with people of similar age and sex from downtown Boston and with a group of young 'intelligent but impoverished' women students in a seminary. They obtained a vast amount of data on childhood background and experience. They followed up the participants with face-to-face interviews every ten years for fifty years. The most recent survey is in a book called *Ageing Well* by George Vaillant. It shows that people surmount the difficulties of their childhood if they have a positive attitude to life. They do well in their professional careers, they have good long-term relationships and widespread interests. People who are miserable complaining wretches have no significant differences in their childhoods, relative to their more successful counterparts, but they achieve the opposite.

My hope for the future is to stay young in body, mind and spirit by looking after myself in all these three areas of life.

Principles:

1 Schools tend to provide little preparation for the major challenges in adult life.
2 A positive attitude and an active mind are reflected in a youthful physical appearance as well as in healthy mental function.
3 Complaining about childhood background and experience gets us nowhere. Memory Lane is a death-trap: we benefit from looking forward rather than backward.
4 Keeping young company keeps us young.
5 Computers have minds of their own but they can be tamed to serve us rather than the other way around.

Action:

1 Recognize that some children have a terrible start at school, let alone in their family backgrounds.
2 Acknowledge that intelligence is largely a natural gift, for which we should be grateful rather than claiming credit for it. Truly intelligent people do not draw attention to it.
3 Maintain a positive attitude, as far as you can, whatever happens to you.
4 Look young by behaving young – when you are able to do so.
5 Keep your mind active.
6 Keep young company.
7 Recognize that it is up to you to surmount whatever difficulties you may have had in your childhood background or upbringing. If you want to do well, and have good long-term relationships and widespread interests, you can. If you want to be miserable and constantly complaining and have a wretched life, you can achieve that.
8 Read George Vaillant's book *Ageing Well*. Stay young by letting the past stay in the past, keeping yourself physically fit and in good shape, avoiding doing things that damage you and by nurturing one special close personal relationship and enjoying yourselves.

Reminder: Live for today.

Notes:

How much longer do I want to live? What do I want to do with the rest of my life? These questions are often on my mind nowadays.

I know that I shall eventually be bereaved in other ways than I have already. I hope I have now had good preparation for that.

I know that I myself will die eventually. I hope that I have now had good preparation for that as well.

I have learned not to look for instant gratification. Some things come in time and they require hard work before they come to fruition.

I make no complaint about my addictive nature, mild dyslexia, mild food allergies, recurrent periodic kidney stones and other physical irritants. These are just the way things are.

I accept my childhood background and experience (they were a long time ago anyway) and I accept the various challenging experiences that I have been through in later life.

I look now to today, as a representative of all my future days. I dare to start again. I dare to learn new things and I dare to try new things. I dare to make mistakes. I dare to try to improve my long-term relationships with my immediate and wider family and with my friends. I dare to make new relationships.

In my work as a counsellor, I look for new ideas and new ways of helping people to develop and achieve their full potential. I don't look back to the glory days. I look forward to even better ones that are still to come. After all, who would be better placed to build on my previous experience?

At present, I have time to reflect and time to think. Previously I was so busy that I hardly had time for either. I am looking now to see what I can do that will be better than anything I have ever done.

But if, at the end of my life, people simply describe me as having been kind, I'll settle for that.

Principles:

1 However short a time we have left to live, there may still be many things that we can do – some for the very first time.

2 The experience of bereavement is eventually universal.

3 The experience of our own eventual death will also be universal. We might just as well become used to that idea and get on with whatever living we still have to do.

4 The demand for instant gratification is a characteristic of petulant children – of any age.

5 We all have problems of some kind or another – but we don't have to go on and on about them, nor use them as excuses for everything that we fail to achieve.

6 Our childhood is over. The fat lady has sung.

7 As has often been said by others, today is the only day we have: yesterday has gone and tomorrow hasn't yet arrived.

8 There is only one way to live – by daring to do so. We should want nothing less, for ourselves and for other people, than to achieve full potential.

9 Personal human characteristics are sufficient epitaph.

Action:

1 Calculate how much longer you have to live (with good health and fortune). Ask yourself what you want to do with that time. Then do it, as well as you can.

2 Accept the inevitability of further bereavement.

3 Gently accept the inevitability of your own ultimate death.

4 Put down the need for instant gratification, if you still have it.

5 Accept whatever physical ailments and other personal difficulties you may have. Make the best of your life, in whatever way you can, despite them.

6 Live in today and focus on developing your human characteristics.

7 Look for new ideas and new ways of helping yourself and other people to achieve full potential.

Values:

I value most:

1 The lives of my wife and children: they represent my primary choices and responsibilities.
2 My own life: I owe it to no one.
3 My principles by which I live my daily life: I do not borrow them from other people. I choose them. I would betray them under duress to save my own life and those of my wife and children, but only if no innocent person's life would be lost in the process. I value my life and therefore I value yours.
4 My mind: I do things to enhance it and I don't do things that would damage it.
5 My health: I do things to enhance it and I don't do things that would damage it.
6 My creativity: my creative output confirms that I am alive.
7 My time: I choose what I do with my life each day.
8 My interests: I have the right to my own enthusiasms.
9 My profession: I have a professional responsibility to those who pay for my services in any sphere of my activity.
10 My friends (including some members of my family): my friends share my values. I develop new friendships as I myself change.
11 My possessions: I am entitled to the product of my labours.
12 My country: I would fight to protect our common culture of tolerance.

These are important values to me.
What values are important to you?

Values:

I value least:

1 My reputation: I judge myself by my own values.
2 My knowledge: I have more to learn.
3 My achievements: some of them were fine – but they are past.
4 My seniority: respect should depend upon behaviour, not upon age or length of tenure of a position.
5 My status: I have none. Therefore I have nothing to lose. My talents, such as they are, go where I go. I alone am responsible for the flowering of my natural ability. No other person, and no social position, can give me a sense of personal value.
6 My physical prowess: this would be a ludicrous value.
7 My 'cool': individuality has substance – fashion has none.
8 My professional group: those I respect are counterbalanced by those I do not, as in any other profession. I set no store by my particular profession. Take away my daily enjoyment in my work and I would find another profession.
9 My political group: I have ideas of my own and I do not accept that might is right. Mere numbers may produce no more than the lowest common denominator.
10 My financial group: my values are determined by what I believe, not by what I purchase.
11 My family as such: I feel no obligation of family ties to those with whom I share few values.
12 Life after death: Currently I am busy and happy in this one.

These are not important to me.
What values are not important to you?

Section 3

Bereavement
and Belief

Reminder: Consider our most important values in life – and try to live by them, one day at a time.

Notes:

After a year of bankruptcy, I was released. My wife, Margaret, and I went to the local county court and paid for my certificate of discharge. Sadly, as she had gone into bankruptcy after me, she was due to remain in bankruptcy for a further four months. Her own relatively small creditors, and the larger ones that she shared with me, were chasing her. I had hoped that the authorities would release her at the same time as me, because there seemed to be nothing to be gained from continuing her bankruptcy, but it was not to be.

During the year we had settled into the Church of England almshouse in Canterbury that was now our home and we had made good friends with the staff and also with the other residents, whose average age was eighty-five. Despite their age, they mostly had active minds and wide interests. We heard very few reminiscences and those we did hear were interesting.

Margaret and I both decided that, whatever our future financial circumstances, we would stay living where we were. One day in the future we would inevitably have to move into relatively secure accommodation. We were already in it so there would be no point in moving twice.

In any case – and God forbid – if either of us were to die, the survivor would be well established already in a supportive community. Had we moved out to the countryside in Kent or back to London, we would have to do all sorts of things for ourselves again. We had no money and therefore we had little prospect of considering any alternative to staying where we were. But our two small rooms and our few pieces of furniture were comfortable and sufficient for our needs. We were happy enough as we were. We had each other. Margaret and I had lived and worked together for virtually the whole of our adult lives. Once I got myself into recovery from my destructive addictive behaviour, we got on well together through thick and thin.

It had been very much to Margaret's credit that our marriage had survived the first twenty-three years of my rake's progress. But in the subsequent twenty-five years we stayed close together, spiritually, mentally, emotionally and physically. Even the terrible losses of our bankruptcy could not tear us apart. As part of our daily routine, we snuggled up close together on the sofa and did the *Times 2* crossword puzzle. The honours were even: each finding the same number of answers to the clues.

When Margaret sat at the computer on her table, she could reach round to hand me a document as I sat on the sofa on the other side of the room. The small dimensions of the room meant that neither of us had to get up. Yet we never argued. In fact I do not recall Margaret ever arguing with anybody. She had clear values and views and opinions and would discuss all sorts of things but hers was a peaceful, loving, gentle spirit. I was so fortunate to live so much of my life with her.

Thoughts:
1 Creditors have a right to try to get their money back.
2 Being bankrupt, after a lifetime of paying one's bills, is wretched, humiliating and frightening – but that's the way it is.
3 Nurturing a long-term close relationship counters the health damage equivalent to smoking fifteen cigarettes a day. People who lack a special relationship may find life a lot more challenging.
4 Whatever the slings and arrows of outrageous fortune, there is always an opportunity to make the best of each day.
5 The close understanding and support of one other human being (or the company of a special pet) can provide much of what is needed to be able to live at peace with oneself and others.

Reminder: We can recover from childhood abuse.

Notes:
As a child, Margaret had a mixed experience of abuse and inspiration. Her father's depression/alcoholism gave her as wretched a life as can be imagined but his insistence that she had the absolute best piano teacher (a pupil of the legendary Solomon) and his encouragement and support in her daily practice, led her to gaining a distinction in Grade VIII of the Associated Board examinations at the age of thirteen, when she played the Chopin Fantasy Impromptu.

Her mother kept the peace and held the family together. Despite having a university degree in French, she slaved in a series of guest houses in order to add to the family income that largely disappeared down her husband's gullet.

Margaret herself took on much of the responsibility of caring for her two younger brothers and her younger sister. When the youngest child was born, Margaret was ten years old and she provided much of his daily care and nurturing.

She remained utterly devoted to her siblings all her life and she herself took on much of the role of keeping the family together. All three of her siblings had distinguished careers, the elder two as musicians and the youngest in the Army.

Ten years after her father's suicide (soon after our marriage and before our first child was born), Margaret did a great deal of work on healing the relationship with her father. She recognized that he had been suffering from an illness (addiction in several outlets) and she understood and forgave him for everything. She always treasured and appreciated the love of music that he had given her.

Depression/alcoholism also affected the father of Margaret's father and he died of it. He was a church organist and he carried his love of music to his younger son who passed it on to Margaret and her siblings. His wife worked for a children's charity but, like Anna Freud, the creator of psychoanalysis for children, she farmed out her own children.

Margaret's father and uncle were given one-way tickets to Australia when they were fourteen and sixteen. They said that they were booed as they walked down the gangplank: Australia thought it had more than enough Poms in difficult economic times. Margaret's uncle stayed there but her father worked on sheep farms and earned the money to come home to England.

By the time I met him, he owned his own house and, generously and forgivingly, provided accommodation in it for his parents.

What is clear to me in this story is the contrast between the creativity and the kindness in the man who was my father-in-law and the abusive drunkenness that illustrated his illness. I wish I had known, at the time that I met him, the insights that I now have. I would have been more understanding of him and kinder to him.

Margaret's mother's insights were more acute than mine. She said to her daughter, my future wife, 'Robert's manner and behaviour are very like your father's in some ways'.

Thoughts:

1 The inner child, beloved of therapists, should be enjoyed and revelled in, rather than pandered to. The responsible inner adult is a more creative companion and guide.
2 Relationships can be healed – with good will – from just one side at any time. However, if the relationship is always one-sided, it will not last happily for ever.
3 Addictive disease runs in some families. Also, people coming from an addictive family tend to marry into another addictive family or set up other relationships with them. In this way, a relatively small genetic pool, of 15% of the population who have addictive natures, is kept ticking over.
4 People who are addicts can none the less be very kind.

Reminder: Life is for living.

Notes:
My own childhood had its own strangeness. My parents were Christian missionaries in India and they farmed me out to guardians in England from when I was ten to when I was eighteen, with one year when we were together (although I remained in boarding school) between the ages of fourteen and fifteen.

I had hoped to be a professional musician but my school did not recognize that as an appropriate subject for study. I got into Corpus Christi College, Cambridge, on a choral exhibition (singing scholarship) and I had hoped to study Music at university – but I lacked the talent to be a professional. I became a doctor, despite at that time having no particular wish to be one. Later I came to love being a general medical practitioner: I enjoyed the human contact.

After just one term at Cambridge, in January 1959, a friend invited me to London to see the Russian art exhibition at the Royal Academy in Piccadilly. Margaret and I met there: I picked her up. I had never done that to anyone before – and never since. From first sight, she was my love.

Margaret came to Cambridge every weekend and sat in the visitors' stalls in chapel while I sang in the choir. After a year we got engaged and after a further eighteen months we got married.

After two weeks' blissful honeymoon in Umhausen, a ski resort in Austria which we enjoyed in July for its Alpine flowers and goat bells, we returned to London, totally penniless. All our wedding present money had gone on the honeymoon. We were both still students and Margaret's local authority stopped her student grant, saying that they did not believe that she would continue her studies now that she was married. They underestimated her professionalism and her commitment. We lived off one student grant and she completed her studies and qualified as a physio-therapist.

Through friends, my aunt found a place for us to live in North Kensington. Our living room, bedroom and bathroom opened onto the communal hall on the ground floor. The tiny kitchen and dining room and another bedroom (which we sub-let to another student in order to help with the rent) were in a basement that was so damp that I took sixteen bricks out of an inside wall with my bare hands. The garden was initially literally a dump but, with broken paving stones free from the local council, I created crazy paving paths around beds that we filled with lovely flowers. (I never knew that freesias could grow in Ladbroke Grove.)

Margaret kept house for both of us on one student grant. In the evenings, after studying conscientiously all day (I was far more cavalier in my own studies at The Middlesex Hospital), she would walk down the Portobello Road, buying cheap food that would otherwise have been thrown away.

We were poor but we had been poor before: we knew no different. In tight times in future years, Margaret knew how to make the best of survival rations.

Having promised our families that we would not have children before I qualified as a doctor, our daughter Nicola was born within one year and our own new family life began.

Thoughts:
1 All childhood experiences are challenging in some ways. Some have greater challenges than others. All trauma can be healed at some time in the future
2 Love at first sight can happen and it can last.
3 Student years may be impoverished yet still magical.
4 Despite childhood experience, we can create our own future if we are prepared to accept the responsibility of doing so.
5 Sheer determination can achieve most things.

Reminder: Love is all you need.

Notes:
Margaret was unswerving in her love and loyalty. She stood by me (supportively) when I tried again to earn my living as a musician – but eventually I lost that unequal struggle. She stood by me (reluctantly) in property and farming ventures that ended in disaster. She stood by me (physically) when I stood for Parliament and failed. She stood by me (fearfully) when I resigned my medical partnership in the group practice that I had created. (I could not see a creative future.) She stood by Nicola and her younger brothers, Robin and Henry, (determinedly) when they had difficulties of their own. She stood by me (encouragingly) when I resigned from the National Health Service and set up in private medical practice.

Only on one occasion, over my rages that accompanied my addictive/compulsive behaviour (especially my eating disorder, my gambling and my uncontrolled spending) did she say that she had had enough. She told me specifically that she would stay with me for the sake of our children but would leave when our youngest child reached maturity.

I had to win her back and I did so by working the Twelve Step programme, first formulated by Alcoholics Anonymous. This was not available to save my mother from her eating disorder, nor two of my grandparents (my father's father and my mother's mother) who had died from depression/alcoholism.

Margaret and I were influenced particularly by various anonymous fellowships. We learned a great deal from Addictions Anonymous (that looks at any or all addictive or compulsive behaviour) and Helpers Anonymous (that sees when the boundary has been crossed between caring and care-taking and when self-effacement and self-denial become destructive). We were particularly fortunate in having the understanding of each other.

In our work with addictive families, Margaret had the supreme gift of being able to comfort, reassure, educate and encourage when people were distressed and frightened. Many family members wrote to me to say that she had saved their lives.

Leaving bankruptcy, I wanted to get back to full-time work. I had no intention of retiring or travelling or generally taking life easy. I wanted to be back in the thick of it. I knew what it was that I wanted to do and, after so many chops and changes in my life, I knew where my skills lay.

Margaret and I agreed that we would work together for three days a week: two in London and one in Kent. She would play her beloved piano and see her special friends on the other four days while I ran a new treatment centre in rented premises in Canterbury. In this way, we worked out a plan to suit both of us.

I began to prepare all the documents that my new staff and I would need when we opened the new treatment centre. Margaret would join us when she came out of bankruptcy – but she would carry that strain on her own until then.

Thoughts:
1 Addicts are not easy people to live with.
2 Addictive families understand other addictive families.
3 Relationships can be healed.
4 Any crisis leaves its mark. However strong and determined we may be, emotional and physical damage are inevitable.
5 Retrospectively we might wish we had done things differently – but would we necessarily have got different results?
6 Life is for living – while it lasts.
7 The strain of bankruptcy should never be underestimated.
8 There may be times when the preoccupations of one partner blind him or her to the emotional needs of the other. That would be very dangerous to the relationship.

Reminder: Versatility and willingness may be offered – but they cannot be demanded from someone else.

Notes:
At each change in my own direction, Margaret learned new skills. She was immensely versatile. In addition to her physiotherapy, she learned all the requirements to be a professional secretary and she took on that role to earn us some more money. That skill benefited me for ever more. When our children were young, she became a Montessori teacher and she also gained a Bachelor of Education degree from London University in the subject of Education. Sadly, I pushed her into becoming a medical laboratory scientist (in haematology) in my private medical practice. She didn't like that: it was too technical and impersonal for her. She came into her own as a family counsellor when we jointly established a Twelve Step treatment centre where we cared for other addicts and their families. She used her own personal insights and experience to help other families who had also suffered the ravages of depression/addiction.

There was a firmness in Margaret's resolve, whatever she did. Her own family and friends, and also our patients and their families, knew that she would never let them down but would stand by them for ever.

Music was the lynchpin of Margaret's whole life. She was not simply musical, as many children are: she was a musician, professional to the core even though she earned her living elsewhere. As a young child she once played on BBC radio's Children's Hour and she played several times in the Wigmore Hall in recitals given by pupils of her teacher. She continued to have lessons all her life. She loved her teachers for what they gave her and they loved her for the appreciation and commitment she gave to them.

She particularly enjoyed playing chamber music with her sister and brother and special friends. Twice a year they would go to music school for professional coaching even though, as an ensemble, they never played in public. The leader of one of our most prestigious orchestras once commented to her that she probably got more real pleasure from her music than he did.

Margaret always got up early to do her first session of daily piano practice. I would wake to the sounds of Bach, Brahms, Beethoven, Mozart, Chopin, Schumann, Mendelssohn, Ravel, Debussy, or whoever she was asked by her teachers to play in order to broaden her repertoire. She was in heaven. So was I.

She loved opera and ballet, concerts and theatre and she took special time every Wednesday evening to go out with friends. Instead of holidays, we had cultural feasts, going especially to Glyndebourne and the London Symphony Orchestra. Each year we gave prizes to young musicians and, in return, they gave recitals in our home. Margaret was devoted in this, and in every other aspect of her life, to providing tangible help for others. She brought peace and gentleness and love to people's lives.

We visited the homes of addictive families and did in-depth work with them to try to turn the whole family around. Wherever we went, she provided loving support to families afflicted in the way that ours had been. The family groups and workshops that she ran (with assistants) were her special gift. She enriched the lives of others.

Thoughts:

1 I was the principal beneficiary of Margaret's love and loyalty. Was ever a man so privileged in life?

2 The arts bring value and depth and happiness into our lives at any time. They provide the wellspring from which creativity and love will flow in abundance.

3 Receiving love comes as a result of giving it away. One-sided relationships are mere infatuation.

4 Enriching the lives of others is a fabulous legacy.

Reminder: Lightning can strike twice in the same place.

Notes:
Sadly, my own addictive nature was never far below the surface. I did too much and I trusted too much and I risked too much. Eventually this destroyed our material lives. Through bankruptcy, we lost our medical practice. In the final six weeks (after forty-two years) Margaret was my only member of staff, doing all the reception work and, in the evenings, typing all the records. We lost our lovely treatment centre that we had created in Kent. Subsequently it was burnt to the ground by vandals. The same fate had earlier beset our lovely country cottage, which was in truth our real home. A complete stranger objected to a television programme to which I had contributed and he destroyed our peaceful haven. For two years we lived in the garage while the cottage was rebuilt. In our final financial debacle we had to sell it and therefore we lost it again, together with our dog and our two cats, who were our constant personal companions and Margaret's special comforters.

We lived out of suitcases in other people's homes for eight months. Finally we lost everything. Margaret never once complained.

As we left our cottage for the last time, we called in to see the priest who had conducted the funeral services for each of my parents. I told her that we had lost our homes, our medical practice and our treatment centre. I anticipated that she might say a prayer. Certainly one was answered: she found us a sanctuary in a Church of England almshouse in Canterbury, the oldest almshouse in the country. Within two weeks we had moved into it. We paid a maintenance charge from our basic state pensions (everything else went to our creditors). Margaret returned to the skilled frugality of our student days and we survived.

In two small rooms intended for single occupation, we comforted and supported each other. A friend kindly bought

214

us two single beds. (Our double bed would not fit into the bedroom through which we had to pass in order to get to the kitchenette and shower room.) The whole flat would fit comfortably inside our previous living room. Yet we were cosy enough and the surroundings were beautiful.

A consultant psychiatrist friend let me use a room in his house in Harley Street and we travelled there and back each week by coach and underground train and on foot. From a previous travelling time of twenty minutes a day, we now spent six hours. Margaret was my secretary in addition to everything else. We saw a few patients and ran one small group therapy session. This covered the expenses and kept our minds active. We had our professional dignity.

Bankruptcy is a horrible process. We limped through it. However, a series of long-standing friends gave us presents or took us out occasionally for meals or to the opera or to concerts. From subsidizing others, we came to be subsidized ourselves. We were grateful for that.

Thoughts:
 1 We had bounced back before. Surely we could do so again. Theoretically, anyone can: it is simply a question of attitude and application. In practice, I make no judgement on anyone else.
 2 The gradual process of progressive destruction is exhausting. So is travel.
 3 Losing treasured possessions is painful. Losing pets is desperate.
 4 To have nothing material to show for the work of two lifetimes was the direct product of my risking-taking – but, without risk, nothing would have been created in the first place. There has to be a balance between these extremes.
 5 There is a time to give to others but we have to recognize that there is also a time to receive. To appreciate other people's generosity gives pleasure to them.

Reminder: Dreams are meant to be dreamed.

Notes:
When, after a standard year, I was discharged from bankruptcy, there was no official or personal fanfare. It just happened. We understood that but, importantly for us, we did not belong to the generation that sees bankruptcy as a non-culpable routine feature of the business cycle. We felt ashamed and distressed.

As soon as I was free, I set up planning the creation of a new in-patient treatment centre: Doctor Robert Rehab Services. Margaret was fully supportive, as always, and she commented that without creative work I would be like a wild bird in a cage. I mapped out for myself a customary seven-day working week. Margaret would provide administrative back-up and she would also continue to run her beloved family group, for which she had incredible talent.

Prior to her taking on the role of Family Counsellor, we had small groups of four or five family members of patients. Margaret regularly attracted thirty, both in London and Kent. Also she ran five-day residential workshops and weekly group sessions for those who acknowledged their own compulsive helping tendencies (doing too much for the addict and thereby contributing to the dependency).

Now I planned to set up training courses for future 'creative coaches' (as I now termed myself), teaching practical counselling skills rather than dry statistics from research studies. Margaret planned to attend those courses, and later contribute to them, as well as working alongside me in our new in-patient services, but each week she would have four full days playing the piano and seeing her friends on day trips.

I found premises in which we could separately house and educate our patients. We would escape from the medical model and see patients more as students. Our belief was that our protégés, as with our trainee coaches, could be helped to learn new skills. They would have the dignity of learning to transpose their existing creative skills, from constructive areas of their lives, into those areas that tended to be destructive.

The premises were part of a lovely hotel that coincidentally had the same name as our honeymoon hotel: I couldn't miss it. It was bound to succeed: the name was too much of a coincidence. I could rent as many of the self-catering cottages in the grounds of the hotel as I might need from time to time.

Out of the blue, I was invited to run a two-week intensive residential programme with a Greek family. Margaret accompanied me and she bought a new swimming costume. In the event I was so busy that we never got out of the house except to go occasionally to restaurants. With four equally disturbed people in the family that we were with, it was wonderful to have Margaret by my side, providing personal support. At night, as always, I wrote.

On returning home, I attended a three-day conference on addiction. I was able to spread the word about our new coaching and training courses. Margaret went to Bournemouth, the town of her childhood and where we were married forty-eight years previously, to see her brother and a family friend, and have some fun and relax.

Thoughts:
1 Shame is a personal concept: it is generated (or not) by individuals. It cannot be forced onto others.
2 The capacity for creativity is always individual – but it is greater when shared with a like mind.
3 There is a time for work – the more demanding it is the more rewarding it is – and also a time for play. There has to be.
4 Planning for the future can be done creatively and enthusiastically at any age and in any circumstances.
5 Coincidences are fun.

Reminder: Live each day as if thy last.

Notes:

Very early in the morning on the last day of the conference, before I was awake, Margaret texted me to say that she was going for a walk along the beach. My return texts throughout the morning received no reply.

The police subsequently posted her as a missing person. Our son Robin, who had attended the same conference in London, drove us to Bournemouth. Our daughter Nicola drove there from her home in Marlborough. When we arrived at Margaret's brother's home in Poole, the police had just arrived to say that they had found a body that resembled our description of Margaret. I went to the hospital morgue to identify her body and to tell her how much I loved her. Robin and Nicola followed me in their own sad personal ceremonies.

My darling wife, my love for fifty-one years and my daily companion at work and at home for forty-eight years had gone. As a family, we comforted each other as best we could.

I chose to go back to Canterbury with Robin to our respective homes. I wanted to be on my own with the spirit of my darling Margaret. I had no wish for comfort or companionship from anyone else. Despite our bankruptcy, with the loss of our homes and offices and the loss of our social and cultural activities and the loss of daily contact with friends, we had been happy together in what we saw as the beginning of a new life. I needed now to be with her in spirit.

Margaret died on a Saturday morning. The autopsy would not be performed until Monday. I waited and I wondered what could possibly have happened to her. As a trained doctor, I knew a whole range of possibilities and I mulled them over.

There was a loving card on the small drop-down table in our kitchenette. In it Margaret told me where my supper was, in case I arrived home first. She wrote out a gratitude list saying, among other things, how much she loved me and our children. I had written her a similar list two weeks previously. We often left loving notes for each other.

We used to play pinch and punch on the first day of each month. We tried to catch each other out on April Fools' Day. We always discussed ideas as well as events and relationships. We matched each other – dare I say, loved each other?

I waited and I wondered.

On the Monday afternoon the autopsy report came through. Margaret had died of a stroke, caused by a subarachnoid haemorrhage. A small artery in the brain had burst. People with this clinical condition sometimes die in their twenties. I had shared fifty wonderful years with my sweet love. I was so fortunate to have enjoyed so many amazing years with her.

Thoughts:
1 We do not know the day of our death. It would be terrible if we did. Far from getting things done that we had previously postponed or forgotten, it is perhaps more likely that we might simply give up bothering
2 It is not possible to live in each other's pockets the whole time. To be really close involves giving each other room to breathe and to be ourselves.
3 Rites of passage inevitably become imprinted on the memory but we need to refresh other, happier, memories repeatedly in order to put the sad formal processes relating to death into an appropriate place that is insignificant alongside all the many beautiful memories of life.
4 To fully appreciate another human being is something that has to be done during that person's lifetime. It is too late afterwards.
5 Waiting and wondering simply has to be done sometimes. There is no avoiding it.

Reminder: Time is eventually the great healer.

Notes:
Our close friend Caroline told me that she had spoken on the telephone with Margaret for over half and hour on the day before she had gone to Bournemouth. Apparently she was her normal happy positive self and she had no physical symptoms.

For the next eleven days I was on the telephone all day, calling or texting friends and breaking the sad news.

I attended meetings of various anonymous fellowships, self-help groups for addicts of one kind or another (or their family or friends) almost every night. I spent time every day with my fellowship sponsor – the guide who, during the previous year, had taken me again methodically thorough each one of the Twelve Steps up to Step VIII (making a list of those whom I had harmed and becoming ready to make amends to them all, except when to do so would injure them or others). Margaret died before I made these direct amends to her in Step IX.

Had the stress of our bankruptcy indirectly caused her death?

I agonized over the full cause of death of my darling Bear.

In one sense all life is unreal. We may try to convince ourselves that we have significance, whereas the observable material fact is that we are merely the dominant species on a speck of dust that is lost in the vastness of the Universe. In another sense, we are spiritual beings, each one of us a part of the Universal Spirit that has no boundaries such as physical form. These two worlds are equally real or unreal. We hear other people's firm spiritual beliefs and utter convictions but they may be little help to us. We have to find our own.

Margaret and I had both recently read Deepak Chopra's book *The Spontaneous Fulfillment of Desire*, from which some of these ideas come. I had made detailed notes of his daily meditations for each day and I used them. They bound me closer to the love of my life. They worked for me.

Previously no one really close to me had died. My mother died at ninety-three, deaf and blind and in pain. It was time for her to go. My father died at ninety-six, his mind leaving this earth three years before his body. The material and personal losses of our bankruptcy were savage but we came thorough them. I wanted to get back to work and to running a successful new enterprise but I had no need of material wealth and other possessions. I have all that I need and all our children are now adults, with children and occupations and homes of their own.

As a bankrupt, Margaret left nothing other than two things that her trustee had allowed her to keep: her ring and her piano. I have no wish to leave anything of greater substance. Our true legacies are our relationships and our ideas. Our bankruptcies were merely preparations for the ultimate loss: life itself.

Thoughts:
1 The initial shock of a bereavement keeps us immune from our true feelings of deep sadness – they come later, some- times in a gentle, accepting way.
2 There are so many practical things that have to be done straight away that we have no time to grieve.
3 Inevitably, our minds go over and over the unanswerable questions of 'why?' and 'how?' and 'what if . . . ?'
4 Also inevitably, we search our beliefs in a way we may not have had to do previously. Yet still we may not find clear answers to our profound questions.
5 The best thing to do is simply to get by from day to day.
6 There is no greater legacy than memories of us held by those we have loved. Properties, baubles and trinkets have no true substance. Creations can be destroyed. Ideas and love have real substance.

Reminder: In the midst of death is death.

Notes:
The first thing I learned on the day of Margaret's funeral was the death of the only son of Margaret's only cousin. Pat and Ken had married three months before us. Now we were joined together again – in our grief, rather than in our happiness.

Margaret's brother Peter flew over from Canada, her sister Hilary came down from Oxford and we all met in her brother David's home in Poole. Together with our children and other family members and lifelong friends of Margaret, such as Peggy our housekeeper, we shared our grief in a simple service at Poole crematorium. Later we shared our fond memories at a reception in Parkstone Yacht Club. Prayers for Margaret had been said that morning in Canterbury Cathedral.

Mary, a long-term friend of all Margaret's family, and David, Margaret's brother, who had each spent time with Margaret the day before she died, told me how happy Margaret had been and how enthusiastic she was for our future. Our daughter Nicola had beautifully organized the funeral and David had read the lesson most movingly. He also sensitively managed the reception.

I reflected on the additional sadness brought to Margaret by her father's death through suicide, poor man, and I knew that she would not want to visit that experience upon her family and loved ones. I felt sad for other families who would have had no such comfort.

Robin had travelled down to the crematorium with his wife. Henry came over from Australia with his wife and daughter and I travelled with them, sharing rare and precious time with them. Our family was very much aware of the love Margaret had shown to all of us and we took our chance as best we could, in her memory, to heal any divisions. Adults make relationships by choice. Children are born into ready-made families (or not). Some divisions are inevitable.

I returned to our home in order to be with Margaret's living spirit, unlike her temporary body, which was appropriately turned to ashes.

Lying in my solitary bed, I recognized that the major part of my life was over. I had no wife, no work of any significance, no office or home that was really my own – other than in terms of physical occupation – and almost no money.

Yet I was determined not to consign myself to history. I asked myself what Margaret would want of me. I found a possible answer to that by asking what I would want for her if our situations had been reversed. I resolved to live the rest of my life to the best of my ability. I felt that I had something to offer, not necessarily the same as previously, but maybe with the extra understanding that my bereavement would bring to my work with other people who were enduring losses of one kind or another.

Thoughts:
1 Death is a fact of life.
2 Families are held together through positive action by individuals: they do not stick together by themselves.
3 No one human being can judge the full emotional state of another. We cannot have sufficient information to be sure of anything.
4 Families can heal their relationships, if they so wish.
5 Grievous loss is inevitable: it is simply a matter of time.
6 Giving up is difficult. Going on is difficult. Life is difficult.
7 Whatever the future holds in store, the present still provides opportunities to create something of value.
8 We learn from experience – if we want to.
9 Losses give us our deepest sense of value. Life goes on in whatever way we choose. We can choose to be demolished or we can choose to allow ourselves to feel our grief to the full and then move on. Spiritually, we choose to live or die.

Reminder: The relationship between any couple is special.

Notes:
Henry came over to the almshouse to spend the next day with me in order to bring me into at least the twentieth century in my computing skills. My tired, sad head would not work with its customary ease and dependability. I could not reasonably expect it to do so. I learned nothing. Understandably my brain was still very much in shock. It needed to heal in its own time.

Margaret had done everything for me. I am what many women would describe as 'a typical man'. Margaret and I shared household chores but she was the organizing force in all my life. I relied upon her. That was the way our relationship worked. Now that she had no body, I could imagine that as being very frustrating for her. I would not wish to trap her spirit with me if she has another journey to follow but I sense her gentle, loving presence guiding me. She giggles at me doing my own typing.

I can manage my simple needs of shopping and preparing meals and I could have coped with my laundry if friends had not offered to do it for me. Keeping my sense of life and my sense of humour was relatively easy, even in this tragic time, because I was born with those attributes, as was Margaret. They held us together, safe in all adversity, and they still do.

But I missed my practical partner and I missed all the lovely personal things. Margaret looked after me. She sensitively corrected me and gently warned me when I got carried away on some madcap idea or other. Now I had to listen to her more acutely than ever before.

I was due to open our new coaching rehabilitation treatment centre just three days after Margaret's memorial service. Our two future senior coaches took on the task of circulating the documents that I had already prepared. To these, in my desperate sadness, I added the notice of the memorial service, the celebration of Margaret's life.

How could we encapsulate Margaret's life in just one hour of celebration? Family and friends would remember her for their own special relationships with her. We had no idea how many of them would attend the service at St Luke's in Sydney Street in South Kensington. This area had been the centre of our personal and professional life for over forty years. What would Margaret's special friends want in the service?

A lot of people knew Margaret and had been helped and loved by her. I myself love her still for all her creative skills and I love her for her considerate and gentle manner. Most of all, I love her just as herself.

In a recent note to her, I had written 'I love you. Thank you for staying with me and for being such a wonderful helpmate. I have so much enjoyed sharing my life with you. We have done so much together and it has been such fun. Cherish yourself. Do not feel any obligation to carry on my work or even my ideas. Live your own life and be true to your own ideas. Enjoy your music and your friend-ships. Tell all our children I love all of them. Be good. Love. Rob'.

Thoughts:

1 It would be silly to expect too much of oneself immedi-ately after a major tragedy.

2 Practical survival is not as difficult as is sometimes assumed.

3 Emotional and spiritual survival are much more chal-lenging.

4 However long and close a particular relationship, no one person ever owns another.

5 Writing notes to each other is a way of showing appreci-ation and care. This should be done while the other person is very much alive. After the other person's death, we are writing for ourselves.

6 Love is a very, very special experience.

Reminder: The Eternal Spirit never dies.

Notes:
I planned to open the memorial service by saying, 'Margaret and I welcome our friends. Each of us here remembers her in our way – as the loving heart of our family, as a pianist, physiotherapist, teacher, family counsellor and true friend. Her physical body died of a stroke but she is still part of me and I am part of her and we are all parts of the Universal Sprit that never dies. I pledge my future personal and professional life to enhancing her very special characteristics of peace, gentleness and kindness. Margaret and I can continue to share our love of music and our work in helping addicts and their families. My intention is to fund annual prizes for young musicians at Glyndebourne and the London Symphony Orchestra, our favourite musical institutions, and to provide premises for the care of addicts and in particular for their families. Through our own individual memories of her and our commitment to her values, Margaret's spirit will live on with each and every one of us.'

I never anticipated that I would be bereaved, at least not in the next twenty years. I had acquired a certain level of learned helplessness. Margaret enabled me to do my most creative work through being my inspiration, my soul-mate and my manager. I feared that I had lost all three in one fatal blow.

In fact the inspiration I gained from her will be with me for ever. Fifty-one years of shared love and experience are ingrained in me. I know Margaret's values: I saw them in the way she lived her life and in the fond, gentle and supportive relationships she made. I desperately miss her as my help-mate: we discussed ideas, we did things together, we were adventurous.

Now, in our flat on my own, with only one physical body between us, I can choose to be lonely and miserable or I can choose to feel Margaret's spiritual warmth. I can imagine that she might be an even greater influence on me now than she ever was in life. I can temper my flamboyance with her caution, my arrogance with her sensitivity.

As my manager, Margaret was simply superb. We co-created our lives but she, in addition to her own creativity, was the firm board from which I was able to spring. I could easily be lost without her – but what a waste that would be of all her investment in me over the years.

Thoughts:

1 To summarize a lifetime in a paragraph is easy when that life is full of love.

2 As Deepak Chopra says, the eyes pick up the light and convert it into electrical signals, the brain interprets them – but who is doing the looking? His idea is that the Silent Witness in each one of is a part of the Universal Spirit that is shared by all of us.

3 Each of us has our own concept of a spiritual life – or not. Some people are so convinced of the truth of their own beliefs that they feel obliged to share them or even impose them. Others are content to leave the mysteries as mysteries but none the less gain comfort from awareness that even our present existence is mysterious.

4 If we find it difficult to work out what the person we lost would like us to do, we can ask what we would like him or her to do if the situation were to be the other way round.

5 Ask ourselves if the other person would like to be thought of with happiness or sadness; to be remembered as he or she was when full of life or at the time of death.

6 Closeness can continue even when physically separated.

7 Personal spiritual influence can last for ever.

8 It is up to each of us to work out for ourselves what we believe. To take on other people's ideas without thought is an abdication of our own privilege of life.

Reminder: Friendship is a gift that has to be treasured in the giving and in the receiving.

Notes:
Margaret made friends. That defined her. She was friendly with four-legged creatures as well as with bipeds. She loved our cats and dogs and she missed having them around in the last year of her life where we lived in a community in which the prospect of every resident having a pet would be overwhelming.

Her human friends blossomed in every aspect of her life. I myself bathed in her friendship and was warmed by it every day. I have to find ways of keeping it. I miss her so dreadfully. I weep for the loss of our shared practicalities and the loss of her tenderness, humour and touch.

To suppress my feelings with medications would be contrary to what I have believed all my life in clinical practice. I want to feel sad. I want to feel lonely, despairing, lost – because only then can I retain the capacity to be happy, exhilarated, enthusiastic.

I look into the empty decades ahead with an awareness that it is up to me to fill them with beautiful activities and relationships. By reaching out to help other people, if they want it, I can gain spiritual refreshment and true friendship, even if only briefly. Hopefully time will expand those tender, precious moments.

This bereavement is the fundamental challenge of my life. With Margaret's continuing friendship (I may not see her but I can feel her influence) and our friendships with family members and professional colleagues and all manner of other lovely people, I shall not allow myself to gorge on melancholy. I want Margaret's spirit to be comforted – not upset – by mine.

Margaret was at the heart of both families: her original family with her sister and brothers, with whom I am increasingly close, and her chosen family with me and our children.

She nurtured us all. Family and friends mattered to her. Professional colleagues and patients mattered to her. The family groups that she created mattered to her. Without her now there is a risk of disintegration. I shall not allow that but I can achieve peace and harmony only if I consciously apply myself to the task.

I do not have Margaret's natural facility for these beautiful characteristics. My addictive nature tends to drive me more to dominate than heal. By contrast, she had the gift of healing human spirits: it is as simple as that. But if it were possible for her to have this gift, then it must be possible for me to develop it – if I focus upon following her example.

Families are difficult. Addictive families are extremely difficult, particularly when stressed and distressed. We could so easily hurt each other and do the opposite of everything Margaret wanted. I want to take on her delicate balance of firmness and gentle tolerance in equal measure. It is needed now more than ever. What she did by nature (and hard work), I have to acquire. I am determined to maintain her legacy of attentive human consideration and generous goodwill and love.

Margaret and I chose each other and we made our relationship work, whereas in a childhood family, there is no choice. She and I grew closer together as we got older. We were closest of all during our year of bankruptcy. I blamed myself for those sad circumstances but she never once blamed me. At times I am attacked by others (it is part and parcel of my professional life, working with addicts) but she never once attacked me. Challenged and confronted me, yes, but never attacked.

Thoughts:
1 Tolerance and human understanding can be learned.
2 We can choose to experience either all of our feelings or none.
3 Peaceful spirits don't ever attack anyone

Reminder: Lives are lived, not lost.

Notes:
I had no factual denial over Margaret's death. I had seen her lifeless body. From my professional work, particularly in the killing fields of addiction and depression, I am familiar with death. I know that she is dead. Even so, I was initially so busy with conversations, telephone calls, texts and emails that I had little time in the day for the deep sadness that accompanies such a profound loss. At night, as ever, I wrote.

I have always lived primarily in the world of feeling. I am comfortable in the world of thought but I am no academic. In my music and in my writing I express my feelings openly. Otherwise, for me, there would be no point in either activity.

When helping people suffering from depression/addiction and from compulsive behaviour of any kind, I see it primarily as a disease of feelings. We who suffer from it know all the cognitive-behavioural reasons why we should not persist in our destructive behaviour (towards ourselves and other people). But we still continue it – until we come to work a daily Twelve Step programme and acknowledge our dependence upon a higher power than self. For me, other people, other units of the Universal Spirit, are my God, my reassurance of relevance.

In the new emptiness of my daily practical life, I have lost my constant physical companion. I weep. I let myself weep.

In our almshouse flat, Margaret and I lived together warmly. We still do so in my mind. If I choose, I can reflect upon all that we have lost – and it is natural to do so – or I can focus upon what we still share. It is certainly true that genuine mutual love never dies: it cannot. Our children lost their mother. Our grandchildren lost their 'Phoebe Granny' (our dog Phoebe distinguishing Margaret from other grandmothers). It was a supremely difficult time for all of us, not just for me. Each one of us in our own way suffered bereavement and searched our souls.

Our daughter Nicola, ever the magnificent organizer, made all the preparations for Margaret's memorial service. We chose the speakers for readings and personal tributes. We chose the priest to deliver the address, the same wonderful lady who had conducted the funerals of both my parents and who found us our almshouse home .

I chose the music for professional musicians to perform. Two anthems came from our wedding service: William Walton's 'Set me as a seal upon thine heart' and William Byrd's 'Ave Verum Corpus', which we used to sing frequently at Corpus Christi College, Cambridge. The third anthem was Patrick Hadley's utterly beautiful setting of 'My beloved spake'. Hilary chose one of their very favourite piano trios, the slow movement of the Ravel. The London Symphony Orchestra provided the players, the two string players being former prize winners, awarded by Margaret and me, in return for which they had given recitals in our home. For the final organ voluntary I chose the Widor toccata that is often used in weddings. I wanted the service to end on a note of triumph.

This was not a recital: it was a personal celebration of music that Margaret loved all her life and that we could share together. The readings and personal tributes by family members and by Margaret's special friends would indeed be very, very special.

Thoughts:
1 Friendships don't just happen. They are created.
2 To weep is to be true to the lost loved one.
3 We can chose to focus upon what we have lost or upon what we shared together in life.
4 A special rite of passage marks the time when we respect and love the one from whom we are now parted. This is a time for calm reflection and also a time for joyous celebration.

Reminder: The world can wait a while for a special person.

Notes:
Trying to keep my mind focused on what to do next in the preparation for Margaret's memorial service and, at the same time, preparing for the opening of the new treatment centre three days later, had been exceedingly challenging while I grieved. I was busy but I did not push down my feelings. I wanted my sad feelings. They were appropriate.

And, while we waited for the day of the memorial service, life went on in its usual way. Nicola surpassed her own high standards in organizing the printing of the service sheets and in arranging all the service particulars while making sure that everybody knew what would happen and how and when.

We still had no idea how many people would attend the service. Many said they would; some said they couldn't. How many people would read the newspaper notices? We didn't know. I went to London the night before the service so that there was no chance of me being held up in traffic. I stayed with one of Margaret's closest friends. I had supported her many years previously when her husband had been killed in a road accident. Now she supported me: we tired the sun with talking and she calmed my fevered spirit in what was among the most gentle but important conversations of my life.

In the morning I had my hair cut. My life had to go on, in its minor routines as well as in the major events. Afterwards, on a beautiful sunny morning, I walked past our former happy home, past the drab empty premises of our former thriving medical practice and down to the church that I went to twice a week for twenty-three years, not for a formal service (we were always in Kent at the weekends) but for early morning meetings of one or another anonymous fellowship in the vestry. I know the church well, not only as a landmark but as a place of spiritual sustenance.

I greeted the early arrivals through my tears and I went on and on doing so until I was told firmly that the service had to start. I took my place at the front and, after the bidding prayers, I took my place at the lectern to read what I had previously prepared.

The service was one wonderfully uplifting moment after another. The music, the readings and tributes, the address and the prayers, all flowed into each other in a wash of radiant colour, given to Margaret as our thanks for what she had given us. For me each and every part of the service was special. The tributes were from special people we know and love. The music was magical. I grieve that I will not hear Margaret play her piano again, except in my mind. The address and prayers were poignant and relevant. Most of all, the presence of so many friends was overwhelming. They gave their time and presence to Margaret as a statement of love that recognized what she had given to them.

We had printed eight hundred service sheets, just to be safe. They ran out. People filled the entire church and half the gallery and they were standing three deep at the back of the nave. It was wonderful that so many people attended the church to say their own goodbyes to Margaret in their own ways.

She was not a public figure. No officials or dignitaries were present. She simply loved people and they loved her.

Thoughts:
1 The bereaved understand the bereaved.
2 People know and treasure love when they experience it.
3 Our familiars are important to us: our friends, our familiar places, our familiar actions – all these give colour to our daily lives. We treasure them.
4 Public figures may also be privately mourned but their memorial services are sometimes mere razzamatazz. The public expression of grief for people not personally known is bizarre.

Reminder: It's all about feelings.

Notes:
The central feature of Margaret's gentle and beautiful life was love. She knew instinctively how to love and she did. After the service, as people gradually drifted away and went about their daily business, I was left on the lawn at the front of the church, wondering what to do next. The fabulous festival, the rite of passage, was over.

Nicola and Robin had left with their families to return to their homes. My brother Andrew had gone somewhere with our close friends from Kent. Nothing had been arranged because there was no need for further formalities. I joined Henry and also Nicola's son Sam and we went for lunch in the Old Brompton Road at La Bouchée, Margaret's and my favourite haunt, and we found Hilary and her partner, David, already there.

During the meal I wandered between the two tables, one representing Margaret's childhood family and the other representing the family that we ourselves had created. Would we ever have reason to meet again? Probably only through me, one way or another. Death inevitably divides – and then unites again only for the next formal departure.

After the meal, Henry drove his wife, Kelly, and their daughter, Allie, and me back to Kent.

I returned to our flat, to be on my own with my darling, beautiful, sweet, lovely girl.

I received over two hundred letters from friends. Replying to them individually by hand was one of the last acts in my process of formal farewell. I owed it to Margaret to be personally considerate to people who had taken the trouble to write to me. Mostly I wrote at night. There would inevitably come a time when the last letter would be written. I feared for that time: it would be so final. After the exhilarating celebration of Margaret's life, came … normality.

Daily life, with all its simple routines and trivialities as well as its responsibilities, resumed much of its customary pattern.

Except for the tears. They turned up whenever they felt like doing so: on one day a misting of the eyes every so often. On another day, forty minutes of sobbing uncontrollably and unashamedly.

Along with Athena, the Goddess of Wisdom in the arts and sciences, and Aesculapius, the God of Healing, I had previously chosen Orpheus, who sorrowfully visited the underworld to search for his lost love, Euridice, to be my archetypes – my spiritual mentors in my earthly journey. I had intended Orpheus to teach me the full meaning of love. He did. Margaret's name, together with mine, was still on the door of our flat. It could stay there. I cried at times in the flat, our two small rooms, but I was not lonely. I missed her dreadfully and yet I was comforted by our familiars.

The funeral and the celebration were inevitably challenging – but I was busy, almost on stage. I know how to survive the challenge of a public performance – and yet, of course, these recent events were infinitely more significant than anything I had previously experienced. Now, in the quieter hours, came an even greater challenge: I simply did not know how I could bear to live without Margaret. Yet I had to learn to do so in order to add further relevance to her life as well as to my own.

Thoughts:
1 Grief is an essentially personal and private process. The formal expressions of public farewell are sometimes moving enough but the individual tender moments come later, on our own.
2 Mythical archetypes may give us more than we bargained for.
3 The routines of daily life give us an opportunity to settle.
4 Having a formal parting ceremony is a helpful rite of passage.
5 Learning to live without someone gives relevance to the lost life, while still letting the tears flow.

Reminder: Family is family.

Notes:
After the celebration of Margaret's life, attended by a thousand of her friends who loved her, I returned to our two-room flat. Without her, it was now too big for me. I missed her company, her warmth, her conversation, her touch, her support, her love. I also missed the many day-to-day things that she did for me. Now I had to fend for myself. I learned how to cope with many things. I did not want to live but I did not want to die. I coped.

I set up a new treatment programme that Margaret and I had planned to run in rented cottages in a local hotel. It closed after nine weeks. I lost all the money that I had earned from giving intensive counselling – in their home abroad – to a family, all of whom were addicts of one kind or another. Margaret, who came with me, had found that experience very distressing. Also, as I got stronger emotionally – from being back at work – she no longer had to support me as much as she had done. She lost a role. She then became more aware of her own distress.

As this crisis gradually unfolded and later came to a catastrophic conclusion, two members of my close family blamed me, saying that I had caused the stress that hurt Margaret. They cut off all contact with me for a year. Others had some contact with me but, for most of my time, I was on my own. Quite often the first person to whom I would speak in a day was at an Alcoholics Anonymous meeting at seven o'clock in the evening. I was lonely. A medical friend had previously offered me the use of a room in Harley Street. Margaret and I used to go to London by coach one day a week The three hour door-to-door journey was tough. I wanted to contact my former patients to let them know where I was and what I was doing but I was denied access to the company mailing list. I had to rebuild my professional life on my own, as best I could.

Thoughts:

1 Professional men often believe that we run the world. We betray our wives or partners when we take their work for granted.

2 It did me no harm to learn how wretched life can be: it often is for many people. We betray them if we disregard that.

3 I betrayed Margaret by asking her to help me in work that she did not want to do. She accompanied me dutifully – and became engulfed in the madness of a particular addictive family. She deserved to be at home, playing her beloved piano.

4 My idea for the new treatment centre was good but it failed in practice. Therefore it was a bad idea. The same principle applies to many aspects of the welfare state. I betrayed the person I loved the most. The welfare state betrays us all.

5 Roles are important. I am very aware – and defensive – of my own role but I betrayed Margaret by being insensitive to hers.

6 Margaret had a vital place in the lives and hearts of all our family members. Their own grief reaction over her various losses has to be accepted and understood. They did not betray me.

7 We were living in what is effectively an old people's home. My loneliness would be commonplace in such institutions, beautiful and supportive though they may be and as ours certainly was. We betray old people if we fail to consider what their lives are really like. However, before they are totally dependent upon care, they betray themselves if they fail to make their own lives less dull. Some do; some don't. I moved on but I might go back in thirty years' time. I would betray myself if I let myself decay before then.

7 I do not use AA meetings as a social function. They are my spiritual medicine. I need them to keep my addictive disease at bay. I would betray all my former staff and patients – and the present ones – if I were to relapse.

8 Denying me access to my own former mailing list certainly betrayed me – but I need to forget that and make a new list.

Reminder: Officials do what officials do.

Notes:

The Official Receiver had expressed no interest in the furnishings and pictures at our cottage in Kent, the final property to go. We had stored them with Emmaus, the charity for homeless men in Dover, and we gave most of our possessions to them to do what the men do – spruce them up and sell them in order to pay for their own keep.

Our few remaining items were transferred to Robin's new treatment centre, which he had skilfully created from the business remnants of our previous centre a few miles away. That former property was now a charred wreck – although Margaret and I never went to see it in that state. Evidently there was nothing left of what she and I had lovingly created. We preferred to remember it as it was.

We went through the bits and pieces which we collected from Emmaus. They were all that was left of the possessions of our professional and personal lifetimes. I kept some books and pictures as keepsakes. I had no room for anything else.

Margaret and I were still being chased by the Council Tax department of the Royal Borough of Kensington and Chelsea for tax that they said was incurred during our time of bankruptcy. They didn't seem to grasp that we had had no say in the disposal of our former property. They took us to court.

Our trustee in bankruptcy also threatened legal action against Margaret and me, saying that we still had legal title to the property of our former treatment centre which, in its wretched state, was still unsold. Surely that should have been sorted out while we were both bankrupt and Margaret still alive.

The Inland Revenue had still not clarified its position on Margaret's income. Bankruptcy and even death do not clear the decks: state bureaucracy is immortal.

Private bureaucracy is little better, the only bank that

provided us with an account (we had no credit card or debit card or cheque book – they themselves issued cheques on our instructions) now charged me £10 on every occasion because they wanted, as a matter of general policy, to discourage the use of cheques.

'Grinding' is the word that best describes the mental process of being chased by officialdom. There is no let-up. (Nor should there be if criminality is involved.) Harassing a bankrupt is a criminal offence – but it seems to be acceptable when government bodies, of one kind or another, do it. Even when the Council Tax people eventually accepted that we should pay nothing, the stress that Margaret and I had endured could not be undone. We had always been resilient – we could not otherwise have looked after addicts for so many years – but this was a dreadful (in the full meaning of that word) experience.

Again I come back to the recognition that I myself had the basic responsibility for looking after my wife and myself. I had neglected that. My clinical work had been worthy (in some people's eyes but not in all) but I failed to run the business. I paid a savage price for that – and my darling Margaret even more so.

Thoughts:
1 Possessions are important: they represent the work it took to create them or purchase them. We appreciate them and we are rightly fond of them.
2 Relationships are even more important. They have to be created and nurtured.
3 Who we are is very much more important than what we do or what we have.
4 The nuts and bolts of routine practical life are exactly that. Life simply goes on.
5 Being harassed by the powers of officialdom, inaccurately or even illegally, is unpleasant in the extreme after a bereavement.

Reminder: Things don't always work out the way we want.

Notes:
An expected new patient failed to materialize in the new treatment centre and I sensed the possibility of further financial and professional collapse. If that were to happen, I had to survive. I felt that I owed that to Margaret and to myself.

On an official form, I ticked the box marked 'widower'.

I had supper with friends. Inevitably and poignantly, there were five chairs. There was also an empty space beside me in the chapel on Sunday mornings in our community service.

There were no casual, chatty conversations on the telephone: my place in other people's lives had changed.

Only in my work and in my writing could I be the person I was before. I focused on that. I went to work each day. I paid the rent and the salaries and I waited. In the first two weeks I waited but nobody came. What was my future destined to be? Would I ever be able to re-establish myself in my counselling work?

I did not have the answers. Should I remain in Kent or try to get back to London?

My enthusiasm was still intact, my energy was only slightly dimmed by loss of sleep. My commitment to helping addicts and their families was as firm as ever. But my tiny financial resources were dwindling each day. I could calculate 'C' day (for calamity or collapse) and I knew it only too well. Even so, I would live my professional dream again – right up until the time when it became a nightmare. The one trainee who had booked on my new training course for creative coaches (my grand new idea) cancelled. My website defiantly tilted at windmills. Did I want to go on? Could I?

I calculated that one thousand people die each day in the UK. That's a lot of bereavement, sometimes in people of my age, sometimes younger, sometimes older. Could I write something of comfort and strength to offer them? Would they want it? I had no one to ask: my constant companion, comforter, challenger and confidante had disappeared into thin air. I very much appreciated all the many things that Margaret did for me while she was alive. I appreciated her even more now.

Supposing I had simply retired, as most people do, when they reach the age of seventy. The property boom was still booming at that time for us. We could have sold out and have been very comfortable and we would have had no debts. When I came out of bankruptcy, I also had no debts – but also no assets.

Supposing I had settled for the quiet life, seeing an occasional patient and doing high-intensity work with families.

Margaret and I had been comfortable in the almshouse and she played the piano in the common room. She was content with the simple life. But I was not: I wanted an active platform from which to speak. Like it or not, nobody listens to people who do not represent something or create something. In any case, I myself do not listen to theorists: I want to see what people can do before I consider their opinions.

But I reflected that if I still wanted to be influential, and to drive forward my ideas on how addicts and their families can be helped, did I really need a public platform, as I believed, or was that merely self-indulgence?

Thoughts:
1 The change in personal status after a bereavement is immediate. There is no escape from that.
2 Determination is admirable – but it does not guarantee a favourable outcome. It may even be destructive.
3 Inevitably we ask ourselves questions that are unanswerable.
4 Hindsight is the most accurate observation point – but it is impossible to reach it in advance.
5 It is easy to confuse personal ambition or desire with what we believe is our right and due.

Reminder: Know thyself.

Notes:
Would various alternative strategies, in providing a less stressful life, have avoided the tragic outcome of Margaret's final year of life? Again I had no one to ask and no answers to provide for myself. I wept in my remorse and in my loneliness.

There is sometimes a sad insensitivity in people who 'know' the answers to the three great imponderables: 'Where did I come from?', 'What am I doing on this planet?' and 'Where am I going afterwards?'. With best intentions some people, with their absolute convictions, leave me more distressed. I respect their right to their own opinions but I do not see their viewpoints as any more than that. For myself I am content with the concept that we are all parts of the Universal Spirit.

In that way, my separation from Margaret is only physical, even though 'only physical' itself is a devastating loss. Throughout her life Margaret influenced me for the better and she still does. She knew how to live: simply, kindly and considerately, warmly, tenderly, compassionately. That is who she was and is. That is her lasting influence upon me while she goes on the next part of her own spiritual journey, whatever it may be.

I have to treasure my life – especially now – as she treasures hers, being the spiritual person she still is. Her relationship with other people, and her influence upon them, is (I assume) equally profound for them in their own way as it is for me. Our children and our grandchildren, her two brothers and her sister and her other relatives, her friends, everyone she knew, had individual relationships with her – and these live on, as mine does.

Being miserable for all the rest of my life would be silly. The pictures of Margaret on my desk smile at me. The picture of her on my iPhone is of her quietly reading a book. The same picture is my screen-saver on my computer. Of course she is with me in my memories and in all the daily reminders of the little things and the unexpected echoes of something she did or said. These happy images will stay with me for ever. I want them.

Other people tell me about their own experience of the death of someone they love. That is kind of them but generally I prefer to discover my own experience in my own way.

I feel sad, lonely and frightened. I am sad for what both Margaret and I have lost but I am also happy for what we shared. I am lonely without her. I miss her conversation, her touch, knowing where she is and what she is doing. Our companionship is not something that I can do for myself.

I fear the emptiness of the years ahead. I hope that I can fill them with my work and with my writing and other contributions in the media but I miss discussing things with Margaret and I miss her own constant innovation, the new ways in which she gently modified her work with addictive families. I miss her piano playing. She became a progressively more sensitive musician as she experienced more of life. I miss her love of her animals, her love of her friends, her love of me.

There is a time to grieve. That time is now and I do not want to suppress it. I am content to live with my feelings – happy or sad.

Thoughts:

1 People who know all the answers may not fully understand the question.

2 One person's experience is not necessarily another's.

3 Feelings can be felt without risk but they are not commands.

4 The empty years ahead will inevitably be filled somehow. We ourselves can choose what we put into them.

5 If there were no grief there would be no happiness. It is the contrast that gives life its richness of emotional colour.

Reminder: Let life take its natural course.

Notes:
What if? Just suppose . . . What might have happened if I had done something or said something different? It was inevitable that I should rack my brain with questions. But I did not have to get stuck on any one of them. There are no clear answers. There is therefore no point in going down any of these routes.

Similarly, there is no point in seeking comfort. It comes by itself, in its own time, in its own way: a sensitive phrase in a letter from a friend, a gentle awareness from someone else in a similar situation, an opportunity to do something useful to help other people when they ask for professional help, the personal acknowledgement that it really is better to have loved and lost than never to have loved at all.

When I feel that someone else's attitude or comment or offer misses the mark, I remember that I have my own personal feelings in my own personal way. What counts, in my view, is the intention of other people, not what they actually say or do.

The deluge of letters, to which I replied out of appreciation rather than duty, are comforting – sometimes specifically and at other times simply as a result of my general awareness that so many people are thinking of my darling Margaret and me. These are the beautiful things that I choose to put into my mind.

Inevitably, utter sadness and despair still flood over me at times. I had started full time work again (for me that had always been a seven-day week for the twenty-three years that Margaret and I had run our treatment centre and it still means that for me now). There can be no days off at the sharp end of work in addiction: care and skill save lives. There is so much variety in my work – looking after all members of a family across the whole spectrum of physical, mental, emotional and social problems – that there is no time to get bored or tired. Without my beloved Margaret by my side, however, I am bereft. As a professional, I try to do my work, creatively and sensitively and I focus my attention on the person seeking my help. As a human being, I weep. I grieve. I long for simple comfort from my wife and I want to give it to her. But that cannot happen.

I spent two hours with a patient who was in a very wretched state. At the end of that time, I knew a great deal about his life, as was right and proper. He knew little of mine, as was also right and proper. This experience inevitably wore me down. I followed it with two hours of instruction on my computer. I remembered very little. The mechanical part of my head still wasn't working.

I was further crushed by the comment that running a treatment centre nowadays involves a lot more than being good as a counsellor or coach. I realized that perhaps the only clinical skill that I believe I really have is now devalued. I need IT skills that I don't possess. I pondered what on earth would become of me if my work were to fail again.

Margaret's eyes, in the happy smiling photograph on my desk, follow me around the room, encouraging me in everything I do and they warm my heart. Thank God she died straight out rather than being left in a physical or mental abyss. I can remember her in the full richness of her life. One moment she was there in all her beauty, calmness and fairness and then . . . she is still with me.

Thoughts:
1 Comfort cannot be forced into us by our own efforts or given to us by other people. It arrives in its own little ways.
2 Professionals deliver the goods, regardless of personal pain.
3 There are inevitably times when stray – or even deliberate – comments will be hurtful. That cannot be avoided. It simply has to be accepted as part of life.
4 Love really is as strong as death – and stronger.

Reminder: Physician heal thyself.

Notes:
I took the sheets and pillowcases off Margaret's bed but I left our teddy bears cuddling each other. I spent days and days on the telephone and writing letters, each event anchoring the sadness more firmly in my spirit. But now I can also re-anchor in my mind the image of Margaret's happy face, giving out simple goodwill and love, as she always did and always will.

I don't know the date of my own death. I shall not bring it on. I have a creative life to lead. I have unfinished work and many, many ideas. We lost virtually all our possessions in our bankruptcy. Now Margaret has lost her physical life and I have lost her physical presence. But nobody – not the creditors, not the Inland Revenue, not governments or accountants or lawyers, nor the occasional accidental insensitivity from other people – can take away my sweetest love. We are as close together as ever before.

My work with people suffering from depression/addiction or any other compulsive behaviour, while at the same time working with their families, is inevitably demanding of myself emotionally. I cannot deal with the destructive experiences of other people's physical, mental, emotional and spiritual lives without at times being harrowed myself. This is the way it has always been in my counselling/coaching work. While still remaining professionally focused on the patients, I cannot do creative work without being mentally, spiritually and emotionally involved in it. To be detached would make my professional life sterile and even irrelevant, merely an intellectual exercise.

I have had twenty-four years of experience of being the catalyst in other people's mental neuro-chemical reactions. Through my interjections, timed and directed primarily for emotional effect, as well as through providing information and stimulation and fresh insights, I enable others to consider whether they want to make changes in their lives or to stay as they are. At the end of each interaction I come out unchanged, ready for the next challenge.

But nowadays, in the ongoing process of my own bereavement, I have to pace myself more carefully and be gentle with myself as well as with the patients. If I get hurt, it will inevitably follow that the patients will get hurt. If I put up emotional barriers, so that I can't get hurt at all, I would – through insensitivity – hurt the patients even more. If I stop doing this work altogether, I would deprive my patients of a significant understanding – and careful – resource. I would also deprive myself of a significant future potential for emotional and spiritual growth that would lead to me doing better work.

Of course there are times when I feel absolutely desperate and cannot see my way ahead. This recent sadness is like no other that I have ever experienced. I feel lost, empty, lonely, useless. As a doctor I am familiar with grief reactions in other people. Consequently I understand what I am going through myself – but this is me, my own weary head and my own broken heart.

I know how to comfort and support other people. Doing so for myself is more challenging: I try in vain to use my devastated spirit to comfort my devastated spirit.

Thoughts:
1 Words and other sounds, images and the stimulation of any of the senses can anchor themselves in our memories. It is up to us to overwrite negative anchors with positive ones.
2 To be creative and committed implies being fully involved, not indifferent nor even impartial, and then refreshed again.
3 In bereavement we comfort ourselves as best we can but we can learn to leave our weary and sad spirits untroubled by careless self-destructive thoughts.

Reminder: Entrepreneurs fail all the time – but it does not stop us from starting again.

Notes:
Of course I thought of suicide. That is natural in my present circumstances. I am beyond caring whether that shocks anybody. But it would cause such grief to my family and friends and they don't need that on top of the loss of Margaret. I have to stay alive and do my best to make something positive from this terrible tragedy.

Friends and family call me – and that is nice – but I find that the most helpful thing is when I call them. I have to make the effort to move, physically as well as emotionally, and that helps me to be nearer to my intended real self, kind and creative even if not yet fully positive and enthusiastic. At least this provides me with some moments of peace in the torment.

Having been through the recent experience of bankruptcy, I am familiar with the way that I personally go through a grief reaction and I know that I have the capacity to get through this tragic bereavement. Therefore I must. All I have to do is to put one foot gently in front of the other each day.

My work supports me when I have any and it saddens me when I haven't. Recently I have been doing some of my most delicate and demanding work ever and I do what I need to do in order to develop it and expand it. At least I know that I haven't lost my touch or my enthusiasm for the work itsef.

For my new treatment centre work I had beautiful premises, keen and experienced staff and exciting new ideas. I knew that this new business was undercapitalized. Of course it was: I had only recently come out of bankruptcy. My staff took some risks in joining me, just as I had taken risks in starting up again. We knew what we were taking on and we went in with every intention of building something that would last.

Surely there is a place for optimism. I have never previously been afraid of a new challenge. I have always been an innovator and I still am. If everything fell apart, I would do something else . . . And that is exactly what did happen. The centre closed after just nine weeks. This was not a disaster – it was a good try. I licked my wounds and I went back to doing the individual appointments that I was already doing in London every Monday and I built on that.

Naturally, I did get tired, partly from not sleeping well and partly from my continuing sadness. Even so, giving up is not what I do. I paced myself carefully during the day and I took on only the work that I could manage responsibly.

I still believed that I had something important to say in the world of treatment for addiction. It is just that I had not yet found the most effective outlet.

Thoughts:

1 Thinking about suicide is a common experience. Planning it or significantly attempting it is not so common. Either way, we should take seriously any conversation in which someone talks about suicide.

2 Talking with someone about the possibility of suicide embeds that idea in the mind of the person considering it. Therefore it should not be mentioned. Instead we can talk about sadness.

3 'Action' is the magic word in raising our spirits: we need to do something physical and get involved with other people in any way we can.

4 There is no such thing as 'failure' when trying our best.

5 Burying grief in work, or drowning it in alcohol or trying to smash it with drugs or food or anything else doesn't work.

6 There is indeed a place for optimism but that does not mean that all ventures succeed and that all hopes will come to fruition.

7 Pacing ourselves gently is the best way forward.

Reminder: Time waits for no man.

Notes:

Yet still there were difficult times. Margaret's elder brother, Peter, and her sister, Hilary, came to the common room of the almshouse to give a piano and violin recital. It was beautiful – but I realized that live music, which had been central to Margaret's whole life, and for much of my own life central to mine, was now leaving my daily experience. Also, I took the chance to ask Hilary to take all Margaret's sheet music and also all her clothes home with her. I kept the bears.

I took stock of my current situation: my wife has died and I do not seek any other relationship at any time (fifty years cannot be put to one side because there are so many anchors involved). I no longer work as a doctor because I would not want to go back to learning all about clinical conditions – such as heart attacks – that I never see or medications – such as antidepressants – that I never prescribe. I have no residential treatment centre and no money to build one and I don't think I want to own and run one any more. I live partly in Kent but most of my friends live in London, which is the centre of almost all of my personal, clinical and cultural interests.

It is difficult not to see all this in a negative light but it is simply a statement of my current reality. This does not mean that it will always be like that but it does mean that I have no choice but to start from here. That is not an encouraging springboard – but it is my reality so I have to get used to it and make the best of it.

However, looking back over my life, I can see that the major events that shaped it came out of the blue: I went up to Cambridge reading Music and I came down with a degree in Medicine, I met Margaret by chance in an art gallery and later, also by chance, I found a field of work (addiction) that I love, even though other doctors tend to run away from it. With all that evidence of the influence of chance in my life, it would be silly of me to imagine that it has no future part to play.

The other reflection that occurs to me is that I have everything that I really need: a secure home paid for through my statutory pension, the opportunity to earn some money in order to buy myself some treats, such as visits to operas, and I have an active mind that has not yet let me down. Also I do have lots of friends who wish me well. I should be so fortunate to be me.

The only downside, that took me by surprise, was sudden pain in my back. Previously I had lost only one day from work every ten years (in a seven-day working week over thirty years) and I had taken a total of only sixty tablets of any kind in my entire life. To be in continuous pain for three months (from osteoporosis: crumbling bones in my spine) left me very insecure. Illness was not in my vocabulary. Nor was age. I wondered whether physical problems were going to be another unwelcome new experience.

Thoughts:
1 Loss is inevitable for each of us. 'The Day the Music Died' is much more than a line from a beautiful song.
2 Mementos are not a sign of sentimentalism but of love
3 Change is the only constant in life.
4 Chance still plays her hand in all of our lives. Be ready for it.
5 Reflection on what we really need and value can be helpful but sometimes the best course of action is to do nothing.
6 We see new opportunities if we search actively for them. They may turn up out of the blue and we would miss them if we were not aware of that possibility at any time.
7 Good health cannot be taken for granted.
8 Ask whose life we would really rather have than our own.
9 Each day has something beautiful to offer us. It is up to us to find it and rejoice in it.

Reminder: Grief is essentially a private process.

Notes:
The final rite of passage was the burial of the urn containing Margaret's ashes. For a week it had been beside her chair, the one in which she usually sat in our flat, while I waited for the engraved stone plaque to be delivered. Now the Prior and I stood beside the hole in the ground that the gardener had prepared and, with two short prayers, the urn was placed in it. Later the plaque covered it. Her sweet life was definitely over. It was difficult to believe that mine was not also at an end.

I could have invited other family members and friends to join the Prior and me at the graveside but I did not want that. All the others had been present at the funeral service or at the celebration of Margaret's life – or both – and I wanted this little ceremony to be just between her and me.

I let the Prior know that, at the time of my own death, I should like Margaret's urn to be disinterred so that my ashes can be buried with hers in our shared grave, with a new shared plaque.

I knew from my time in bankruptcy (it is just a word until it is experienced in real life) that, tough and resilient though I am, there was absolutely nothing that I could do to move my thoughts, my feelings and also my physiology along. My thoughts got stuck in ruts, going back and forward, desperately trying to move on but failing to do so. My feelings varied from day to day. Far from making progress, I found that I paid an emotional price the following day if ever I had a good day. My body developed crazy rhythms of its own, with sleep patterns being particularly disturbed. The effects of cortisol, the stress hormone, became practical realities rather than interesting items in a medical textbook. Trembling, twitching, sweating, peeing and losing weight were constant unwelcome physical companions. I knew them well from our time of bankruptcy. Now I got to know them yet again. I simply had to wait for time to work its healing magic, as it had done (eventually) previously. The difference on this occasion was that in my bankruptcy I was determined to make progress and create a new life. Now, in my bereavement, I was not sure that I wanted any life at all. Suicide was not an option but I had to go through the mental, emotional and physical processes of a grief reaction without any clear picture of what I would have at the end of it all.

Thoughts:

1 A long-term relationship is created each day: it doesn't just happen through the passage of time. All relationships have difficult times but working through those difficulties strengthens them.

2 Reflecting over the full length of a relationship is not possible at first after a bereavement. The overwhelming sense of loss crowds out every other mental and emotional experience.

3 There is a high mortality rate in the surviving partner after a bereavement, specifically through accidents or suicide but also through natural causes such as heart attacks or strokes. It is as if the body simply gives up trying.

4 There is nothing sensible or comforting that can be said to someone who is grieving. Even at the best of times it is impossible to know precisely what someone else is thinking or feeling. To attempt to say something comforting or reassuring risks interfering in that person's private grief. It is best to say little or nothing and just be. Helping with practical things is always appreciated – just doing them rather than saying 'Do let me know if there is anything that I can do for you', which leaves the bereaved person begging for favours. Even then, however, it is the kind thought that really matters.

5 Maybe we do not know what the future will bring – or even if we have one – but it might yet surprise us with its beauty. We shall find out only if we give it a try.

Reminder: Hope springs eternal.

Notes:
I have always been very good at using time well. I value it. I don't waste it. Now it mostly disintegrated. I lost my discipline. I would wake up at four in the morning and struggle to get back to sleep. Later in the day I would fall asleep after meals. That pattern simply isn't me.

I think part of the problem is that I do not have sufficient work to keep me busy the whole time. I could fill up the time with work that I do not want to do but I'm sure that would create even worse problems. Again I was stuck in a mental and emotional situation that was outside my control. I was not the master of my own head. It worked perfectly well when I was actually at work but it did not readily understand the terms 'relax' or 'let go'.

I have meditation books and I know how to use Neuro-Linguistic Programming techniques of self-hypnosis but my head was not interested in any of that: it did its own thing. I have studied positive psychology and I like it very much but it didn't do anything for me now. I've done Mindfulness and Motivational Enhancement and Choice Theory, as well as Cognitive Behavioural Therapy, Rational Emotive Behaviour Therapy and Dialectical Behaviour Therapy. I teach these therapies to trainees. They are fine for heads that are not drugged. Mine was drugged – with melancholy. I had been hammered and I had no choice but to accept that. People who have been in a similar situation would understand me perfectly well. People who have not shared this experience probably don't.

Fortunately, I am very familiar with that understanding, or lack of understanding, because it is exactly what happens in addiction. People who are addicts of one kind or another understand other addicts. Other people do not understand us at all – and, reasonably enough, usually don't want to.

So, in my bereavement, I do not expect to be understood. There is no comfort. I accept that. I do not say there is no hope. There is plenty of hope. It just isn't ready to show itself in abundance just yet. It will come, along with spontaneity, creativity and enthusiasm, when they are ready. That will be when my head is ready, when it has gone through the necessary processes of grieving. That takes time.

Thoughts:

1 Shock causes disorientation. Shell shock caused disorientation in the First World War. Bereavement causes similar shock now (and always has done). The shocked troops in the First World War were not understood – and they were shot as cowards. We need to be more understanding of ourselves and of each other nowadays.

2 'Pull yourself together' is not a kind comment to give oneself and, in any case, it cannot be obeyed after a bereavement. We need to be as understanding of ourselves as we would be of other people.

3 Melancholy is a drug that comes from within the brain, probably mediated through neurotransmitters or hormones. We should respect brain biochemistry rather than fight against it or confuse it by giving it even more drugs, such as pharmaceutical or recreational substances.

4 Non-medical therapeutic approaches of one kind or another can be very helpful when the brain is in a fit state to be able to react appropriately to them.

5 There is no point in looking for instinctive understanding from people who cannot give it. They may not have had any similar experience.

6 Hope comes in its own good time. It is worth waiting for.

7 Spontaneity, creativity and enthusiasm are the hallmarks of a life well lived. Bereavement initially totally negates all of these beautiful characteristics but they return when the grieving process has taken its due time.

Reminder: There is a future to be found – if we want it.

Notes:
After four months I was still deeply shocked, living largely on autopilot. I did what I needed to do each day in order to keep body and soul together. I made no attempt to jolly myself along or to engage in social activities. I took life as it came.

I continued to go to London on one or two days each week to do counselling work in my rented room in Harley Street. I was stimulated by that work: it kept my mind alive and it showed me that I still had something valuable to offer to other people through my professional work.

Financially, my life was precarious. I could survive on my state pension because my living expenses were very small. However, if I were to do any significant work, I would have to pay to establish my professional base: I would have to find the premises and staff and buy all the equipment and get the necessary management and marketing systems in place. I had done all that several times before so I should be able to do it again. I therefore learned how to use a laptop and I enjoyed developing new skills. For fifty years I had relied upon my wife and my secretaries. Now, for many things, I had nobody but myself to call upon and I had to learn how other, less privileged, people survive in the real world.

Fortunately, Margaret and I had made many friends over the years and many people wished me well. Josh, who had known both of us well, wanted to learn my counselling skills. He sat in on my consultations and I bought his computing skills so that he could keep his body and soul together.

Together we looked at ideas: a radio series, a book or two, a tie-up with a newspaper in some way, some podcasts, a public lecture – all designed to promote my work as a counsellor and lead towards establishing a treatment programme of some kind. Turning the dreams into reality would be challenging but the alternative would be to do nothing – and that would be the end of my life, as I see it. Clearly I would have to move back into London. It is my natural home. There would be nothing to stop me – except having no money, no borrowing capacity and no accommodation. These were significant challenges but they had to be resolved. Another friend, Pete, introduced me to a charity which might provide a home, similar to the one I had in Canterbury, and I followed through with that idea. I would be leaving Margaret's ashes behind in Kent – but her spirit would be coming with me. Further conversations with her sister Hilary convinced me that I should move on. Otherwise my own ashes would be joining Margaret's before I was ready.

Thoughts:
1 There is no hurry to move on – at any age. It is better to wait until the shock of bereavement has settled.
2 There is no point in trying to jolly ourselves along. It wouldn't work. Take life as it comes and allow yourself to experience whatever feelings are natural in each situation.
3 The words 'Money isn't everything' can only be said by those people who have plenty of it.
4 Generating new ideas is a function of willingness to do so. Anyone can have ideas. Turning them into practical reality is a function of hard work and being prepared to take risks. Looking towards developing new skills can be very exciting.
5 The world is a harsh place for many people, not only for the bereaved. Making friends pays dividends.
6 Dreams based in reality avoid becoming our worst nightmares.
7 Doing nothing is what some people choose to do. That is their right, so long as they can support themselves.
8 We deserve to be remembered by what we are in life, not simply through what we do.
9 We ourselves decide when we are ready to die – or not.

Reminder: Despair not.

Notes:
Gradually, as the denial phase of bereavement wore on, the anger and depression phases came in.

I don't do anger. I know how to do fury and rage but I haven't done that for many years, since beginning to work the Twelve Step recovery programme, first formulated by Alcoholics Anonymous. I have no sense of anger towards God or Fate. There is no point in that. I have no sense of anger towards other people. There is nothing to be gained from that. However, I do know how to be sad – very sad. I suppose this sadness can be anger turned inwards against myself.

I have plenty to be angry about towards myself. In the week before she died, Margaret had told several people how she was keen to work alongside me in our future work and how happy she was in her own life, with her special friends and her family therapy group and her piano. Only I know how much more attentive I could have been to her. I was so wrapped up in myself and in my own ideas and plans. I feel very sad about that.

Reflecting over the fifty years of our relationship, I feel very happy that Margaret and I had so many wonderful times together. The sadness that I feel now will never displace that joy and laughter and simple pleasure. The warmth of our love for each other was clear for all to see – and many people commented on it. So it is natural that I should be sad and lonely in my grief. I have no wish – nor capacity – to change that.

I have no idea what time will bring to me. I don't want to know until it comes. I need no reassurance or hope from other people. I'll wait. My future will come to me all in good time and in its own way. All I have to do is to let each day bring whatever it brings. There is nothing to be gained by trying to force anything. In the meantime I observe others. I see the young students, living it up, as we used to do. I don't envy them. Our student days were great but I do not wish to repeat them. I see the young adults going about their daily work, establishing their careers and bringing up their young children. I don't envy them either – I've done that.

I also see people who are in a far worse state than mine: the young mother dying from motor neurone disease, the old lady bent double with osteoporosis, the lady whose husband has Alzheimer's Disease and who is completely exhausted from looking after him, the man whose wife has recurrent falls. I am fortunate to have only the problems that I know I have.

Yet still I grieve, I weep, I miss the love of my life. I feel desperately lonely and sad without her.

Thoughts:
1 Each of us goes through our grief reaction in our own way. The standard textbook patterns of grieving may not apply to us.
2 Denial does wear off in time: we become fully aware of the truth.
3 There is no obligation to be angry. It is a choice. 'Letting it all come out' is not necessarily helpful at all.
4 Regret and remorse are inevitable.
5 Remember the good times and cherish them.
6 Projecting into the future is counter-productive.
7 No good comes from wearing ourselves out with worry.
8 Of course there are many other people in far worse states than ours. That gives us an opportunity to be sympathetic and kind to them. It does not diminish our own sadness. It could not: it is ours. We experience it in our own way.
9 The depth of the grief that we feel is determined by the depth of the relationship we lost. Someone who has had many relationships may feel less of a sense of loss than someone who has had just one – but I don't know: I can judge only how I feel. This is the lowest I have ever been.

Reminder: Life is still for living.

Notes:
Four and a half months after Margaret's death, I still had no positive wish to live. However, I had no wish to die. So I just went through each day, following my usual routines.

The one thing that did brighten me up was my work. I enjoyed seeing people who wanted my help. I enjoyed doing what I could do to help them to find positive ways of looking at moving their own lives forward. I enjoyed improving my own skills by practising them. I recognized that this aspect of my life was something that need not change at all. Obviously it was very different, working without Margaret by my side, but there had often been times when she was working in one room while I was working in another. There was therefore no reason, practically or psychologically, why I should not continue to work as I had done previously when she was somewhere else.

I had tried to work in Kent but it hadn't worked out. In simple terms, my work is capital city work: that's mostly where it comes from, that's where my friends and colleagues are, that's where I feel at home, that's where I have lived all my adult life. If I were to centre my life in Kent I would lose all of that and, in effect, lose my own personal primary remaining reason for living.

The standard advice is that people who have been bereaved should make as few immediate changes as practicably possible. In my case the major changes had been in the previous year, in my bankruptcy. The change I now contemplated – going back to live and work full-time in London – was a reversion to where I was before, rather than a change to somewhere completely new.

Living full-time in London again would be likely to be very different to my previous style of living but I had little choice if I wanted to move in order to stay alive spiritually. I had spent too long living out of suitcases and being dependent on the generosity of friends. I was homeless and I applied for council housing. I also applied to be put on the housing waiting list of a London charity to which I had been introduced.

At the same time, I looked at doing things that I had never done before, such as writing articles and blogs for a newspaper, doing after-dinner speeches and public lectures and doing a radio series on addiction. Also, I wanted to build up my counselling work from one day a week to a full working week. I wanted to use my experience and skills as best I could.

I cannot say that I recaptured my enthusiasm but at least I am giving it a chance to return when it feels right for it to do so.

Thoughts:

1. The absence of a negative feeling – rather than the presence of a positive one – is good enough to begin with.
2. Staying with familiar routines is a way of getting through each day when we don't know how we will feel from one day to the next.
3. Continuing an existing activity – an occupation or a hobby – is a sensible way of moving forward while changing very little.
4. Too many changes, or a dramatic change, can be exceedingly unsettling at a time when a sense of stability and security are particularly needed.
5. Taking forward, into the future, some aspect of our previous lives is helpful in providing a gentle continuity. In this way we are able to connect the two phases of our lives – before and after the bereavement – in a helpfully seamless manner.
6. Practising a previous skill keeps our minds alive.
7. Making a mistake is not a disaster: we can learn from it.
8. Getting stuck in a rut is a disaster at any age and in any situation.
9. First take action– any positive action. Subsequently you will find that enthusiasm will follow.

Reminder: Friends provide friendship.

Notes:
Margaret made and kept many personal friends. She kept them by staying in touch with them. I was lazy in that respect. I was at times more interested in building my professional skills – and even an empire – than in building friendships. Margaret did both, proving to me and to everyone else that it is possible.

Fortunately, my work – both in the medical practice and in the treatment centres – did bring me many friendships. People were grateful for what Margaret and I had done over the years in trying to help them. Consequently, at this low point in my personal and professional life, I had the encouragement of many friends. This made a huge contribution to my well-being, my peace of mind.

I had no doubt that I could still do my work at the peak of my capacity. The difficulty lay in finding out how to deliver a service that people wanted and that they could afford. The continuing general economic crisis in the country didn't help.

I looked at the prospect of working for someone else but nobody was looking at me. Other people were concerned for their own survival and they were cutting back on staff rather than building them up. I had previously been offered opportunities to work for 'a share of the profits' but there had been no offer of an interim salary or payment of expenses and there was no guarantee of how the profits would be determined when I had no control over the company expenses.

For thirty years I had worked in the private sector, paying my own way and receiving nothing from the government or from private medical insurance companies. I already lived in the real world but now I had no resources whatever on which to draw, other than what I could create for myself. I had to remember that there are very many other people in exactly that situation.

There is nothing to be gained – and a great deal to be lost – in burying my head in my grief or hiding my body under my duvet.

I want to keep my friends as my friends, not lose them by asking them to bail me out: there would be no clear end to that process. I have to retain my dignity. In any case, if I were to lose my friends and become a burden to them, I would jeopardize the goodwill from which patients are referred to me. I would kill the goose that has the potential to lay golden eggs – or any eggs at all. Somehow I have to hold my nerve, do what I can each day, look at new ideas, get rid of any sense of self-pity or blame and move forward bit by bit if at all possible.

Thoughts:
1 Friendships have to be created and maintained. They do not just happen.
2 The purpose of friendships is for them to be mutually enjoyable. They wither and die if they become one-sided.
3 The private sector is the real world. It is excellent preparation for difficult times.
4 Retreating from the world – in any way – causes even more difficulty.
5 There is no shortage of people who will take advantage of those who are down.
6 There is also no shortage of possible friendships, provided that we are prepared to make the necessary investment.
7 Geese lay golden eggs in fairy tales. In real life we have to be sure to nurture, rather than abuse or take for granted, any goose that comes our way.
8 Holding our nerve is difficult at the best of times – but we need to do this most of all when we are on the floor. That is what separates the men from the boys.
9 Self-pity and blame are utterly self-destructive.

Reminder: Love will find a way.

Notes:
Everything I know about love, I learned from Margaret. She had the gift of loving people. She practised it. Her childhood was dreadful but, instead of reacting with resentment, she gave understanding and love. In our married life I made dreadful demands on her but again she responded with understanding and love. It would be easy to assume that she was loving by nature – and I think she was – but that would have worn out unless she rekindled it every day. If there is just one thing that I want to do in the rest of my life, it is to be like her in this way – to love people simply because it is a lovely thing to do.

I doubt that I shall ever love again in an individual sense. I was not particularly loved in my childhood – my parents weren't around for most of it. I had no other loves (just a couple of infatuations) in my adult life. I don't know how to begin to love anyone other than Margaret. We shared so much. We had so many common interests. We had so many experiences together. We created so much together, feeding off each other's talents.

My feeling now is primarily one of privilege. I have loved and been loved. I don't know how many other people can say that to the same depth. I have been incredibly fortunate to have had that wonderful heart-warming sense of love for so long. Fifty years of love cannot be taken away from us now. It is still very much alive.

So what of my future? Am I destined to be alone and lonely for ever? Shall I ever hold anyone in my arms again? And, if I were to do so, would it work? Would it mean anything? How on earth would I begin to get to know someone else in even a fraction of the ways in which I knew my darling wife? I cannot begin to answer these questions now. I do not even want to consider them. I mention them only because of my profound sense of loss. I miss my sweet love. I miss her dreadfully.

I know perfectly well that people do make successful second relationships – and more. Maybe some of their first relationships were as close as ours – but that is impossible for me to judge and there is no way that I can be comforted by someone else's experience. Each of us, in our bereavement, simply has to go through it in our own way. Anyway, right now I'm not looking for a new relationship and I have no intention of looking for one.

But Margaret, secure in my personal love, was able to love many other people in a special individual way. I hope that I can do that even in the absence of a personal love. It should be possible.

Thoughts:
1 Love is a spiritual feature of life. It cannot be willed into existence, nor achieved through applying our minds to it.
2 No one can ever judge anyone else's experience of love.
3 Resentment kills love and kills the capacity for love. We can learn to have loving natures – if that is what we want.
4 I assume that the longer a close relationship the greater the loss in bereavement and the greater the difficulty in considering having any other relationship.
5 Problems in childhood may not necessarily have any future relevance whatever to our capacity for close relationships as adults.
6 The sheer number of shared experiences – and little habits – in a long-term relationship binds the partners together.
7 It is a privilege to love and be loved. There is plenty of hard work to be done in achieving that relationship but it is a privilege none the less to have had that experience even once.
8 The future must be left to take care of itself – unhurried. Rushing off into the arms of someone else would be a recipe for a great deal of pain.
9 A close personal relationship does not guarantee the capacity to have a generally loving nature – but it helps.

Reminder: It is more constructive to imagine a positive future than a negative one.

Notes:

We all live inside our own heads. We talk to ourselves (usually silently) all the time. When there is nobody to talk to at home it is only too easy to produce one negative thought after another.

I have been so used to having Margaret with me every day of my life, both at work and at home, that I am overpowered by the silence after her death. I sense her with me, of course, and I can guess how she might react to particular situations, but mostly I get on with my life as best I can and I don't get tied up in complex circular conversations with myself.

Looking to the future, I find that I still do what I have always done: either I see everything coming up roses or going down the drain. I miss Margaret's balanced judgment – even if I stupidly ignored it on many occasions. Nowadays, when I need her viewpoint more than ever, I haven't got it. I have to imagine it and I try to develop a feel for her straightforward perspective. She knew how to keep things simple, whereas I tend to be a compulsive complicator.

Even with that caution, I still find myself tending to be eternally pessimistic – until I break out in a flurry of super-optimism. That being said, I have to be fair to myself and acknowledge that my predictions over this last couple of desperately destructive years have been totally accurate. If only I had been equally perceptive over the possibility of Margaret's death, I might have been able to do something to prevent it or, at least, be more sensitive in my own behaviour towards her. But there's nothing I can do about that now. I have no choice but to accept the cruel facts.

My problem now is to find a way of making sensible judgments at a time when I feel least able to make them. I look into the future and I see nothing. I see no personal life and I see no professional life. Clearly that cannot be a balanced judgment – but that's what my head tells me. Therefore I have to fall back on the awareness gained from my work with addicts like me: we know that our heads sometimes tell us lies – but we don't know when.

The solution has to be simply to take life one day at a time, put in the footwork on whatever project is in hand and then let go and let God (or 'Good Orderly Direction') sort out what happens next. I am very familiar with all the sensible recommendations given in treatment programmes (I should be by now, after twenty-three years of running one) but I still find it difficult to put them into practice myself. Perhaps we all do.

Thoughts:

1　Self-talk is not pathological: it is not only commonplace, it is vital. We need it in order to ensure that we consider options rather than behave totally impetuously.
2　The loss of a soulmate is an immense loss. How on earth can we replace such a close relationship and partnership?
3　We each have our own way of 'staying in touch' with the person who has died. No one has the right to dictate an absolute true way to anyone else.
4　It is unlikely that we shall suddenly change our natural way of doing things after we have been bereaved. We therefore have to take into account that we have lost our external correcting mechanism and we need to take note that we may not be very good at correcting ourselves.
5　Acceptance of cruel turns of fate is easier said than done – but that's the way it has to be.
6　A bruised head is not capable of producing balanced judgments. We have to wait (as best we can) for time to heal the emotional bruises. Simple, trite, exhortations are still the best because they work. Even so, theory is easy but practice is difficult.

Reminder: Sensitive times need sensitive management.

Notes:
I am only one of many people grieving the loss of Margaret. I need to remember this because sometimes their grief spills over into insensitivity towards me. They are simply expressing their own sadness but sometimes it comes out as exasperation or irritation with me.

I forget things. I don't reason well. In my work I function very clearly but I find personal conversations difficult: they go too near the 'crumple button' (when anything – kind or critical – said to me is likely to make me crumple). This is hardly surprising: I am going through the very worst time of my life at the very time when there is nobody beside me to support and comfort me.

Practical things are challenging at times. Shopping and preparing meals are just part of the routine but anything outside my familiar activities can throw me, even if the answers that would clear my hazy head are only a couple of clicks away on my laptop.

Emotional challenges can be very unsettling. Nobody has actually said that the wrong person died – but I feel that myself so it would not be surprising if other members of our family felt it as well. Whether this is true or not, there is nothing I can do now about all the uncertainties and unanswered questions. I have to live with them.

Several friends have commented that I should remember how much help I have given to other people during my life and that I should therefore allow myself to be helped now and simply take life easy. That would kill me. I suppose I never really thought that I was helping people: I was doing my professional work, which happened to be in a 'helping' profession. I want now to get back into full-time work. It is not simply my comfort zone or even a retreat from reality. I enjoy doing it: my work has never been 'work'. It takes nothing out of me: it gives a great deal to me. The thought of retiring has never entered my head. Margaret had her piano and her special friends and her family group. I had a rich variety of stimuli in my work.

I do not feel that I have missed out on life by not spending time watching television or playing with grandchildren or joining in local activities. I am still in a time of peak productive capacity. I can do all those other things later, when I am ready for them – which I'm not.

Without Margaret's steadying hand, our family and friends have lost some sense of direction. We are all a bit lost without her – probably me most of all, totally lost. I can't stay lost for ever but I don't think it hurts me to stay in my shocked state for a bit.

Thoughts:
1 A time of grief is unsettling for everybody who was close to the person who has died. We may have to give understanding and care at the very time that we most want to receive it.
2 We can control only our own behaviour – and even that is difficult to manage at times. Other people's behaviour is always out of our control, not only at times of grief – but we become more sensitive to it then.
3 Being bereaved is a double calamity: we lose the one we love and, at the same time, we lose our companion and comforter.
4 We need to be understanding of ourselves in our loss. Our heads do not work with their customary ease: they clog up.
5 In their own grief, family members and friends may at times make some things more difficult for us rather than easier. We simply have to understand that – and accept it if we ourselves are going to be able to move through our own grief process.
6 Well-meaning family members and friends may offer us their pearls of wisdom and their blueprints for our future but we do not have to buy into them if we don't want to.
7 Accepting that we are still in a shocked state is a necessary part of the healing process.

Reminder: We are as helpless as we choose to be.

Notes:

I am perfectly capable of looking after myself in all sorts of ways – but I don't want to. The consequent problem is that I don't get any better at doing the things that I don't want to do. I find myself asking the same questions again and again. I cause my various advisors to become exasperated and I exasperate myself.

In a long-term relationship there may be a division of labour that becomes accepted as the way that things are usually done. Deprived of my partner, I have a forlorn hope that things will somehow do themselves and that difficulties will sort themselves out. But that isn't what happens in reality. Problems mount if they are not dealt with straight away. New skills remain in the pending file. A hang-dog expression can easily become a habit, a plea that somehow someone will help me out of my adopted incompetence in an unobtrusive – perhaps magical – way.

I know perfectly well that I need to brighten up in order to give myself the best chance of getting things to go my way. The problem is that I don't really know what way I want to go. As a result I remain a bit lost, helpless, pathetic – and that simply isn't me or, at any rate, not the me I used to be. This is perhaps the most difficult feature of my grief reaction: I'm not myself any more. I'm not even half of me. I'm not efficient in the way that I used to be. Time disappears. I don't mope but I don't look forward to anything because at present I have no vision of what my life could be like.

In my younger days I was always looking forward to creating new things – and I went on and did exactly that. Today I have no clear image of what I could create, particularly because my bankruptcy left me with no borrowing capacity. I have always built new ventures on borrowed money (eventually too much). Now I can't – but maybe something else will stimulate me.

But first I need to get the new ideas – and that isn't going to happen unless I brighten myself up. It really is a vicious circle.

I am often advised to chill out, to do nothing at all for a time. I know – and Margaret knew – that I would die very quickly if I were to follow this advice to relax and rest. If I were to stop, I doubt that I would have the capacity to start again.

I find the contrast between London and Kent very wearing. I see London as being full of potential for me, whereas I see nothing for me in Kent: London is where I belong. Yet there is a world of difference between potential and actual achievement. I am going to have to move on in my life – but I don't want the hassle of doing so. In a few sad months I have learned to be helpless. I can't afford that. Like it or not, I've got to wake myself up – otherwise I shall die and join Margaret before my due time.

Thoughts:
1 Action, as always, is the magic word. If we stop taking an active part in life, we will lose whatever enthusiasm and skill we had.
2 Learned helplessness is exasperating for everyone – those doing it and the people trying to dig us out of it. Even so, we need to be understanding of ourselves and recognize that this can be part – a potentially fatal part – of our grief reaction.
3 Difficulties do not go away on their own. Their resolution requires thought, planning and application.
4 Becoming incompetent is a choice – a bad choice.
5 Being sorry for ourselves is understandable in tragic situations but, in time, other people get fed up with us if we stay stuck in self-pity.
6 Brightening ourselves up cannot be done to order but we can avoid doing the opposite – glooming ourselves down.
7 Following other people's advice may not be sensible: they may not know what makes us tick.
8 Dying before our time is not what we are here to do.

Reminder: Ultimately we have to look after ourselves.

Notes:

There is a limit to what I could reasonably expect family and friends to do for me – or that they would want to do. They have lives of their own. My parents lived into their nineties. So could I. That would be an enormous burden on other people if I were to make no provision for myself. At my age, and having only recently come out of bankruptcy, this is no small task for me to undertake.

I have never previously acknowledged my age. There was no reason to do so. I was fit and healthy and I had very stimulating work and a great deal of personal and professional support. Now, at the age of seventy-three, I have none of these things. A collapsed vertebra in my lower back caused persistent pain for many months, particularly when walking – which was my main way of getting about – and when carrying even a light shopping bag. Also I had difficulty finding a comfortable position for sleep. A friend suggested that the problem was psychological, as a result of carrying the weight of the world on my shoulders. Perhaps it was. However, an MRI scan showed significant derangement and I was given treatment for osteoporosis (thinning of the bones). Working a seven-day week for the last thirty years, I had been physically fit and very active. Now I have to get used to the fact that bits of me are falling apart.

My head continues to be my greatest concern. I can think logically and carefully but I still do not know what would be best for me in my personal and professional future. Friends are immensely kind and generous but ultimately I have to make decisions for myself at the very time when I am most insecure.

After twenty-six years of abstinence from all mood-altering substances, I went to meetings of various Anonymous Fellowship groups almost every day. I did not want to relapse back to any of my former addictive behaviour. As with using antidepressants, possible short-term relief might be followed by long-term pain. That would be a very severe price to pay.

I make no attempt to deny or suppress my feelings to myself, although I am careful not to put too great a burden on other people in expecting them to calm my emotional storm.

I do whatever work comes my way and I look for more. I write articles, contribute to broadcasts, keep up my blogs and podcasts, give public lectures, arrange to train someone else's staff ... and so on. I am determined to have a future, not just a past.

Thoughts:
1 Families have responsibilities of their own. Taking on the long-term care of relatives is too great a burden when these relatives are capable of looking after themselves.
2 Coming out of bankruptcy (or something equally awful), and into a bereavement, is difficult at a time of general economic or other crisis – but that's the challenge that may have to be faced. There may be no alternative other than to do whatever we can each day.
3 Age is largely – but not totally – an attitude of mind.
4 Physical and psychological issues compound each other. It would be silly, or even dangerous, to assume that a particular problem is either totally physical or totally psychological.
5 Other people – friends and family and even doctors – may not understand us when we say that our heads are not our own, that we find it difficult to make clear decisions, but that's the way it is when we are still working our way through a grief reaction.
6 The kindness and generosity of friends are life-savers.
7 Those of us who are addicts of one kind or another can never forget that we need to maintain our recovery.
8 Denying or suppressing our feelings damages ourselves. Dumping them on other people damages our relationships.
9 Live in the present; remember the past; create the future.

Reminder: Timing is everything.

Notes:
As a musician or as a speaker, I know the importance of timing. The trick is to focus on the listener rather than upon what I believe I am putting over. Delivery is as significant as content.

As a doctor, I also know the importance of timing. Get that wrong in the practice of health care and all sorts of disasters can occur. Conversely, correct timing can be highly influential. For example, the second injection in a series of inoculations has to be given after a particular time interval in order to achieve the maximum beneficial effect.

As someone familiar with addictive behaviour, I know the significance of the timing of traumatic incidents. When a second trauma arrives at a time when the individual is already sensitized by a previous trauma, the effect can be dramatic.

This is what I believe happened to me. I had only just come out of bankruptcy, having lost everything that my wife and I had created in our lifetimes, when I was struck down by her death. The combination of the two events, one soon after the other, was devastating. Being bereaved when I was already on the floor – or just beginning to try to get up – was a terrible blow.

I have always prided myself on my resilience. I survived the separation from my parents for most of my childhood. I survived changing subjects from Music, my first love, to Medicine. I survived sixteen years of professional disillusion and frustration in the National Health Service before breaking out on my own into the creative but risky area of private practice. I survived the rejection of my ideas on the treatment of addiction by most of my colleagues. I survived bankruptcy with my spirit intact but I feel desperately sad over taking my darling wife down with me. But then I was suddenly left with an inner emptiness, the depth of which I had never experienced before.

My sweetheart died at the very time when I was least able to cope with the loss of her love, her companionship, her support and challenge, her beauty and intelligence, her friendliness and her humour. On top of that was a harsh accusation that my thoughtlessness had caused my wife's death through stress. Close relationships were broken off at the very time when I needed them and wanted to focus upon healing rather than upon further divisions. Compounding all this, were my continuing financial insecurity and my uncertainty over where I should live and how I could work. And then my back gave out so that I could walk only one hundred yards at most and couldn't carry anything at all heavy. I dared not ask myself what else might go wrong or happen to me.

Thoughts:
1 Things happen when they happen. We may not have much choice – if any – in their timing.
2 Successive traumas do not simply add to themselves (1, 2, 3, 4 . . .), they multiply (1, 2, 4, 16 . . .).
3 Previous resilience is beneficial but it can be sorely tested.
4 Sometimes we may view our own behaviour with a tolerance and rationalization that we would not extend to other people. At other times we may be excessively critical of ourselves.
5 Sometimes, in their own grief, people who are close to us may do almost the worst possible things to us. For our own sanity, we have no choice but to accept that situation and run with it as best we can.
6 The strength of the relationship between two people cannot be judged, other than superficially, by anyone outside it.
7 The older we are, the more losses we inevitably experience. As Shakespeare said, 'When sorrows come, they come not single spies but in battalions'.
8 Predicting – or guessing – the future is a pointless exercise. Our challenge is to be able to shape it. Maybe the best is yet to come.

Reminder: Negativity is boring.

Notes:
There comes a time when sympathy runs out. Other people do not want to be dragged down by the effort of supporting and comforting me indefinitely. The telephone calls become less frequent. The invitations begin to dry up. Life moves on for these other people – and it has to do so for me as well.

This transition cannot be achieved by determination. That would be false and very damaging psychologically. It has to come about naturally. First of all I have to have pleasant, rather than critical, self-talk. I have to stop damaging my own spiritual recovery. I have to ask myself whether I want to be miserable for the rest of my life or give myself some chance of happiness. I therefore can choose to do things that are likely to make me happy. Or not.

Two years from the time that I called in the liquidators, eighteen months from the time of being made bankrupt and six months from the date of my bereavement, I recognized that I really might live on for many years – maybe another quarter of my lifespan – and that there is no point in spending them in perpetual misery. Anyway, I would lose all my friends. Also I would lose my society, my familiars that give my life its particular colour.

I continued to keep my mind alive by doing the crossword and codeword puzzles in *Times 2* each day and by reading and writing. I made the best use of my time with other people, having interesting conversations rather than going over the same sad ground again. I focused on finding out what interested them. (In this respect Dale Carnegie's book *How to Win Friends and Influence People* is still the best 'How to . . .' book of all.)

I looked at opportunities for my personal and professional future. I dreamed of having colleagues and staff and I did everything I could to help that dream become my reality. Interestingly, I found that the stimulus to looking in new directions was as a result of finally having no other choice: I saw that my former life was definitely over. I had to free myself from the constraints of my memories and let go of my determination to prove anything to anybody. My future direction would have to be as new as when I changed subjects from Music to Medicine. There is no need for me to change subjects so dramatically but I would need to change my focus and look for new developments, rather than modifications of what I had done before.

On a personal basis I shall love Margaret for ever – of course I shall – but there are other people I can love in different ways. There is no disloyalty in that. The mistake would be in rushing into a new close relationship and getting hurt even more. I can wait. In the meantime I can enjoy good company.

Thoughts:
1 The patience, understanding and forbearance of other people is not inexhaustible.
2 Let nature – our own nature – take its course.
3 We can learn to talk back to our internal critical and negative voices. We can put (sensible) positive voices in their place.
4 We can treat ourselves with the same consideration and courtesy that we would hopefully give to other people.
5 We need to make a realistic appraisal of our mental and physical life and its likely time span – and then act on that. Keeping our minds active is even more important than being physically fit.
6 Creating new positive relationships is vital.
7 Dreams can become reality only if we give them a chance.
8 When we lose absolutely everything there is only one way to go: somewhere new. It could be very exciting.
9 True love is eternal. It can never be put at risk by a new relationship. The only risk is in hurting ourselves. A new love would be different but it would be love none the less.

Reminder: Faith is elusive. Practical steps and positive relationships can work wonders.

Notes:
At a time of despair we have a number of choices. We can leave the earth physically, by committing suicide. We can leave it emotionally by taking antidepressants or other pharmaceutical or recreational drugs. We can leave it mentally by abandoning reason and adopting absolute beliefs of one kind or another. We can leave it spiritually by becoming zombies, taking no further interest in a creative and enthusiastic life. Or we can do the best we can to get by from day to day, taking life as it comes.

As time went on in my bereavement, I found that my sense of loss remained as it had been at the start. I would not expect anything different. Fifty-one years of shared life cannot be shrugged off or diminished in any way. I would not want it to be.

But this does not mean that my life no longer has any relevance. I had twenty-one years of life before I met Margaret. I did exist. I can do so again – and I want to do far more than merely exist: I want to live life to the full again in whatever way I can.

Yet the grief process cannot be hurried. It takes its own time in its own way. I am very fortunate in many ways. I need to express my gratitude for that, in the same way that Margaret did regularly – and, as I noted earlier, just before she died. I am grateful for the wonderful years we spent together. Many people never have such a privileged experience. I am grateful for having children. Again, many people do not. I am grateful for having a wide circle of friends. I am grateful for having had so many stimulating interests over the years and a career that is still active. My life can be as full in future as I want it to be. But right now I feel the sense of loss more than I feel anything else. I deal with it by accepting it. I can live through it. I do not have to run away from it or pretend that it isn't there. I grieve still.

I do not envy people who have a religious faith. I think they lose as much in life as they gain. By having a fixed viewpoint, they may miss out on the full wonder involved in not knowing answers and still being amazed by questions. On the other hand, I do not criticize them: we each have a right to our own views – and no right to impose those views upon other people.

So, from day to day, I focus upon doing practical things – looking after myself in simple personal ways, doing my work as well as I can, keeping in touch with old friends and making new ones, maintaining my previous interests and keeping a look out for new possible growing points. There is so much to do in a day.

And then, in my quiet times, I wonder where Margaret's spirit is now and I wonder what will happen to me when I die, as inevitably I shall one day.

Thoughts:
1 Suicide solves nothing, as far as we can tell, and it would be sad to discover – after the event – that this really is true.
2 Antidepressants and other drugs of one kind or another solve absolutely nothing. They merely make life into a blur.
3 We should treasure our whole range of feelings as the essence of being alive.
4 Reason and faith are mutually exclusive but we should, none the less, be respectful of others in their choice.
5 Life is for living. Without creativity and enthusiasm there is no life of any appreciable value.
6 The level of loss that we feel in our bereavement exactly matches the level of excitement and love that we shared.
7 Grieving takes time. Death can wait.
8 By expressing gratitude for what we have had, we make it more likely that we can have more in our lives in future.
9 There is a time to ponder, reflect and wonder.

Reminder: The way we see things can change in an instant.

Notes:
I went to look at a part of London in which I might be able to get accommodation from a charity. It was grim. I felt desperately sad at realizing how much I had lost in recent years and how few options I had now in many fundamental issues in my life.

Later in the day I went on a training course in a particular psychological approach that interests me. This was also grim. The subject was the treatment of a young woman whose partner had hanged himself in their flat two weeks previously. The edited video recordings of her sessions lasted over an hour and a half.

In the evening I went to the Barbican to see the Donatella Flick young conductors competition with the London Symphony Orchestra. Hearing Wagner's *Liebestodt* (Lovedeath) was grim for me. It is one of my very special pieces of music – but there was no Margaret beside me. In fact I had heard no music, live or recorded, at all since Margaret's death. It had been such an important part of our lives together that I found it too painful to experience it without her.

Then I reflected and I had an epiphany:

In the immediate vicinity of the prospective accommodation was every facility that I could possibly need – and very smart too. It was only further away that the area was rough – and that will get better in time. Buses and the Underground were right next door. Medical facilities, a gym, a computer training room and other communal facilities were part of the premises and there was a large and pleasant garden. I had blinded myself in not 'seeing' all these important and lovely things straight away.

In the training course I had watched one of the most skilled therapists I have ever seen. I learned a huge amount from him. In the evening I had found myself in very congenial company and the music was blissful. The winner of the competition brought me new insights into Wagner's music and I shall treasure them.

In one day I had experienced three separate events in which I had first of all had negative impressions and then turned them into very positive ones. It was the workings of my own head – not just the outside circumstances – that needed to be firmly re-evaluated. My grief was colouring all that I saw. I would have to come through that if I wanted to enjoy any future happiness.

Thoughts:
1 The brain is a physical, chemical and electrical structure that changes physically in response to what we do with it.
2 The same place or event can make very different impressions on us at different times in different moods.
3 We can feel wretched for ever if we choose to do so.
4 Changing the outside world will have no beneficial effect for us unless we sort out the inside world of our perceptions.
5 The process of adjusting our moods, and our ways of seeing things, happens naturally. We can get in the way of this process and hinder it but we cannot force it to work faster or go in the direction we want. All we have to do, as we gradually come through our grief reaction, is to be aware that the way we see things is not necessarily the only way.
6 Depression is customarily thought of as a noun, a thing that happens to us. It is not: it is a verb (I depress... etc). We gain power over it when we recognize that, however much we may resist the concept, we create it ourselves through our own perceptions, our own choice of how we look at things.
7 We cannot come to this realization straight away. It will happen in time, when we see it for ourselves.
8 Other people cannot help us to go forward by encouraging us or through being strict with us. We ourselves have to make the move.

Reminder: All of life is a transition from one state to another.

Notes:
Slowly I began to recognize that my life would never be the same as it had been. My relationships were already changing. Friends who knew us primarily as a couple stopped inviting me on my own. Others who were primarily Margaret's friends gradually disappeared. Some of my own friends also wandered off. Perhaps they assumed that I would lose my spark and become a bore or even a burden. However, against this trend, were some lovely people who went out of their way to be friendly and supportive. Often I was surprised by their identity: they had not necessarily been close friends with us previously but they certainly became close friends to me now.

Professionally, I soon discovered that my status had dropped. As I was no longer a working doctor, it was as if I hardly counted at all. I had no office of my own, nor staff, and therefore it seemed to me that I had been put into a new category: 'poor Robert'. This was tedious because I did not feel that way at all.

I saw myself as being in a transition – moving from one lifestyle to another, finding my way in uncharted territory. I was living an adventure that had been forced upon me by Margaret's untimely death but it was an adventure none the less and I have always been an adventurer. In that capacity I had no wish to be 'brave Robert'. I just wanted to be 'Robert', with no other description attached. Fortunately I had some very special friends who saw me in exactly that light. They wanted me back on my feet, in a home of my own in London and doing the counselling work that I find most challenging and rewarding. But it was clear that none of this was going to come to me by itself: with the significant help of these special friends, I had to go out to get it.

Yet still my head, understandably, went its own way as my grief continued to unfold. There were days I was still very

very sad. On one occasion in London I retraced the steps that Margaret and I had taken when we walked along Piccadilly on the day that we first met. This time, I could not get into the Royal Academy of Art because I did not have a ticket to the current exhibition. Nor could I go down the steps in the tube station entrance where I first spoke to her: it was cordoned off. It was as if I was being shown firmly that I had to live in the present and future, not in the past. I wanted to do both – but it wasn't possible. I wept. What else would I do? I was in transition but I had not already arrived anywhere.

Thoughts:

1 Some changes in life are so great that they cause total upheaval. That's just the way it is.
2 Friends have their own lives to live and their own journeys to make. We don't own them.
3 Special friends may turn up out of the blue in surprising form.
4 The professional world can be savage. If we are not perceived as having anything of value to offer right now, we may simply be dropped. That's also just the way it is.
5 To be on the receiving end of pity is undignified and irksome.
6 Adventurers are probably born rather than made, but on some occasions we all become adventurers, whether we like it or not. Then we sink or swim: it's up to us.
7 It's all right to be sad. And it's all right to cry.
8 Memory Lane may be unhappy but it can help us to move on. We cannot live in the past – at all – however much we might like to do so. It would cripple our future.
9 Life may at times present us with some very clear – and very painful – experiences and images. We can run away from them or learn from them. Transitions are difficult because they are so uncertain. We may have no idea where we are heading. We need simply to get by from day to day.

Reminder: Enthusiasm (from the Greek *en theos*) means 'God within'.

Notes:

I had lost so much. How could I possibly be enthusiastic? The answer to that question is seen by asking another: What would happen to me if I were to lose my enthusiasm?

When I feel enthusiastic, I come to life: the spirit of God inside me inspires me and lights me up. When I am out of touch with the spirit of God inside me I lose my enthusiasm.

Of course, it is exceedingly difficult to be enthusiastic when my whole world is falling apart – but that is what I have to find the courage to be. False hail and heartiness would be a disaster, precisely because it is false. The concept of 'fake it to make it' never works. I have to look for opportunities to create new things and to be kind and supportive and encouraging to others. It is only by reaching out to help others – if they want it – that I myself can be helped through taking my mind off my own troubles and preoccupations. I have to get out of my own way and let God (my ethics, values and principles, not necessarily a religious God) direct my life.

I am familiar with loss, dreadful loss. Yet my enthusiasm survives. I shall create and love again – in new ways. Daily I experience grief and despair but I do not let them kill me. I do not take mood-altering substances, prescribed or otherwise, because they would cloud my mind and spirit and I don't want that.

I have a life to live, work to do, friendships to make and (with help) spiritual recovery to maintain and enhance by doing whatever I can to enable my personal experience to be helpful to others. There is no reason why my enthusiasm, my God within, should let me down unless self-obsession shackles me again. To go back to such self-destruction would be a wretched fate.

The living death of being without enthusiasm, or being

drugged into a state of nonchalance, is not for me. I have a richer life to live than that. I can develop an attitude of gratitude, irrespective of whatever may be happening in my life.

It is not necessary to try to create – or capture – enthusiasm. It is there inside me anyway, regardless of what may be happening to me in the outside world. All I have to do is to keep to my daily routines and be aware of old pitfalls and new opportunities. I can worry myself to death if I choose to do so. Or I can focus on the good things that occur each day. The choice is mine.

One product of my work with addicts is that I have seen how we destroy ourselves through our own self-will run riot. If I don't damage myself, I have a good chance of coming through this difficult time and making something really positive in the rest of my life.

Another product is that I see myself as having a responsibility to show that what I have previously said about hope and resilience in recovery is not merely theory but is a practical foundation that is totally dependable when I need it.

Thoughts:

1 Enthusiasm is inside each and every one of us – if we choose to look for it and nurture it.
2 The spirit of God inside us is seen in our enthusiasm. It brings us to life. We do not have to be enthusiastic about anything in particular, we can simply meet each new day with an awareness that beautiful things happen all the time and we can be part of them.
3 We do not need to be grateful only when specific things happen. We can develop an attitude of gratitude. It is up to us to find ways of benefitting from any situation – even if only to learn from it – and see how we can use our experience to benefit others.
4 Courage is not the absence of fear: it is persistence despite loneliness, insecurity, doubt and fear.

Reminder: On the far side of despair is acceptance.

Notes:
There are times when one difficulty piles in upon another. The end result is not so much that I give up under the cumulative weight of my various challenges but rather that I don't see the point of going on. I want the life I had before and that cannot be. I would like something like it – or even better – but I can't see the shape of it. I know that I can take on any destructive thing that comes my way if I am able to see a positive future goal. Where there is no light ahead, I am left only with self-discipline – the driving force that lies between the blankness of a day when customary comforting routines have disintegrated and the day of ultimate annihilation, survival or peaceful acceptance.

It is easy to judge a situation that we are not actually in or have ever been in. Trite observations and facile exhortations and advice, given with the best of intentions, are counter-productive: they make things worse.

From the inside of my bereavement, I got beyond considering what was my best option: I simply stayed alive from one day to the next. 'Depression' is too easy a word (it means too many different things) to describe this inner void. A more telling word would be 'despair'.

For me, as an addict, taking antidepressants in this situation would trap me again in dependency on mood-altering substances. That would compound my difficulties. A questionable short-term gain would be followed by long-term significant losses in autonomy. My real self – the part of me that is creative and enthusiastic (and which is very much still present on good days) – would be submerged.

The advantage of allowing myself to feel despair is that I keep open the possibility of feeling exhilaration. I feel that simply by getting from day to day (with the practical support of friends, who want to see me get back to my former productive self, and the spiritual support of attendance at regular meetings of the anonymous fellowships) would give me the opportunity not simply to survive but also to grow. In essence, the principles that I rediscover each day are, firstly, that – as John Donne said – no man is an island and, secondly, that we keep the spiritual sustenance that we give away. The more I involve myself in sensitively reaching out to help others the more I myself feel spiritually enriched.

Gradually I came to accept that, just as my childhood is over but I can none the less learn from it, so the same is true for a major part of my adulthood. But not all of it: I still have a lot of living to do. Repeatedly I come to learn these same lessons, each time with greater conviction. I accept that I can make of my future life whatever I want to make of it. This principle is the same as it always was, regardless of age or of loss.

Thoughts:
1 Some days are difficult days: that's just the way it is. Sometimes the difficulties are cumulative: they mount up progressively. That's also just the way it is.
2 The point in going on living is precisely because we do not know our future. Ultimately it is ours to create, just as our past was ours to create, regardless of the circumstances of our upbringing or adult life.
3 Keeping on going forward, even when there is no clear future, keeps open the possibility of future happiness and creativity.
4 Despair is not a fatal condition: we can come through it and be stronger as a result of it.
5 Running away into the soft comfort of dependency achieves nothing whatever that is positive.
6 Involvement with other people is the key to a happy future.
7 We can learn from our experience rather than repeat it.
8 The same lessons may need to be learned again and again.
9 All life is what we choose to make of it.

Reminder: Body and mind work closely together.

Notes:

I am well aware that there is a high mortality rate in early bereavement. Forty per cent of men and twenty-six per cent of women die – mostly from physical illnesses – within three years of the death of their partner. Whatever the death certificate may say, the true cause of death would appear to be a broken heart.

I have absolutely no intention of being an interesting statistic. Of course my heart broke. It will never heal from that desperate wound. Margaret and I were together for so long – the whole of our adult lives. However, neither of us owned the other. We had many friends and family members who each owned a part of each of us, although we belonged to ourselves and gave ourselves primarily to each other. Now that we are physically separate, our spirits live on but we have to treasure whatever existence we now have. Otherwise we would fail to value in full the life we had together, let alone value whatever we have now. Our time together was precious. Our time apart can also be precious as we each develop our new understanding of what we are to be and what we are to do now.

For myself, I believe that I still have important work to do and important new relationships to make and important previous relationships to heal and nurture. My recent experience of bereavement will be the most valuable experience of all in my professional work as a counsellor. How could it not be? I have plumbed the depths of sorrow as never before. I have learned the true meaning of profound grief and loss at first hand. Maybe I shall specialize in grief counselling. I don't know. I think I need to look after myself first of all, before I look after other people.

For people who work in other areas, there will be the same depth of understanding but it might be applied personally rather than professionally.

Physically I gradually picked up. After six months my back

pain became a nuisance rather than a burden. My blood pressure went back to being that of a twenty year old. My pulse rate became slow and regular again. Pretty well everything went back to normal – except my sleep pattern and that had never been very good. My weight remained stable and I continued to do my daily exercise routine. My hope was that this would restore my energy and my enthusiasm and optimism to their previous levels. Well I suppose it did to some extent and at least I did not get worse. To do better than that would be to expect miracles.

Yet miracles do happen – every day – and I experience more than my fair share. I am grateful for each and every one of them. I spend time with lovely people, I see and hear lovely things, I do lovely things. There is a lot of love in my life – because I welcome it. I am as youthful as I choose to be: I am not a statistic.

Thoughts:

1 The date of our death is largely in our own hands. If we avoid doing unhealthy things and indulge in healthy things, the chances are that we shall be healthy.

2 We can grieve ourselves to death if we choose to do so – but that would be sad when there is so much more to appreciate in life.

3 Nobody owns anybody. We are responsible for ourselves.

4 We value the past and the future when we treasure the present.

5 Each one of us can find a benefit – in our own professional or personal relationships – from the experience of bereavement.

6 It is worth repeating that we can restore our physical health by doing healthy things and by avoiding doing unhealthy things. That will inevitably improve our emotional and mental health, if only by preventing it from getting worse.

7 Miracles do happen if we look for them. We should expect them.

8 We can choose optimism and enthusiasm, love and youth.

Reminder: Time passes.

Notes:
I found it progressively more difficult to be in our flat on my own. I am not solitary by nature and I did not want to become so by habit. I like living and working with other people. In fact I was living in a community – but it was a retired community and I was not retired. I still wanted to be in full-time work. I went to London by coach once a week but, with three hours travel each way. That was tiring rather than stimulating even though I enjoyed doing the work. In the rest of the week I taught myself to touch-type, became more computer-literate and I wrote.

I wondered whether I should write professionally, earning some money to enable me to have the occasional treat such as a trip to the opera – but who would give me a job when there are so many young and talented writers looking for work? I wondered what else I might do and I always came up with the same answer: get back to living and working in London, doing the work that I most enjoy – my work with addicts of one kind or another.

Friends told me that I could stay in their home in Chelsea when they weren't there – which was most of the time – and I did. Then the work began to appear, apparently from nowhere (not primarily from my previous patients). As my assistant, Josh, worked to get us further up the Google listings, we began to get new patients through the Internet. Like it or not, I had indeed joined the twentieth century, if not yet the twenty-first.

A friend from Holland asked me if I would help to train the staff in a new treatment centre and I accepted enthusiastically. Josh and I spent three days lecturing and running group therapy, psychodrama and Neuro-Linguistic Programming sessions. We loved it.

Fortunately, so did our hosts and we were invited to return at a later date when they could organize themselves to take full advantage of our time with them. From being a supposed spent force, I was suddenly in full harness again.

I began to re-establish my professional contacts and, most importantly for my own sake, I got back to the early morning meetings of various anonymous fellowships and I met many of my previous friends and made new ones.

The Royal Borough said that they would not be able to give me a home because I was not technically homeless: I had a home even if it was in the wrong place for me. The charity to which I had applied said that it was unlikely that I would be offered a place in the next twelve months. It looked as if the candle of my dream would quickly be snuffed out. But, now that I was back in my long-term haunts, friends kept helping me in one way or another (sometimes very generously), and new patients kept arriving. I began to look for premises that I could rent so that I could say, as Paul Newman did at the end of The Hustler, 'I'm back!'.

Thoughts:
1 There are better things to do in life than to sit in the gloom, waiting for the grim reaper to call. Retirement is an attitude of mind, not a function of age.
2 People need people.
3 Doing what we do best is probably what we should do, rather than trying something totally new.
4 Being in the place where we are already known is probably more likely to bear fruit than somewhere totally strange.
5 Friends are a product of previous investment of time and thought.
6 Work comes as a result of planning and sheer hard graft.
7 We get back what we put out – the good just as much as the bad.
8 Vitality, creativity, energy and enthusiasm never die – but they do have to be present in the first place: they cannot be rekindled if there is no original spark.

Reminder: Opportunities do not always come twice.

Notes:
My friend Pat decided to help me to find a flat. She downloaded a sheaf of particulars from agents' websites, we sorted through them and I gave each flat a series of point counts on location, cost, size, facilities, floor level and so on. This narrowed the field to just one. I telephoned the agent, we met him on a Sunday and took the flat on just one inspection. I paid him a hefty number of weeks' rent in advance, in order to avoid embarrassing friends by asking them to provide me with a financial reference after my bankruptcy, and the flat – one room and a shower room – was mine. Buying new furniture was easy: there was limited space.

This studio flat is just round the corner from my wife's and my previous home and one hundred yards from our previous office. I am back where I belong, in the very centre of my known world. Might there be other opportunities? Yes, of course. Might the agent have seen me coming as a right sucker? Yes again. But that's too bad. My alternative, as I saw it, was to die a slow death from inactivity. I love the pace, the noise, the hustle and bustle of South Kensington. I've done so for forty-five years; it's in my blood. I don't want to look anywhere else – and, as a former general medical practitioner, I am very familiar with the property in the area. This is the flat I want and I've got it.

Previously I owned a great stretch of freehold property. Now I am renting one small room. But that's not the point: I'm on my way back to the life I am used to, the life I want again. I don't want an empire and flocks of staff. I've done all that and I don't want to repeat it. I don't want to do anything that would require registration with authorities of one kind or another. I've had enough of bureaucracy. The rest of my life is for me and for my friends and for the people I see in my work. I am delighted to be a taxpayer again, rather than a pensioner but, apart from that form of contribution to the state and the wider community, I have no intention of being a servant or slave again. I have a life of my own to live.

My work picked up. It did not grow specifically from my previous work: it came more from the website that my assistant, Josh, created and from people who heard about me through my further exposure in the media. My one room costs three times what I had to pay for the flat in the almshouse in the country – but it's mine because I earn the money that pays for it, rather than because it is given to me in a state pension. Coming up to seventy-four, I have no wish to be patronized or pandered to. I'll pay my own way and hold my head high. The chronic pain from osteoporosis in my spine persists a bit but that's life. There are many worse things that could happen to me – and maybe some of them will. But I have my personal dignity, in the way that I see it, and that matters to me.

Thoughts:
1 Opportunities come to those who look for them.
2 There is no substitute for enthusiasm.
3 Risks can lead to catastrophes. I, of all people, know that – but a life without risk is no life at all.
4 We each have our own passions. We have to stay true to them.
5 Each one of us has our own sense of a spiritual home – the place that brings us to life. That is our personal choice and privilege.
6 To pick ourselves up again, we do not necessarily have to do what we did before. Starting in a completely new field might be too great a challenge – and not much fun – because we might run the risk of dreaming of what we had before. But finding new ways of exploiting our tried and tested skills can be very exciting.
7 There is surely a time when we owe nothing to anybody and we can simply be ourselves. Perhaps that time should be whenever we ourselves choose (at our own expense).

Reminder: Move on.

Notes:

I went to Kent to collect my belongings and say goodbye to friends. The first part was straightforward enough: there were a lot of pictures but not much else. The beds and the sofa and armchair were too large for my new flat so I gave them away. My desk and chair, two glass trolleys and some lamps were the only items of furniture that I could take with me as tokens of the life that Margaret and I had shared together. Like it or not, I was at the beginning of a new adventure.

Saying goodbye to friends in the almshouse was easy. I had not known them long or well, although they had been very friendly to us. On some days the first person I would speak to was at seven o'clock in the evening at a meeting of an Anonymous Fellowship. I knew – and the other residents knew – that I needed to be back in the swim with my own community in central London, where nine o'clock in the evening is not bedtime but the time for the second part of our day to begin.

Saying goodbye to personal friends whom I had known for forty years was more difficult. The invitations to come down for a weekend at any time were genuine enough but I knew that I would never go back. I would not want to do so. As with India, the country of my birth, I would not want to reflect upon how things used to be. I need to move on.

One close friend chose to tell me that Margaret would be alive today if I had behaved differently. I have to accept that family members and close friends have their own grief reactions, of which anger is a stage. I also have to accept that they may be right. Bankruptcy is very stressful and Margaret had raised blood pressure, despite her peaceful disposition. Either way, Margaret and I had no cross words at all during our time in the almshouse, despite having only two small rooms. I know that to be true.

Saying goodbye to the lovely landscapes of East Kent was very difficult. We had been there for over forty years. I had so many happy memories, so many associations. No more would I vary my way home so as to seep in the gorgeous countryside. No more would I search for the different species of wild orchid that are found particularly in 'our' valley. No more would I drive anywhere – I had no further need of a car.

Saying goodbye to Margaret's gravestone was a sad final gesture but no more than that. I choose to remember her in life. She comes with me wherever I am, even now.

Thoughts:
1 There is no point in staying stuck in the past. We can treasure our happy memories but we have to move on
2 The life that we share with our loved ones is in our minds – how we think, discuss, converse, play and laugh.
3 Life is never over until it's over – and perhaps not even then. The body dies but the spirit lives on in our memories. There are practical alternatives – for anybody other than those in the final phase of terminal illness – to being in God's waiting room.
4 Hermits and solitary monks live in isolation with their God. The rest of us need people around us to keep us sane.
5 Moving on means exactly that.
6 It is always a greater – and more appropriate – challenge to judge ourselves than to judge other people. However, when we are on the receiving end of someone else's judgment, it does us no harm to consider that it might be accurate.
7 Wants have to be differentiated from needs.
8 Life comes in phases. There is no reason why the next phase should be less exciting or rewarding than the last.
9 The countryside and the city are equally beautiful to those of us who appreciate both.

Reminder: Time does not stand still.

Notes:

I could not simply pick up the reins from where I had put them down almost two years earlier. Although the Official Receiver had still not sold my medical practice premises, I had no money and did not want them anyway. Nowadays they are just a building. Without the staff and the patients – and in particular without Margaret – they are just a hollow shell.

I did not want to work as a doctor any more. The increasingly restrictive regulations of the Care Quality Commission and the General Medical Council make medical practice so regimented that there is no place for innovation. Doctors nowadays have to do what various Big Brothers tell them to do. That is not my style. I want to create, not follow obediently in the wake of politicians, bureaucrats and placemen.

But the world of counselling has also been under increasing regulation. There are, of course, good reasons for that – but the results are restrictive of the good as well as of the bad. Again my instinct is to stay small. I suppose I could simply call myself a 'Friend' – which is what, in effect, I am. I do not prescribe drugs. I do not have beds in which to confine people. I do not employ staff. I do not use dangerous techniques. I simply listen and discuss. To regulate that really would bring in the era of the Thought Police.

I remember the humourists, Flanders and Swan, saying – in the age of satire that stripped the veneer off life – that their job was to put it back. I feel that my future job is to put the humanity back into clinical care.

I am gradually coming to terms with my new status. I do not see myself as an ex- anything. I am as I am now. I am no longer a registered doctor. I am no longer married. I am just me. The status 'me' is totally acceptable. I don't want to be anything other than myself. I do not wish to belong to a corporate body. I do not seek the protection of the herd. I want to have the fun of generating new ideas and revelling in finding new ways of doing things. I need other people – other originals – to join me in this quest but I do not need to be told what to do.

All this is a part of coming back to life after my bereavement. I still have a life to live and I'm going to live it.

Thoughts:

1 The more time we take out from active participation in anything, the more difficult it is to get back into it.

2 People bring buildings to life. Without the bicker and banter of humanity in all its variety, the buildings are nothing other than expensive status symbols.

3 We have a choice to lead or to follow. True leaders do not generally choose to be politicians or bureaucrats or placemen.

4 Some regulation is necessary so that we do not have to carry arms in order to protect ourselves, our families and our property – but that is its only justification. Otherwise the restriction of freedom is too constricting and repressive.

5 Whatever our age and whatever stressors may land on us, we still – if we choose – have the capacity to think and act for ourselves.

6 If we do not have problems to solve, we shall not have the stimulus and reward of solving them.

7 There is always a place for human kindness in any activity.

8 If we see ourselves as an ex- something we shall always be an ex- something (or nothing at all). To be simply ourselves today is a great achievement, worthy of a lifetime's thought and work.

9 It takes time to come back to life after a bereavement – but it will not happen at all if we do not put our minds to it. If there is life still to be lived, we can have real pleasure in discovering what it might bring to us.

Reminder: A phoenix can rise from the ashes but Icarus rose too close to the sun and crashed back to earth.

Notes:

My work gradually strengthened, both in quantity and in quality. The more established I became, the more patients came to see me. The more work I did, the more confident I became. I soon felt that I was back at my peak and capable of developing even further. I had new ideas and I was keen to put them into practice. I felt that all my previous personal and clinical experience was a preparation for what I could now do.

Increased work meant increased income. This was gratifying because I like to be independent. During my year of bankruptcy I had some very kind help from friends but otherwise I had to provide for myself, and for my wife, as best I could. Our children have responsibilities of their own. Clearly they would not be able to help me in the future so I would have to look after myself.

I asked myself what savings I would need to accumulate in order to feel secure. I had no answer to that. I realized that there is no financial sum that provides a sense of emotional security: it is a personal concept. I decided that I would simply do whatever work comes my way, spend as little as possible by taking on no staff and building no empire, save what I could and keep things as simple as possible.

Yet I overlooked the fact that I am an addict. As soon as I began to do well, I began to dream the same dreams that I had dreamed before. I forgot that they had become nightmares. Fortunately, this time round, I had no borrowing capacity even though my positive account meant that my bank were for ever offering me 'products' – ways for them to take my hard-earned money. My close friends, Josh and Pat, told me very clearly that they would not tolerate me going on a spending binge. If I did so, they would not support me in my madness. To see my own madness has always been difficult:

it is for all addicts – that's why we group together in Alcoholics Anonymous or similar 'Fellowships'. We see ourselves reflected in the mirror of the group. I went to even more meetings – for my sanity.

Another good thing that came out of the blue (after lots of hard work putting myself in the right place to be seen) was exposure in the media and opportunities to write, speak and train. I enjoy that work every bit as much as running a treatment centre and there are no financial risks, no bureaucratic entanglements and no staff to pay for and supervise.

Even so, my addict head still wondered if I might buy myself back into former glory. However, I may still have enthusiasm and lots of energy but I am so fed up with government regulation that I have no wish whatever to do anything that would lead me into that minefield again. I'll stay small, profitable, self-sufficient – and at peace with the world.

Thoughts:
1 Creative work soothes the spirit and satisfies the soul.
2 The weight of the years slips away when new adventures invigorate the mind and brighten each day.
3 Yesterday is gone. Today brings opportunity to create tomorrow.
4 Money is everything: it provides security and independence. As Mark Twain said, 'I've been rich and I've been poor and – believe me – rich is better'. Profitability is heaven.
5 Families have their own agenda. Friends are by choice – and tend therefore to be both supportive and appropriately challenging.
6 Addicts do not see ourselves at all well.
7 Opportunities come to those who look for them and prepare for them.
8 Bureaucracy stifles creativity.
9 Small is indeed beautiful and self-sufficiency is honourable.

Reminder: Losses may or may not be irretrievable.

Notes:
Sorting out my belongings, I came across the nightie that my wife had worn on our honeymoon almost fifty years ago. I had not known that she had kept it. Suddenly, out of the blue – or pink to be precise – I was reminded of the most tender and gentle moments of our lives. That demolished me.

Later I discovered that I must have thrown away my favourite photographs of my darling wife. In transferring my possessions from Kent to London, I had used black bin-liners – the same ones that I used for rubbish to be thrown away. Clearly I had got them mixed up. I felt desolate over my stupidity. Mistakes happen but that was too big to take without crying my eyes out yet again.

I also lost my framed degree certificates from Cambridge. I was proud of them but they are only bits of paper. I still have the degrees themselves. By contrast, any reminder of Margaret is still – and always will be – a personal treasure. A lifetime of a close relationship is not over until the lives of both participants are over.

Margaret's loving nature was the glue that held our lives – and our family – together. Some of our family relationships disintegrated without her. I had hoped to be her proxy (as well as continuing to be myself) but it did not work out that way. Some close relatives blamed me for her death. There was no chance of me persuading them to believe otherwise.

I lost the love of my life, my daily companion, my mementos of her, our family life, our social and cultural life, our shared sense of humour, everything that I held most dear and, inevitably, my physical health. I had been through the suicidal phase of my grief reaction. Now I was in purgatory: a spiritual void. How much more loss could I take? Would I ever again feel enthusiastic? Would I have the opportunity to channel it constructively?

Yet still I had so much: my work, my experience, my friends and colleagues, my ideas and my commitment to creativity. Maybe some of my losses would soften in time. I have to hope so.

Then the photographs and my degrees turned up: I had not thrown them away after all. That one event brightened me up considerably because it not only restored my lovely keepsakes, but showed me that good and beautiful things can happen even in the midst of utter despair.

Margaret's family remained close to me. Surely they would have been the first to pillory me if there had been any suggestion that I had been in any way responsible for her death – but they did not blame me at all. They comforted me even in their own great loss. They, together with Josh and Pat in particular but also other friends and family members, put me back together. However, they could only achieve that if I myself was committed to life – and I am. I want to live my life to the full and to do my very best to be worthy of all that Margaret had invested in me.

Thoughts:

1 There is no protection against sudden reminders of the former happiness that is now lost for ever.

2 There is also no protection against mistakes: they happen.

3 There is no shame – and a lot of benefit – in letting the tears flow. Grief needs to be expressed rather than suppressed, even many months after the bereavement.

4 'Till death us do part' refers only to physical, rather than personal or spiritual, relationships.

5 Families grieve in their own way – and nothing changes that.

6 Losses mount up. There seems to be no end to them.

7 One small happy event might be an indication of more to come.

8 Know who your real friends are – and stick with them. Then make new ones as well.

Reminder: Life begins whenever we want it to begin.

Notes:
My new work continued to expand. It is new in the sense that I work with one assistant in a single room, rather than with over a hundred staff in three separate sizeable institutions. It is also new in that I am working mostly one-to-one (actually two-to- one) rather than mostly in group therapy sessions, although I continue to do some. However, the work itself is the same as it had been except that I no longer work as a doctor. I had loved being a doctor but it is time to move on. Hopefully, I shall never need to move on from counselling/coaching work.

My new office is a delight, the necessary size for my limited needs and right in the centre of my social and spiritual universe.

My new agents – for my writing and broadcasting – are perfect for me. They encourage and correct me in equal measure, just as Margaret had done in a personal capacity.

My new friends join my previous friends. I no longer go to Kent but this leaves me free to enjoy London at the weekends, something I have not done in forty-five years. In fact I no longer go anywhere. London has everything I want. I sold my car – and saved a lot of money and reduced my risks.

I suppose it was inevitable that I would find a new special person (I loathe the term 'partner' because it seems so lacking in commitment) with whom to share my personal life. I am not a solitary: I don't do well on my own.

Pat is my own age and she is a widow. Margaret and I knew her and her husband. She lives in South Kensington, in Onslow Square, where we used to live and, before her husband died, she worked in Kendrick Mews where we subsequently lived and worked. She publishes travel books so we very much share a literary interest. Mutual friends – of which we have many – say that we are meant for each other. Neither of us would take that for granted: any relationship requires hard work if it is to last.

Friends invited me to supper and I took Pat with me for the first time. I felt proud to have her on my arm. Pat's own friends are very kind to us, accepting that we give something very special to each other. Ultimately we each create our own relationship. Whatever came before was different: valuable and treasured and never forgotten or put aside – but different.

I now earn sufficient money to be financially independent, provided that my health holds good, so I can look myself in the eye and make my own terms in life. I can afford to make my own choices. I can build for the future.

Thoughts:

1 Downsizing is not fearful: it can provide greater security. The way back will only be successful if it is also the way forward.

2 Financial independence leads to all other independence.

3 Working hard is not necessarily productive: working smart is.

4 There is a time to move on in some fields of work but not in others. Changing some aspects of our work may provide continuing stimulus and reward.

5 Disaster strikes when wants exceed needs and outstrip resources.

6 Search out opportunities for growth – but think about them before rushing into them.

7 Use professionals for professional work.

8 Location, location, location is always what matters for property.

9 Friends are special. Special friends are even more so. Finding someone special may require no more challenging a task than seeing, in a new light, the friends we already have.

10 Building a long-term relationship requires long-term work. New relationships have to be genuinely new, rather than mimic previous ones. Anyway, that's more fun.

Reminder: Today is always the first day of the rest of our lives.

Notes:

My darling Bear, my sweetest love, my wonderful girl, I love you more than ever. I miss you dreadfully. I cannot imagine that the rest of my life will continue to be without you beside me in the flesh, not only in the spirit – but so it will be.

We had such happy times together. We had difficult times as well, but none so difficult as these.

I love you, I love you, I love you. I shall love you till the sun goes out.

I have no wish to live without you but I must. I have to continue what we created together. I cannot betray all those lovely people who took us to their hearts and trusted us when we said that 'this too shall pass'.

Your spirit is with me now, as I write this final chapter in the story of our beautiful lives together and of your sad death that separated us – and of my absolute determination to be worthy of you now and for the rest of my life. I shall not let you down.

In the first few days after your death, I prayed that God would take me too. He didn't. Perhaps you wouldn't allow it. Now I pray to live – to create, enthuse and inspire if I can.

In my consulting room, the centre of my creative life, your photographs are with me every day. I remember so clearly when each was taken: the first on the beach at Bournemouth, being blown about on the January weekend when you first introduced me to your family, our wedding photographs in all our innocence and hope, the photograph of all our family in our fineries at a wedding at the Guards' Chapel, you in your study at the cottage, nestling up to our ginger cat (whose name cannot be repeated in public) and, finally, you holding your beloved black cat Beatle in blissful harmony together.

I wish, I wish I could hold you once more. I wish I could hear your friendly voice and your divine piano playing.

I have tried my best to keep the family together. I have tried my best to take each day as it comes. I do try each day to bring your gentle spirit alongside mine in my work when troubled individuals or families come to (you and) me for help.

I love Pat in a different way from the love I share with you. She looks after me and protects me as you do. She keeps me alive as you do. She supports and challenges me as you do. – All in her own special way. I love her for her, just as I love you for you. Whereas you and I shared a love of Chopin and Schumann, Pat and I share a love of Strauss and Wagner.

The values and ideals that you and I created together live on.

One day I too shall die – not yet, I hope: I have a lot of living still to do. When my time comes, I hope that some people will remember me in the way that so many remember you – as someone who tried to be kind and creative and to bring peace and happiness into their lives.

What is death? I don't know. I don't want to know. I'll meet it when it comes. For now, I'll live my life in the only way I know – giving it everything I have.

> Be with me, my sweetheart. Help me and let me comfort you.

> Be mine, as I am yours.

> God bless you, my darling.

> God bless you, my love.

> God bless you, my sweetest Bear

Reminder: No good deed goes unpunished.

Notes:
Everyone working in the front line in a helping profession knows that we shall pay a price for that. We all know it but we still come back for more – and more.

I am now back in the area of London that I love. I have a new wife, a new home, a new office, a new style of work, new opportunities, new interests and new social activities. I am making new friends. I love my new life every bit as much as I loved my old life. In fact I consider that I am privileged to have had two lives: my former life that is now largely over and my new life that is just beginning at the tender age of seventy-five.

I loved being a doctor. I enjoyed my work as a GP and I loved the patients I looked after – some for forty years. I don't want to be a doctor now. There is no opportunity to create: the fun has gone. GPs in the National Health Service now make a lot of money. I don't want it at the price of working for the state.

The private sector is little better because Big Brother is even more intrusive than in the state sector – because he doesn't understand that people can actually want to work and to do good work, even if the financial rewards are unpredictable. He snoops into everything. I believe that independence – the essence of private practice – is being progressively eroded every minute.

I loved my work in my treatment centre. Nowadays I do more or less the same work on my own. Big Brother puts me off ever considering running a substantial organization again.

I loved Margaret as much as anyone could love anyone. I was desperately sad to have caused her so much pain through all our losses. She never once complained. She took each day as she found it.

Now I am blissfully happy with Pat. We have a wonderful life together and we also take each day as we find it.

Thoughts:

1 My first life is finished. I don't want it back. I have moved on.

2 My second life is great. I'm learning so much and doing so much that I'm enjoying every minute.

3 The time in between my two lives was difficult but nobody ever said that life would be easy at any time. Two friends in particular – Josh and Susan – helped me through. I had known them for only a short time but they were rock solid in their personal support and friendship every day. I have been to each of their homes only once. Their help was that they understood what I wanted from life. Many other friends have been very kind to me and I love them for that. But it was Pat who fully brought me back to life again.

4 I am now free from family ties and responsibilities. I think it has been a mistake in the past for me to ask for help from close family members. They have their own agendas, as they are entitled to. From now on I shall have the same personal expectations of family members as I have of friends. I do not accept that family should take pride of place in affection or consideration. My experience has been that water is sometimes thicker than blood. We should live primarily for ourselves, doing what we want to do, being considerate to others – and giving to them when we feel like it.

5 The thing that I find most stimulating about my future is that I have no idea what it will be. I imagine that I shall continue my counselling work. Hopefully Big Brother cannot get his grasping mitts onto that but, if counselling is suffocatingly regulated in future, I shall call myself a coach or even a friend. I shall do more writing and perhaps try my hand at a novel. I might sketch out a musical. My guiding principle in all of this will be 'Why not?'

6 One day I shall die. I do not look forward to the process but I do look forward to what comes afterwards – precisely because I do not know what form it will take. But supposing this life is all there is. I would settle for that: it's wonderful.

Epilogue: A zest for life.

The final wishes of Thomas Hardy's Mayor of Casterbridge have this conclusion:

'. . . and that no flours be planted on my grave and that no man remember me. To this I put my name.'

There are times in my life when I would have said the same. Today is not one of them.

The sense of life within each one of us seems to differ. I have a burning desire to go on living, not just existing but adventuring, creating and loving. With a few blips, I've always been like that.

I refuse to allow the circumstances of my past to dominate my present and future. I see my past as training for my future. I hope to learn from all my experiences – tragic or exhilarating, frightening or calming, wretched or rewarding – and then move on.

Patients consulted me as a doctor because they were in physical or emotional pain or because they were frightened. My task was to examine, investigate, assess and recommend.

Reflecting upon my own life and observing my actions and reactions, I see a zest for life. That is my diagnosis on myself. My strongest recommendation is that I should continue as before, to keep taking the human spiritual medicine that has served me so well.

Let others choose to depress themselves with morbid preoccupations, if they have nothing better to contemplate. Or let them resort to the temporary solace of a chemical nirvana. I shall not.

My loyalties were abused. I have endured crises and cruel turns of fate. Now I move on. I have better things to do than to ruminate on the injustices of my life.

I have too much living to do to waste my remaining days looking backwards rather than forwards. Life is for living and I intend to do exactly that – to live my life to the full, one glorious day after another.

I have no interest nowadays in looking back at betrayals and crises. What on earth would be the point in doing that?

Three years after my bankruptcy and banishment from my social and professional familiars, I am back in South Kensington, living and working in the centre of my own universe.

Two years after my bereavement, I am very happily remarried. I had never imagined that it would be possible to love again at such depth. My life is full of music again. I write. I broadcast. I spread my ideas in whatever way I can and I generate new ones. Pat is right alongside me in all of these activities.

I have the same energy that I had when I was a student – and a lot more experience to guide me towards positive creative expression, rather than silly haphazard flamboyance.

Looking to the future, I want to focus my attention primarily on developing a progressively closer loving relationship with my wife, Pat. We already share important values. We knew that before we got married. Now we want to share experiences – to go to the opera, ballet, theatre and cinema, to travel and explore, to do the daily crossword and codeword, to watch our favourite shows on DVDs, to hold hands in the street.

We shall both continue to do our creative work for as long as we are able to do so. The thought of retirement wouldn't enter either of our heads. If, for some reason, we cannot continue our present work, we'll do something else.

I feel young again because I am young again. My birth certificate says I am 75. It lies. I feel 35 and I behave 25.

I take Sir Thomas More as my guide:

'Happy the man, and happy he alone, he who can call today his own. He who, secure within, can say, "Tomorrow do thy worst, for I have lived today".'

Lightning Source UK Ltd.
Milton Keynes UK
UKOW02n1342010916

281990UK00002B/6/P